# Fully Abstract Models of Programming Languages

**Allen Stoughton**
School of Mathematical and Physical Sciences
University of Sussex

# Fully Abstract Models of Programming Languages

Pitman, London

John Wiley & Sons, Inc., New York, Toronto

PITMAN PUBLISHING
128 Long Acre, London WC2E 9AN



First published 1988

Available in the Western Hemisphere from
John Wiley & Sons, Inc.
605 Third Avenue, New York, NY 10158

ISSN 0268-7534

**British Library Cataloguing in Publication Data**
Stoughton, Allen
Fully abstract models of programming languages.—(Research notes in theoretical computer science, ISSN 0268-7534).
1. Programming languages (Electronic computers)—Syntax 2. Programming languages (Electronic computers)—Semantics
I. Title II. Series
005.13 QR76.7

ISBN 0-273-08788-6

**Library of Congress Cataloging in Publication Data**
Stoughton, Allen.
Fully abstract models of programming languages / Allen Stoughton.
p. cm.—(Research notes in theoretical computer science)
Bibliography: p.
Includes index.
ISBN 0-470-21041-9 (U.S.)
1. Programming languages (Electronic computers)—Semantics.
I. Title. II. Series.
QA76.7.S739 1988
005.13—dc19 87-34472



Reproduced and printed by photolithography
in Great Britain by Biddles Ltd, Guildford

# Contents

# Preface

This monograph presents a language-independent theory of *fully abstract* denotational semantics of programming languages—models that identify program fragments exactly when they are operationally interchangeable—and uses this theory to show the existence or nonexistence of such models for several example programming languages. It is intended for researchers in programming language semantics, and is mathematically self-contained: only naive set theory and some very basic notions of category theory are assumed. Some familiarity with universal algebra and domain theory would be helpful, however.

This monograph is a revision of the author's Ph.D. thesis [Stou], which was submitted to the University of Edinburgh in August, 1986. It is a pleasure to acknowledge many stimulating discussions with my thesis supervisor, Gordon Plotkin. Numerous conversations with Marek Bednarczyk, Ilaria Castellani, Peter Dybjer, Matthew Hennessy, Kim Larsen, David McCarty, Robin Milner, Peter Mosses, Andrew Pitts, K.V.S. Prasad, Edmund Robinson, Dave Schmidt, Oliver Schoet and Colin Stirling, as well as particular talks with Gérard Berry, Evelyn Nelson and Glynn Winskel, were also helpful. Special thanks are due to Gérard Berry, Peter Dybjer and David McCarty for critically reading my thesis, and to Gérard Berry, Rance Cleaveland and Andrew Pitts for their comments on a draft of this monograph.

I was financially supported by a University of Edinburgh Studentship and research fellowships from the Department of Computer Sciences of Chalmers University of Technology and the Science and Engineering Research Council of Great Britain.

*To Jan*

# 1 Introduction

## 1.1 Program Equivalence and Full Abstraction

Notions of program equivalence are fundamental to the theory and practice of programming languages. They are the semantic basis for program optimization and can be used to justify the correctness-preserving transformations that are employed by program manipulation systems. Notions of program equivalence are generally substitutive in the sense that the results of embedding equivalent terms (program fragments) into a context (a term with "holes" in it) are also equivalent. Thus a programmer can replace fragments of a program by equivalent terms without considering the details of the whole program.

Program equivalences are typically defined according to the following paradigm. Terms that are considered to be directly executable and observable are designated as *programs*, and their behaviour is defined. Then two terms are defined to be equivalent if and only if (iff) they have the same behaviour in all program contexts, i.e., iff one can be replaced by the other in any program without affecting the behaviour of that program. Thus term equivalence is reduced to program behaviour.

The distinction between terms and programs is often suggested by the syntactic categories of programming languages. For example, in an imperative language with statements and expressions the statements might be taken to be the programs, reflecting the view that expressions can only be executed as parts of statements. For languages with block structure, i.e., in which identifiers can be statically bound, it is common to take the closed terms as the programs.

By the behaviour of programs we mean the actions of programs that are visible to external observers. Program behaviours for a deterministic programming language might simply be functions from inputs to outputs, whereas behaviours for languages with communicating processes might consist of communication histories. Much depends upon the level of detail that external observers are allowed to see.

It is also possible to consider notions of program ordering, i.e., notions of when one term should be considered less defined, or convergent, than another. Program orderings are typically defined by ordering the set of program behaviours and then defining one term to be less than another iff the behaviour of the first is less than that of the second in all program contexts.

Program behaviours and their orderings can be defined as abstractions of both operational and denotational semantics, although the literature is currently biased toward the use of operational semantics. Examples of the use of denotational semantics in this way are given in this monograph. Often there are multiple natural notions of behaviour that can be defined via a given semantics. Examples of behaviourally defined program orderings and equivalences can be found in [Mil1], [Mil3], [Plo1] and [HenPlo1].

Once a notion of program equivalence has been selected for a programming language, its properties must be determined and proof techniques found. Denotational semantics, as developed by Scott, Strachey and their followers (see [Stoy] for an introduction and extensive references), is a suitable framework for these activities. The idea is to reduce the equivalence of terms to the equality of their semantic values in appropriate models, i.e., to semantically capture the notion of program equivalence. Thus it is necessary to work with models that are *equationally correct* (or simply *correct*) in the sense that only equivalent terms are identified (mapped to the same semantic value). Models with the ideal property that exactly the equivalent terms are identified are called *equationally fully abstract* (or simply *fully abstract*).

Similarly, one can judge denotational semantics with reference to notions of program ordering. A model is said to be *inequationally correct* with reference to a program ordering iff one term is less than another in the program ordering whenever the meaning of the first is less than that of the second in the model, and *inequationally fully abstract* iff one term is less than another in the program ordering exactly when the meaning of the first is less than that of the second in the model.

For models to be useful for reasoning about program equivalences or orderings, it is necessary that their structure be understandable independently from those equivalences or orderings; informally, we call such models *natural*. For example, models synthesized using the standard constructions of denotational semantics are generally natural, in contrast to term models, i.e., models constructed from equivalence classes of terms, etc.

The idea of judging denotational semantics with reference to predefined notions of program ordering and equivalence is due to Milner [Mil1] and Plotkin [Plo1] and has been studied, for a variety of programming languages, by Abramsky, Berry, Curien, Hennessy and others. Research on full abstraction can be divided into two categories:

(i) The synthesis and analysis of natural models.

(ii) The theoretical study of the conditions under which fully abstract models exist.

We consider each of these in turn.

For many programming languages, the standard techniques of denotational semantics yield natural models that are too concrete, i.e., correct but not fully abstract. Many common language features, such as functions of higher type, concurrency, storage allocation and data abstraction, are problematic. This phenomenon was first noticed in connection with a simple applicative programming language, based upon the typed lambda calculus, called PCF (Programming Computable Functions). Plotkin [Plo1] showed that the natural continuous function model of PCF is correct, but not fully abstract, with reference to its standard notion of program equivalence, which is based upon the total evaluation of closed ground terms. This lack of full abstraction is due to the presence of certain "parallel" elements in the model, which are not realized by terms in the programming language. In fact, Plotkin showed that if a "parallel conditional" is added to the language then the continuous function model of this extended language is fully abstract. The problem of finding a natural fully abstract model of the original language is still open, although much progress has been made by Berry, Curien and Winskel [BerCurLév]. A byproduct of their work is the *sequential algorithms* model of PCF [BerCur], which is fully abstract with reference to an alternative notion of program equivalence that is sensitive to the order and extent of evaluation of function arguments. See [BerCurLév] for an excellent survey of this and other research into the full abstraction problem for PCF.

Other examples of the search for natural fully abstract models can be found in [HenPlo1], which considers a simple parallel programming language, [Abr1] and [Abr2], which treat a nondeterministic applicative language with infinite streams, and [Bro] and [HalMeyTra], which deal with Algol-like languages. Many open problems exist.

The difficulty of finding natural fully abstract models for many programming languages has led to the theoretical study of the conditions under which fully abstract models exist. Proofs of the existence or nonexistence of fully abstract models of programming languages are relative, of course, to what count as models of those languages. Positive results spur on the search for natural models, whereas negative ones indicate that the class of models being considered must be widened.

The study of the existence of fully abstract models can be carried out within the framework of initial algebra semantics [Sco][ADJ1][CouNiv]. Programming language syntax is specified in this framework by many-sorted signatures, whose sorts and operators correspond to the syntactic categories and constructs, respectively, of programming languages, and models are universal algebras whose carriers have certain order-theoretic structure and whose operations preserve that structure. Usually the carriers are taken to be complete partial orders (cpo's) and the operations continuous functions, but it is also possible to work with weaker notions of continuity [AptPlo][Plo2] or to generalize from partial orders to categories [Leh][Abr2]. The meanings assigned by models to iteration and recursion constructs are normally required to be least fixed points of appropriate unary derived operations. For example, the meaning of a while-loop *while E do S od* should be the least fixed point of *if E then S*; – *else skip fi*. Many additional requirements may be set for models of particular programming languages, e.g., extensionality for models of applicative languages.

Positive results are typically proved via term model constructions. Such techniques were first used by Milner, who constructed a fully abstract model of the combinatory logic version of PCF [Mil2]. His construction was simplified and applied to the typed lambda calculus version of PCF by Berry [Ber1]. Similar techniques were used by Hennessy and Plotkin to construct fully abstract models of two variants of CCS [HenPlo2][Hen]. These term model constructions proceed, roughly, as follows. One designates certain terms as "semantically finite", orders them by the language's notion of program ordering, and then makes them into an $\omega$-algebraic cpo, using the familiar ideal completion. An algebra is then defined using this cpo as its carrier. In Berry's construction, the syntactic projections $\Psi_n M$ of arbitrary terms $M$ are taken as the semantically finite terms.

Recently, Mulmuley has considered the problem of connecting the continuous function model of the combinatory logic version of PCF with Milner's fully abstract model [Mul]. Using operationally defined inclusive predicates, he defines a fully abstract model as a retract of the complete lattices version of the continuous function model and then removes the top elements from this model, thus yielding Milner's model. In this ingenious construction the unwanted, parallel functions are retracted either to wanted, sequential ones or to the top elements. Thus the technique is not applicable to the usual continuous function model, which is based instead upon cpo's; since the complete lattices model is less abstract than the cpo model [Plo1], this may be seen as a disadvantage. In addition, Mulmuley's retraction does not preserve function application, and thus is not a homomorphism of algebras, and his retract model is not a combinatory algebra, because of the interaction between the $K$ combinators and the top elements.

The first negative result was proved by Apt and Plotkin [AptPlo] for a nondeterministic imperative programming language with random assignment, i.e., the facility for choosing an arbitrary natural number and assigning it to a variable. They prove that there does not exist a fully abstract model that is based upon cpo's and continuous functions for this language. This is because there are programs (such as the one that chooses a natural number and then decrements it until it becomes zero) that always terminate, but whose finite approximations all have the possibility of divergence. They are able, however, to give a natural fully abstract model that is based upon a weaker notion of continuity. Abramsky, following this work, has proved a similar negative result for a nondeterministic applicative programming language with infinite streams [Abr3].

## 1.2 A Theory of Fully Abstract Models

All of the research described above has focused on full abstraction for specific programming languages. In this monograph we try to develop a theory of fully abstract models of programming languages that is applicable to programming languages in general. The goal is to develop a unified framework in which simpler proofs of the existing positive and negative results can be given and new results can be proved. The following paragraphs summarize the contents of the monograph.

We begin by building a mathematical framework for studying full abstraction, based upon initial algebra semantics. As models we take *complete ordered algebras*, i.e., many-sorted universal algebras whose carriers are sort-indexed families of complete partial orders and operations are continuous functions. Following [CouNiv], every signature is required to contain a distinguished nullary operator $\Omega$ of each sort, which stands for divergence or nontermination, and is interpreted as the least element of its sort in every model. Although programming languages rarely contain such constants explicitly, many languages for which divergence is possible in all syntactic categories do contain terms that the constants $\Omega$ can be modelled after, e.g., *while true do skip od*, in some imperative languages. **Chapter 2** consists of the definitions and theorems concerning universal algebras and ordered algebras that will be needed in the sequel. In particular, we prove several quotienting and completion theorems that will be used in term model constructions.

**Chapter 3** is devoted to the definitions and elementary properties of full abstraction and least fixed point models. We consider three kinds of full abstraction (and also correctness): *equational*, *inequational* and *contextual*. The first two are as described above, and the third is the natural generalization of equational full abstraction from ordinary terms to contexts. Formally, notions of program equivalence are congruences over the term algebra, and notions of program ordering are substitutive pre-orderings over the term algebra in which the maximally divergent terms $\Omega$ are least elements. Least fixed point models are intended to assign iteration and recursion constructs meanings that are least fixed points of appropriate unary derived operations. Such requirements are formally expressed in our framework by *families of least fixed point constraints*, which specify that the meanings of certain terms should be least upper bounds of the meanings of certain directed subsets of the ordered term algebra. We also consider contextually least fixed point models, which are the natural generalization of least fixed point models from terms to contexts.

In **chapter 4** we study two programming languages within our framework. The first is the combinatory logic version of PCF, and the second is an imperative language with explicit storage allocation and higher and recursive types, which we call TIE. We give denotational semantics for both of these languages, define notions of program ordering and equivalence as abstractions of these models, in a uniform manner, and show that the models are inequationally correct with reference to these notions of ordering. In contrast, the model of PCF is already known not to be fully abstract, and we conjecture that neither is our model of the second language.

In **chapter 5** we give necessary and sufficient conditions for the existence of correct and fully abstract models, for each of the three kinds of correctness and full abstraction. The condition for the existence of inequationally fully abstract models is the cornerstone of these results. An inequationally fully abstract model of a programming language exists iff its notion of program ordering satisfies the constraints in the closure—under the operations of the term algebra—of its family of least fixed point constraints. Showing the necessity of this condition is straightforward. Its sufficiency is proved via a term model construction: the ordered term algebra is quotiented by the notion of program ordering, and then embedded into a complete ordered algebra in a way that preserves the least upper bounds corresponding to the constraints in the closure of the family of least fixed point constraints. The chapter concludes with several theorems concerning the existence of initial objects and the nonexistence of terminal objects in various categories of models.

**Chapter 6** consists of simplified proofs of the negative results of [AptPlo] and [Abr3], using the condition for the existence of equationally fully abstract models given in chapter 5. Although our theory is directly applicable to Abramsky's nondeterministic applicative language with streams, we prefer to work instead with a nondeterministic imperative language with infinite output streams. Since the streams of our language are unreadable, in contrast to those of Abramsky's language, we achieve a slight sharpening of his result. The notions of program equivalence for the languages of this chapter are defined via operational semantics, and no model-theoretic reasoning is used in the proofs of the negative results.

In **chapter 7**, we investigate two approaches to obtaining fully abstract models from correct ones. In the first, we use the condition for the existence of inequationally fully abstract models given in chapter 5 in order to develop useful necessary and sufficient conditions involving the existence of correct models. In the second, we consider the possibility of collapsing correct models, via continuous homomorphisms, to fully abstract ones. We show that this is not always possible—indeed the natural continuous function model of PCF provides a counterexample—but give sufficient conditions for its possibility. Both of these approaches yield fully abstract models for the languages introduced in chapter 4, and, more generally, for languages whose notions of program ordering and equivalence are defined as abstractions of models using the technique of chapter 4. In the case of PCF, we are able to continuously collapse the reachable inductive subalgebra of the continuous function model to Milner's fully abstract model, thus providing a pleasing, algebraic solution to Mulmuley's problem of relating these models.

Finally, in **chapter 8**, we consider the limitations of the monograph and the corresponding possibilities for further research.

# 2 Universal Algebras and Ordered Algebras

This chapter introduces the definitions and theorems concerning universal algebras and ordered algebras that are the basis of the monograph. We begin, in section 2.1, by describing the (mostly standard) conventions of notation and terminology that will be followed in the sequel.

Sections 2.2 and 2.3 deal with the basics of many-sorted algebras and ordered algebras, respectively. Most of the definitions and theorems in these sections are both standard and straightforward and detailed references will not be given. Those readers who are interested in the history of these ideas are referred to [Grä], for the universal algebra, and [Sco], [ADJ1], [CouNiv] and [Nel], for the work on ordered algebras. The exception to this is the definition and treatment of "unary-substitutive pre-orderings", which I believe to be new (see definition 2.2.23).

Section 2.4 consists of a completion theorem and two quotienting theorems for ordered algebras. The completion theorem is a variation of that of [CouRao] and concerns the embedding of ordered algebras into complete ordered algebras in such a way that *certain* existing least upper bounds are preserved. For our results in chapters 5 and 7 we must preserve sets of existing least upper bounds that cannot be described by the usual families of subsets [CouRao] (subset systems in the terminology of [ADJ2] and [Nel]), which are defined uniformly for all ordered algebras. As a result, we work with families of subsets that are associated with individual ordered algebras. The quotienting theorems are taken from [CouNiv] and [CouRao].

## 2.1 Mathematical Conventions

We identify the set of natural numbers $N$ with the ordinal $\omega$, so that $0 = \emptyset$ and $n = \{0, 1, \ldots, n-1\}$, and write $Tr$ for the set $\{tt, ff\}$ of booleans.

Function space formation, $X \to Y$, associates to the right and function application, $f\,a$, to the left. We sometimes write $Y^X$ for $X \to Y$. For $f: X \to Y$ and $X' \subseteq X$, $f\,X'$ is $\{\, f\,x \mid x \in X' \,\} \subseteq Y$, the image of $X'$ under $f$, and $f|X'$ is $\{\, \langle x, y\rangle \in f \mid x \in X' \,\}: X' \to Y$, the restriction of $f$ to $X'$. For a set $X$, $id_X: X \to X$ is the identity function, and for $f: X \to Y$ and $g: Y \to Z$, $g \circ f: X \to Z$ is the composition of $f$ and $g$. The $n$th iterate,

$f^n$, of a function $f: X \to X$ is defined by $f^0 = id_X$ and $f^{n+1} = f \circ f^n$.

For a set $X$, the set $X^\star$ of finite sequences of elements of $X$ is $\bigcup_{n\in\omega} X^n$, and the set $X^\infty$ of finite and infinite sequences of elements of $X$ is $X^\star \cup X^\omega$. For $a \in X^\star$ (respectively, $a \in X^\omega$), $|a|$, the cardinality of $a$, doubles as the length of $a$. Furthermore, $\subseteq$ doubles as the is-a-prefix-of relation on sequences. We write $\langle x_1, \ldots, x_n \rangle$ for elements of $X^n \subseteq X^\star$; in particular, $\langle\,\rangle = \emptyset \in X^0$ is the empty sequence. For $a \in X^\star$ and $b \in X^\star$ (respectively, $b \in X^\omega$), the concatenation of $a$ and $b$, $a\,b \in X^\star$ (respectively, $a\,b \in X^\omega$), is

$$a \cup \{\, \langle n + |a|, x \rangle \mid \langle n, x \rangle \in b \,\}.$$

The product $D_1 \times \cdots \times D_n$ of sets $D_1, \ldots, D_n$, $n \geq 0$, is $\{\, \langle d_1, \ldots, d_n \rangle \mid d_i \in D_i \,\}$. Thus, if $n = 0$ then $D_1 \times \cdots \times D_n = \{\langle\,\rangle\}$. The projection functions $\pi_i: D_1 \times \cdots \times D_n \to D_i$, $1 \leq i \leq n$, are defined by $\pi_i \langle d_1, \ldots, d_n \rangle = d_i$. More generally, the product $\prod_{x\in X} A_x$ of an $X$-indexed family of sets $A$ is

$$\{\, \rho: X \to \bigcup_{x\in X} A_x \mid \rho\, x \in A_x, \text{ for all } x \in X \,\}.$$

The projection functions $\pi_x: \prod_{x\in X} A_x \to A_x$ are defined by $\pi_x\, \rho = \rho\, x$, and we often write $\rho[x]$ for $\pi_x\, \rho$. For $x \in X$,

$$-[-/x]: (\prod_{x\in X} A_x) \times A_x \to (\prod_{x\in X} A_x)$$

is defined by

$$\pi_y\, \rho[a/x] = \begin{cases} a & \text{if } y = x, \\ (\pi_y\, \rho) & \text{otherwise.} \end{cases}$$

We write $\mathcal{P} X$ for the powerset of a set $X$, i.e., the set of all subsets of $X$.

A binary relation over a set is a pre-ordering iff it is reflexive and transitive, a partial ordering iff it is an antisymmetric pre-ordering, and an equivalence relation iff it is a symmetric pre-ordering. If $R$ is a relation over $X$ then we write $R^\star$ for the reflexive-transitive closure of $R$. If $\leq$ is a pre-ordering then we write $\geq$ for its inverse ($x \geq y$ iff $y \leq x$). Other examples of the notation for inverses are $\succeq$ for $\preceq$ and $\geq_f$ for $\leq_f$. Note that the inverse is not always the exact mirror image of the original ordering. If $\equiv$ is an equivalence relation over $X$ then $X/{\equiv}$, the quotient of $X$ by $\equiv$, is $\{\, [x]_\equiv \mid x \in X \,\}$, where $[x]_\equiv$, the $\equiv$-equivalence class of $x$, is $\{\, x' \in X \mid x' \equiv x \,\}$. Sometimes we drop the relation $\equiv$ from $[x]_\equiv$.

As we will make extensive use of many-sorted algebras, we will frequently need to manipulate families of (structured) sets. Many operations and concepts extend naturally from sets to families of sets, in a pointwise manner. For example, if $A$ and $B$ are $X$-indexed families of sets, i.e., functions with domain $X$, then a function $f: A \to B$ is an $X$-indexed family of functions $f_x: A_x \to B_x$, $x \in X$; $A \subseteq B$ iff $A_x \subseteq B_x$, for all $x \in X$; and $(A \cap B)_x = A_x \cap B_x$, for all $x \in X$. We will make use of these and other such extensions without explicit comment.

We often give *inductive definitions* of sets, i.e., we define a set $X$ to be the least set (under the subset relation) satisfying certain closure conditions. A proof by *induction over* $X$ of a proposition $\forall x \in X\, \phi(x)$ consists of showing that the set $Y = \{\, x \in X \mid \phi(x) \,\}$ satisfies the closure conditions, since, by the leastness of $X$, we can then conclude that $Y = X$. Induction over the natural numbers and structural induction over term algebras (see definition 2.2.5) are special cases of this general principle.

## 2.2 Many-Sorted Algebras

This section contains the definitions and results concerning many-sorted algebras that will be used in the sequel. We begin with the definitions of signatures, algebras, homomorphisms and subalgebras. The initial or term algebra is then defined, followed by the definition of reachability. Substitutive and $\Omega$-least pre-orderings over algebras are then considered. Next, derived operations are introduced, leading to the important notion of unary-substitutive pre-orderings. Several results relating unary-substitutivity and substitutivity then follow, and the section concludes with two lemmas concerning the relations over the term algebra that are induced by relations over algebras.

**Definition 2.2.1** A *signature* $\Sigma$ consists of a set of *sorts* $S$, a set of *operators* $\Sigma$, and a function from $\Sigma$ to $(S^* \times S)$, which assigns *types* to operators. We write $s_1 \times \cdots \times s_n \to s'$ for $n$-ary types $\langle\langle s_1, \ldots, s_n \rangle, s' \rangle$; unary types $\langle\langle s_1 \rangle, s' \rangle$ are written $s_1 \to s'$, and nullary types $\langle\langle\,\rangle, s'\rangle$ as $s'$. In addition, each signature contains a distinguished nullary operator $\Omega_s$ of type $s$, for each $s \in S$. We often drop the sort $s$ from $\Omega_s$.

The operators $\Omega_s$ may be thought of as representing divergence or nontermination.

**Definition 2.2.2** A $\Sigma$-*algebra* $\mathcal{A}$ is an $S$-indexed family of sets $A$ (the *carrier* of $\mathcal{A}$) together with an *operation* $\sigma_{\mathcal{A}}: A_{s_1} \times \cdots \times A_{s_n} \to A_{s'}$, for each $\sigma \in \Sigma$ of type $s_1 \times \cdots \times s_n \to s'$. A *homomorphism* $h: \mathcal{A} \to \mathcal{B}$ over algebras is a function $h: A \to B$ such that for all $\sigma \in \Sigma$ of type $s_1 \times \cdots \times s_n \to s'$,

$$h_{s'}\, \sigma_{\mathcal{A}}\langle a_1, \ldots, a_n \rangle = \sigma_{\mathcal{B}}\langle h_{s_1}\, a_1, \ldots, h_{s_n}\, a_n \rangle,$$

for all $a_i \in A_{s_i}$, $1 \leq i \leq n$.

We use uppercase script letters ($\mathcal{A}$, $\mathcal{B}$, etc.) to denote algebras and the corresponding italic letters ($A$, $B$, etc.) to stand for their carriers. We often drop the algebra $\mathcal{A}$ from $\sigma_{\mathcal{A}}$, and write $\sigma$, $\sigma\, a$ and $a_1\, \sigma\, a_2$, instead of $\sigma\langle\rangle$, $\sigma\langle a\rangle$ and $\sigma\langle a_1, a_2\rangle$, for nullary, unary and binary operations, respectively. As usual, if $\Phi(-)$ is an operation on algebras then we write $\Phi(A)$ for the carrier of $\Phi(\mathcal{A})$.

**Definition 2.2.3** For algebras $\mathcal{A}$ and $\mathcal{B}$, $\mathcal{A}$ is a *subalgebra* of $\mathcal{B}$ iff $A \subseteq B$ and for all $\sigma \in \Sigma$ of type $s_1 \times \cdots \times s_n \rightarrow s'$ and $a_i \in A_{s_i}$, $1 \leq i \leq n$,

$$\sigma_{\mathcal{A}}\langle a_1, \ldots, a_n\rangle = \sigma_{\mathcal{B}}\langle a_1, \ldots, a_n\rangle.$$

If $\mathcal{A}$ is an algebra and $B \subseteq A$ then by *$B$ is a subalgebra of $\mathcal{A}$* we mean that $B$ is closed under the operations of $\mathcal{A}$. We write $\mathcal{A} \subseteq \mathcal{B}$ for $\mathcal{A}$ is a subalgebra of $\mathcal{B}$.

A consequence of this definition is that $\mathcal{A}$ is a subalgebra of $\mathcal{B}$ iff $A \subseteq B$ and the inclusion map from $A$ to $B$ is a homomorphism from $\mathcal{A}$ to $\mathcal{B}$. Note that the $\subseteq$ relation over the class of algebras is a partial ordering.

**Definition 2.2.4** If $f \colon \mathcal{A} \rightarrow \mathcal{B}$ is a homomorphism then $f\, \mathcal{A}$, the *subalgebra of $\mathcal{B}$ induced by $f$*, consists of $f\, A$, together with the restrictions of the operations of $\mathcal{B}$ to $f\, A$.

The set $f\, A$ is closed under the operations of $\mathcal{B}$, since if $\sigma \in \Sigma$ has type $s_1 \times \cdots \times s_n \rightarrow s'$ and $a_i \in A_{s_i}$, $1 \leq i \leq n$, then

$$\sigma_{\mathcal{B}}\langle f_{s_1}\, a_1, \ldots, f_{s_n}\, a_n\rangle = f_{s'}\, \sigma_{\mathcal{A}}\langle a_1, \ldots, a_n\rangle.$$

Note that $f$ is also a homomorphism from $\mathcal{A}$ to $f\, \mathcal{A}$.

**Definition 2.2.5** We define the *term algebra* $\mathcal{T}_\Sigma$ (or simply $\mathcal{T}$) as follows. Its carrier $T$ is least such that if $\sigma \in \Sigma$ has type $s_1 \times \cdots \times s_n \rightarrow s'$ and $t_i \in T_{s_i}$, $1 \leq i \leq n$, then $\langle\sigma, \langle t_1, \ldots, t_n\rangle\rangle \in T_{s'}$. If $\sigma \in \Sigma$ has type $s_1 \times \cdots \times s_n \rightarrow s'$ then the operation $\sigma_{\mathcal{T}}$ is defined by $\sigma_{\mathcal{T}}\langle t_1, \ldots, t_n\rangle = \langle\sigma, \langle t_1, \ldots, t_n\rangle\rangle$.

A standard result then easily follows.

**Lemma 2.2.6** *The term algebra $\mathcal{T}$ is initial in the category of algebras and homomorphisms.* $\square$

**Definition 2.2.7** For an algebra $\mathcal{A}$, we write $M_{\mathcal{A}}$ (or simply $M$) for the unique homomorphism from $\mathcal{T}$ to $\mathcal{A}$. An element $a \in A_s$, $s \in S$, is *denotable* iff there exists a term $t \in T_s$ such that $M_s\, t = a$.

Here $M$ stands for "meaning" and can be thought of as the meaning or semantic function from syntax to semantics. An easy application of lemma 2.2.6 is that $M_{\mathcal{A}\,s}\, t = M_{\mathcal{B}\,s}\, t$, for all $t \in T_s$, $s \in S$, if $\mathcal{A}$ is a subalgebra of $\mathcal{B}$.

**Definition 2.2.8** An algebra $\mathcal{A}$ is *reachable* iff $M_{\mathcal{A}}\, \mathcal{T} = \mathcal{A}$, i.e., every element of $A$ is denotable.

An equivalent definition is that an algebra is reachable iff it has no proper subalgebras. An obvious consequence of this definition is that $\mathcal{T}$ itself is reachable.

We now consider several kinds of relations over algebras.

**Definition 2.2.9** If $\mathcal{A}$ is an algebra and $R$ is a relation over $A$ then $R$ is *substitutive* iff the operations of $\mathcal{A}$ respect $R$: for all $\sigma \in \Sigma$ of type $s_1 \times \cdots \times s_n \to s'$ and $a_i, a'_i \in A_{s_i}$, $1 \leq i \leq n$,

$$\text{if } a_i\, R_{s_i}\, a'_i, 1 \leq i \leq n, \text{ then } \sigma\langle a_1, \ldots, a_n\rangle\, R_{s'}\, \sigma\langle a'_1, \ldots, a'_n\rangle.$$

As usual, substitutive equivalence relations are called *congruences.*

It is easy to see that if $\leq$ is a substitutive pre-ordering over $\mathcal{A}$ then $\leq \cap \geq$ is a congruence. Note that if $R$ is a substitutive pre-ordering (respectively, partial ordering, equivalence relation) over $\mathcal{A}$, and $\mathcal{B}$ is a subalgebra of $\mathcal{A}$, then the restriction of $R$ to $B$ is a substitutive pre-ordering (respectively, partial ordering, equivalence relation) over $\mathcal{B}$.

**Definition 2.2.10** If $f: D \to E$ is a function over sets then the *equivalence relation over $D$ induced by $f$*, $\equiv_f$, is defined by: $d_1 \equiv_f d_2$ iff $f\, d_1 = f\, d_2$.

If $f: \mathcal{A} \to \mathcal{B}$ is a homomorphism then $\equiv_f$ is clearly a congruence over $\mathcal{A}$. We make use of this definition in giving the next one.

**Definition 2.2.11** For an algebra $\mathcal{A}$, the *congruence over $\mathcal{T}$ induced by $\mathcal{A}$*, $\approx_{\mathcal{A}}$, is $\equiv_{M_{\mathcal{A}}}$.

Note that if $\mathcal{A} \subseteq \mathcal{B}$ then $\approx_{\mathcal{A}} = \approx_{\mathcal{B}}$.

**Definition 2.2.12** If $\mathcal{A}$ is an algebra and $R$ is a pre-ordering over $A$ then $R$ is *$\Omega$-least* iff for all $s \in S$ and $a \in A_s$, $\Omega_s\, R_s\, a$.

We will extensively use both $\Omega$-least substitutive pre-orderings and congruences. Note that if $\mathcal{A}$ is an algebra and $R$ is a relation over $A$ then there is a least $\Omega$-least substitutive pre-ordering containing $R$, as well as a least congruence containing $R$.

As there are no constraints concerning the $\Omega$ operations on congruences, it is not surprising that not every congruence is induced by an $\Omega$-least substitutive pre-ordering, as the next lemma shows.

**Lemma 2.2.13** *There is a signature $\Sigma$ and a congruence $\approx$ over $\mathcal{T}$ such that there is no $\Omega$-least substitutive pre-ordering $\preceq$ over $\mathcal{T}$ with the property that $\approx = \preceq \cap \succeq$.*

**Proof.** Let $\Sigma$ over $S = \{0,1\}$ have the following operators:

(i) $\Omega_0$ and $a$ of type 0;

(ii) $\Omega_1$ of type 1; and

(iii) $f$ of type $0 \to 1$.

Let $\approx$ be the least congruence over $\mathcal{T}$ with the property that $\Omega_1 \approx_1 f\,a$. Then, no other unequal terms are congruent.

Suppose, towards a contradiction, that a $\preceq$ as in the statement of the lemma exists. Then

$$\Omega_1 \preceq_1 f\,\Omega_o \preceq_1 f\,a \preceq_1 \Omega_1,$$

showing that $\Omega_1 \approx_1 f\,\Omega_0$—a contradiction. $\square$

We now consider derived operators, which are defined via the free algebra over a set of generators.

**Definition 2.2.14** For an $S$-indexed family $X$ of disjoint sets of *context variables* not occurring in $\Sigma$, $\Sigma(X)$ is the signature formed by adding nullary operators $x$ of type $s$, for each $x \in X_s$, $s \in S$, to $\Sigma$. The $\Sigma$-algebra $\mathcal{T}_\Sigma(X)$ (or simply $\mathcal{T}(X)$) is the restriction of $\mathcal{T}_{\Sigma(X)}$ to a $\Sigma$-algebra. For $x \in X_s$, we simply write $x$ for $\langle x, \langle\rangle\rangle \in T(X)_s$.

We often use the letter $c$, for "context", to stand for elements of $T(X)$. The standard result that $\mathcal{T}(X)$ is the *free algebra generated by* $X$ now easily follows.

**Lemma 2.2.15** *Define $f: X \to T(X)$ by $f_s x = x$. If $\mathcal{A}$ is an algebra and $g: X \to A$ then there exists a unique homomorphism $h: \mathcal{T}(X) \to \mathcal{A}$ such that $g = h \circ f$:*

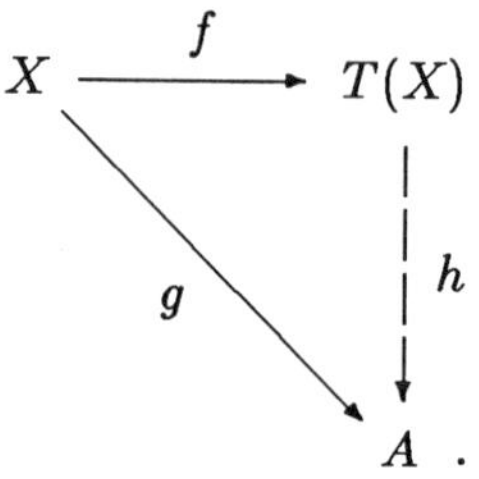


□

**Definition 2.2.16** For a signature $\Sigma$, $V_\Sigma$ (or simply $V$) is an $S$-indexed family of disjoint, countably-infinite sets of *context variables* not occurring in $\Sigma$. We often view a set $Y$ of variables ($Y \subseteq \bigcup_{s \in S} V_s$) as the $S$-indexed family of variables $Y'$ defined by $Y'_s = V_s \cap Y$.

**Definition 2.2.17** A *derived operator* of type $s_1 \times \cdots \times s_n \to s'$ is a pair

$$\langle c, \langle v_1, \ldots, v_n \rangle \rangle,$$

where the $v_i \in V_{s_i}$ are distinct variables and $c \in T(\{v_1, \ldots, v_n\})_{s'}$. We write $c[v_1, \ldots, v_n]$ for derived operators $\langle c, \langle v_1, \ldots, v_n \rangle \rangle$. For an algebra $\mathcal{A}$, the *derived operation*

$$c_{\mathcal{A}}[v_1, \ldots, v_n] \colon A_{s_1} \times \cdots \times A_{s_n} \to A_{s'}$$

is defined by

$$c_{\mathcal{A}}[v_1, \ldots, v_n]\langle a_1, \ldots, a_n \rangle = h_{s'}\, c,$$

where $h \colon \mathcal{T}(\{v_1, \ldots, v_n\}) \to \mathcal{A}$ is defined via lemma 2.2.15, by taking $\{v_1, \ldots, v_n\}$ for $X$ and defining $g$ by $g_{s_i}\, v_i = a_i$, $1 \le i \le n$.

We write $c$ for $c[v_1, \ldots, v_n]$ when the order of the variables is clear from the context, and we often drop the algebra $\mathcal{A}$ from $c_{\mathcal{A}}$. A derived operator $c[v_1, \ldots, v_n]$ of type $s_1 \times \cdots \times s_n \to s'$ is a *projection* iff $c = v_i$ and $s' = s_i$, for some $1 \le i \le n$, and a *constant* iff $c \in T_{s'}$.

The next three lemmas show how derived operators can be constructed from constant and projection derived operators and ordinary operators.

**Lemma 2.2.18** *Suppose $\mathcal{A}$ is an algebra and $a_i \in A_{s_i}$, $1 \le i \le n$.*

(i) *For each projection $v_i[v_1, \ldots, v_n]$ of type $s_1 \times \cdots \times s_n \to s_i$,*

$$v_{i\mathcal{A}}\, \langle a_1, \ldots, a_n \rangle = a_i.$$

(ii) *For each constant* $t[v_1, \ldots, v_n]$ *of type* $s_1 \times \cdots \times s_n \to s'$,

$$t_{\mathcal{A}}\langle a_1, \ldots, a_n\rangle = M_{s'}\, t.$$

**Proof.** (i) is immediate from definition 2.2.17, and (ii) is a simple structural induction over $T$. □

**Lemma 2.2.19** *If* $\sigma \in \Sigma$ *has type* $s_1 \times \cdots \times s_n \to s$, $c_i[v_1, \ldots, v_m]$, $1 \leq i \leq n$, *are derived operators of type* $s'_1 \times \cdots \times s'_m \to s_i$, $\mathcal{A}$ *is an algebra and* $a_j \in A_{s'_j}$, $1 \leq j \leq m$, *then*

$$(\sigma_{T(\{v_1,\ldots,v_m\})}\langle c_1, \ldots, c_n\rangle)[v_1, \ldots, v_m]$$

*is a derived operator of type* $s'_1 \times \cdots \times s'_m \to s$ *and*

$$(\sigma\langle c_1, \ldots, c_n\rangle)_{\mathcal{A}}\langle a_1, \ldots, a_m\rangle = \sigma_{\mathcal{A}}\langle c_{1\mathcal{A}}\langle a_1, \ldots, a_m\rangle, \ldots, c_{n\mathcal{A}}\langle a_1, \ldots, a_m\rangle\rangle.$$

**Proof.** Immediate from definition 2.2.17. □

**Lemma 2.2.20** *If* $c[v_1, \ldots, v_n]$ *is a derived operator of type* $s_1 \times \cdots \times s_n \to s$, $c_i[v'_1, \ldots, v'_m]$, $1 \leq i \leq n$, *are derived operators of type* $s'_1 \times \cdots \times s'_m \to s_i$, $\mathcal{A}$ *is an algebra and* $a_j \in A_{s'_j}$, $1 \leq j \leq m$, *then*

$$(c_{T(\{v'_1,\ldots,v'_m\})}\langle c_1, \ldots, c_n\rangle)[v'_1, \ldots, v'_m]$$

*is a derived operator of type* $s'_1 \times \cdots \times s'_m \to s$ *and*

$$(c\langle c_1, \ldots, c_n\rangle)_{\mathcal{A}}\langle a_1, \ldots, a_m\rangle = c_{\mathcal{A}}\langle c_{1\mathcal{A}}\langle a_1, \ldots, a_m\rangle, \ldots, c_{n\mathcal{A}}\langle a_1, \ldots, a_m\rangle\rangle.$$

**Proof.** An easy structural induction over $T(\{v_1, \ldots, v_n\})$. □

Two standard lemmas concerning derived operations now follow.

**Lemma 2.2.21** *Homomorphisms preserve derived operations and derived operations respect substitutive pre-orderings.*

**Proof.** Both parts of the lemma are easy structural inductions over $T(X)$, for appropriate sets of variables $X$. □

**Lemma 2.2.22** *If* $\mathcal{A}$ *is a subalgebra of* $\mathcal{B}$ *then for all derived operators* $c[v_1, \ldots, v_n]$ *of type* $s_1 \times \cdots \times s_n \to s'$ *and* $a_i \in A_{s_i}$, $1 \leq i \leq n$,

$$c_{\mathcal{A}}\langle a_1, \ldots, a_n\rangle = c_{\mathcal{B}}\langle a_1, \ldots, a_n\rangle.$$

**Proof.** Immediate from lemma 2.2.21 and the fact that the inclusion map from $A$ to $B$ is a homomorphism from $\mathcal{A}$ to $\mathcal{B}$. $\square$

It is now possible to define a weaker notion of substitutivity that, as we shall see, arises naturally.

**Definition 2.2.23** If $\mathcal{A}$ is an algebra and $R$ is a pre-ordering over $A$ then $R$ is *unary-substitutive* iff all unary derived operations respect $R$: for all derived operators $c[v]$ of type $s \to s'$ and $a, a' \in A_s$,

$$\text{if } a\, R_s\, a' \text{ then } c\langle a\rangle\, R_{s'}\, c\langle a'\rangle.$$

We could, of course, define the notion of *n-substitutive* pre-orderings, which would be respected by $n$-ary derived operations, but we have no use for this generality in the sequel.

A consequence of lemma 2.2.22 is that if $R$ is a unary-substitutive pre-ordering (respectively, partial ordering, equivalence relation) over $\mathcal{A}$, and $\mathcal{B}$ is a subalgebra of $\mathcal{A}$, then the restriction of $R$ to $B$ is a unary-substitutive pre-ordering (respectively, partial ordering, equivalence relation) over $\mathcal{B}$. If $\leq$ is a unary-substitutive pre-ordering over an algebra $\mathcal{A}$ then $(\leq \cap \geq)$ is a unary-substitutive equivalence relation over $\mathcal{A}$.

We now define an operation that will be employed in the definitions of notions of program ordering and equivalence of chapters 4 and 6.

**Definition 2.2.24** If $P \subseteq S$, $\mathcal{A}$ is an algebra and $R$ is a pre-ordering over $A|P$ then $R^c$, the *contextualization* of $R$, is the relation over $A$ defined by: $a\, R^c_s\, a'$ iff $c\langle a\rangle\, R_p\, c\langle a'\rangle$, for all derived operators $c[v]$ of type $s \to p$, $p \in P$. If $R$ is a pre-ordering over $A$ then $P$ will implicitly be $S$ in the definition of $R^c$.

Subsets $P \subseteq S$ can be thought of as consisting of program sorts, and derived operators $c[v]$ of type $s \to p$ as program contexts. Thus if $R$ is a relation over $T|P$ (programs) then two terms are related by $R^c$ iff they are related by $R$ in all program contexts.

The next lemma shows that, as might be guessed, $R^c$ is always a unary-substitutive pre-ordering.

**Lemma 2.2.25** *If $P \subseteq S$, $\mathcal{A}$ is an algebra and $R$ is a pre-ordering (respectively, equivalence relation) over $A|P$ then $R^c$ is the greatest unary-substitutive pre-ordering (respectively, equivalence relation) over $\mathcal{A}$ whose restriction to $P$ is included in $R$.*

**Proof.** It is easy to see that $R^c$ is a pre-ordering over $A$ and that it is symmetric if $R$ is symmetric. The inclusion of the restriction of $R^c$ to $P$ in $R$ follows from the existence of projection derived operators $v[v]$ of type $p \to p$, for all $p \in P$. Next, we show that $R^c$ is unary-substitutive. Suppose $a_1 \, R^c_s \, a_2$ and $c[v]$ is a derived operator of type $s \to s'$. We must show that $c\langle a_1 \rangle \, R^c_{s'} \, c\langle a_2 \rangle$. Let $p \in P$ and $c'[v']$ be a derived operator of type $s' \to p$. Then, $(c'\langle c \rangle)[v]$ is a derived operator of type $s \to p$ and

$$c'\langle c\langle a_1 \rangle\rangle = (c'\langle c \rangle)\langle a_1 \rangle \; R_p \; (c'\langle c \rangle)\langle a_2 \rangle = c'\langle c\langle a_2 \rangle\rangle,$$

by lemma 2.2.20, and by the assumption that $a_1 \, R^c_s \, a_2$. Finally, suppose $R'$ is a unary-substitutive pre-ordering (respectively, equivalence relation) over $\mathcal{A}$ whose restriction to $P$ is included in $R$; we must show that $R' \subseteq R^c$. Let $a_1 \, R'_s \, a_2$. If $p \in P$ and $c[v]$ is a derived operator of type $s \to p$ then $c\langle a_1 \rangle \, R'_p \, c\langle a_2 \rangle$, and thus $c\langle a_1 \rangle \, R_p \, c\langle a_2 \rangle$. Thus $a_1 \, R^c_s \, a_2$, as required. □

It is easy to see that if $P \subseteq S$, $\mathcal{A}$ is an algebra and $\leq$ is a pre-ordering over $A|P$ then $(\leq \cap \geq)^c = (\leq^c \cap \geq^c)$.

**Lemma 2.2.26** *If $\equiv$ is a unary-substitutive equivalence relation over an algebra $\mathcal{A}$ and $\leq$ is a pre-ordering over $A$ that induces $\equiv$ then $\leq^c$ also induces $\equiv$.*

**Proof.** Since $\leq^c \subseteq \leq$, $\leq^c \cap \geq^c \subseteq \equiv$. For the opposite inclusion, suppose $a_1 \equiv_s a_2$, $s \in S$. To show that $a_1 \leq^c_s a_2$, let $c[v]$ be a derived operator of type $s \to s'$. Then $c\langle a_1 \rangle \equiv_{s'} c\langle a_2 \rangle$, since $\equiv$ is unary-substitutive, and thus $c\langle a_1 \rangle \leq_{s'} c\langle a_2 \rangle$. Similarly, $a_2 \leq^c_s a_1$. □

The next lemma shows that, as mentioned above, unary-substitutivity is weaker than substitutivity. In fact there is even a unary-substitutive equivalence relation over an algebra such that every congruence over that algebra induces a different pre-ordering over $T$.

**Lemma 2.2.27** *There is a signature $\Sigma$, an algebra $\mathcal{A}$ and an $\Omega$-least unary-substitutive pre-ordering $\leq$ over $\mathcal{A}$ such that:*

(i) *$\leq$ is not substitutive;*

(ii) *The unary-substitutive equivalence relation $\equiv = \leq \cap \geq$ is not substitutive; and*

(iii) *There does not exist a congruence $\equiv'$ over $\mathcal{A}$ such that*

$$M_s \, t_1 \equiv_s M_s \, t_2 \text{ iff } M_s \, t_1 \equiv'_s M_s \, t_2,$$

*for all $t_1, t_2 \in T_s$, $s \in S$.*

**Proof.** Let $\Sigma$ over $S = \{0, 1, 2\}$ have the following operators:

(i) $\Omega_0$ of type 0;

(ii) $\Omega_1$, $x$ and $y$ of type 1;

(iii) $\Omega_2$ and $z$ of type 2; and

(iv) $+$ of type $0 \times 1 \rightarrow 2$.

Define the algebra $\mathcal{A}$ as follows. Its carrier $A$ is defined by $A_0 = \{\Omega_0, w\}$, $A_1 = \{\Omega_1, x, y\}$ and $A_2 = \{\Omega_2, z\}$. All of the nullary operations have themselves as their values. The operation $+$ is bistrict with reference to the $\Omega$'s, i.e., $a + a' = \Omega_2$ if $a = \Omega_0$ or $a' = \Omega_1$; on non-$\Omega$ elements, it is defined by $w + x = z$ and $w + y = \Omega_2$. Note that the element $w$ of $A_0$ is not denotable. Let $\leq$ be the least $\Omega$-least pre-ordering over $\mathcal{A}$ such that $x \leq_1 y \leq_1 x$:

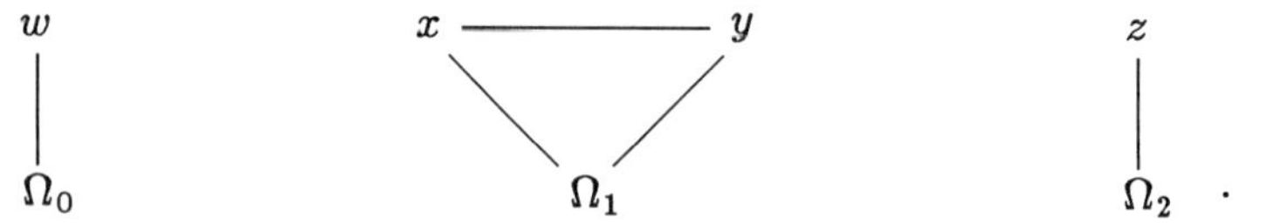


Clearly the constant and projection unary derived operations respect $\leq$. This leaves $(v + \Omega_1)[v]$, $(v + x)[v]$ and $(v + y)[v]$ of type $0 \rightarrow 2$ and $(\Omega_0 + v')[v']$ of type $1 \rightarrow 2$. Since $+$ is bistrict, $v + \Omega_1$ and $\Omega_0 + v'$ respect $\leq$. The unary-substitutivity of $\leq$ then follows, since

$$\Omega_0 + x = \Omega_2 \leq_2 z = w + x$$

and

$$\Omega_0 + y = \Omega_2 \leq_2 \Omega_2 = w + y.$$

(i) will follow immediately from (ii), and (ii) immediately from (iii). For (iii), suppose that such an $\equiv'$ exists. Then,

$$\begin{aligned} x \equiv_1 y \;&\Rightarrow\; x \equiv'_1 y \\ &\Rightarrow\; z = w + x \equiv'_2 w + y = \Omega_2 \\ &\Rightarrow\; z \equiv_2 \Omega_2, \end{aligned}$$

which is a contradiction. □

As might be guessed from the proof of the previous lemma, a sufficient (but not necessary) condition for a unary-substitutive pre-ordering over an algebra to be substitutive is that the algebra be reachable. As an aid toward proving this, we first give a characterization of substitutivity, which will also be used in section 2.3.

**Lemma 2.2.28** *Let $\mathcal{A}$ be an algebra and $R$ a pre-ordering over $A$. Then, $R$ is substitutive iff for all derived operators $c[v, v_1, \ldots, v_n]$ of type $s \times s_1 \times \cdots \times s_n \to s'$, $n \geq 0$, and $a, a' \in A_s$, if $a \, R_s \, a'$ then*

$$c\langle a, a_1, \ldots, a_n\rangle \, R_{s'} \, c\langle a', a_1, \ldots, a_n\rangle, \text{ for all } a_i \in A_{s_i}, 1 \leq i \leq n.$$

**Proof.** The "only if" direction follows from lemma 2.2.21 and the reflexivity of $R$. For the "if" direction, suppose $\sigma \in \Sigma$ has type $s_1 \times \cdots \times s_n \to s'$, and $a_i, a_i' \in A_{s_i}$ have the property that $a_i \, R_{s_i} \, a_i'$, $1 \leq i \leq n$. We must show that

$$\sigma\langle a_1, \ldots, a_n\rangle \; R_{s'} \; \sigma\langle a_1', \ldots, a_n'\rangle.$$

If $n = 0$ then $\sigma \, R_{s'} \, \sigma$, since $R$ is reflexive; so, assume that $n \geq 1$. Since $R$ is transitive, it is sufficient to show that

$$\begin{aligned} \sigma\langle a_1, \ldots, a_n\rangle \;\; & R_{s'} \;\; \sigma\langle a_1', a_2, \ldots, a_n\rangle \\ & R_{s'} \;\; \sigma\langle a_1', a_2', a_3, \ldots, a_n\rangle \\ & \vdots \\ & R_{s'} \;\; \sigma\langle a_1', \ldots, a_n'\rangle. \end{aligned}$$

We show a representative step in this chain:

$$\sigma\langle a_1', \ldots, a_{i-1}', a_i, a_{i+1}, \ldots, a_n\rangle \; R_{s'} \; \sigma\langle a_1', \ldots, a_{i-1}', a_i', a_{i+1}, \ldots, a_n\rangle.$$

Let $v_i \in V_{s_i}$, $1 \leq i \leq n$, be distinct variables. Then,

$$(\sigma\langle v_1, \ldots, v_n\rangle)[v_i, v_1, \ldots, v_{i-1}, v_{i+1}, \ldots, v_n]$$

is a derived operator of type

$$s_i \times s_1 \times \cdots \times s_{i-1} \times s_{i+1} \times \cdots \times s_n \to s',$$

and thus

$$\begin{aligned} & \sigma\langle a_1', \ldots, a_{i-1}', a_i, a_{i+1}, \ldots, a_n\rangle \\ = \;\; & (\sigma\langle v_1, \ldots, v_n\rangle)\langle a_i, a_1', \ldots, a_{i-1}', a_{i+1}, \ldots, a_n\rangle \\ R_{s'} \;\; & (\sigma\langle v_1, \ldots, v_n\rangle)\langle a_i', a_1', \ldots, a_{i-1}', a_{i+1}, \ldots, a_n\rangle \\ = \;\; & \sigma\langle a_1', \ldots, a_{i-1}', a_i', a_{i+1}, \ldots, a_n\rangle, \end{aligned}$$

since $a_i \, R_{s_i} \, a_i'$. □

**Lemma 2.2.29** *Unary-substitutive pre-orderings over reachable algebras are substitutive.*

**Proof.** Let $R$ be a unary-substitutive pre-ordering over a reachable algebra $\mathcal{A}$. We make use of the characterization of substitutivity given by lemma 2.2.28. Suppose $c[v, v_1, \ldots, v_n]$ is a derived operator of type $s \times s_1 \times \cdots \times s_n \rightarrow s'$, $n \geq 0$, $a, a' \in A_s$, $a_i \in A_{s_i}$, $1 \leq i \leq n$, and $a \, R_s \, a'$. Since $\mathcal{A}$ is reachable, there are $t_i \in T_{s_i}$ such that $a_i = M_{s_i} \, t_i$, $1 \leq i \leq n$. Then, $(c\langle v, t_1, \ldots, t_n \rangle)[v]$ is a derived operator of type $s \rightarrow s'$, and

$$\begin{aligned} c\langle a, a_1, \ldots, a_n \rangle &= (c\langle v, t_1, \ldots, t_n \rangle)\langle a \rangle \\ &R_{s'} \; (c\langle v, t_1, \ldots, t_n \rangle)\langle a' \rangle \\ &= c\langle a', a_1, \ldots, a_n \rangle, \end{aligned}$$

since $R$ is unary-substitutive. □

Combining lemmas 2.2.25 and 2.2.29 we have that if $P \subseteq S$, $\mathcal{A}$ is a reachable algebra and $R$ is a pre-ordering (respectively, equivalence relation) over $A|P$ then $R^c$ is the greatest substitutive pre-ordering (respectively, congruence) over $\mathcal{A}$ whose restriction to $P$ is included in $R$.

This section concludes with two lemmas concerning the relations over $T$ that are induced by relations over the carriers of algebras.

**Lemma 2.2.30** *Suppose $P \subseteq S$, $\mathcal{A}$ is an algebra, $R$ is a pre-ordering over $A|P$, and $Q$ is the pre-ordering over $T|P$ defined by*

$$t_1 \, Q_p \, t_2 \textit{ iff } M_p \, t_1 \, R_p \, M_p \, t_2.$$

*Then $R^c$ is a unary-substitutive pre-ordering over $\mathcal{A}$, $Q^c$ is a substitutive pre-ordering over $\mathcal{T}$, and*

$$t_1 \, Q^c_s \, t_2 \textit{ iff } M_s \, t_1 \, R^c_s \, M_s \, t_2,$$

*for all $t_1, t_2 \in T_s$, $s \in S$.*

**Proof.** The substitutivity of $Q^c$ follows from lemma 2.2.29, and

$$\begin{aligned} t_1 \, Q^c_s \, t_2 \;\; &\text{iff} \;\; c\langle t_1 \rangle \, Q_p \, c\langle t_2 \rangle, \text{ for all } c[v] \text{ of type } s \rightarrow p,\ p \in P \\ &\text{iff} \;\; M_p \, c\langle t_1 \rangle \, R_p \, M_p \, c\langle t_2 \rangle, \text{ for all } c[v] \text{ of type } s \rightarrow p,\ p \in P \\ &\text{iff} \;\; c\langle M_s \, t_1 \rangle \, R_p \, c\langle M_s \, t_2 \rangle, \text{ for all } c[v] \text{ of type } s \rightarrow p,\ p \in P \\ &\text{iff} \;\; M_s \, t_1 \, R^c_s \, M_s \, t_2, \end{aligned}$$

for all $t_1, t_2 \in T_s$, $s \in S$. □

**Lemma 2.2.31** *Suppose $\mathcal{A}$ is an algebra, $R$ is a pre-ordering over $A$, and $Q$ is the pre-ordering over $T$ defined by*

$$t_1 \, Q_s \, t_2 \text{ iff } M_s \, t_1 \, R_s \, M_s \, t_2.$$

(i) *If $R$ is unary-substitutive then $Q$ is substitutive.*

(ii) *If $Q$ is substitutive then*

$$t_1 \, Q_s \, t_2 \text{ iff } M_s \, t_1 \, R_s^c \, M_s \, t_2,$$

*for all $t_1, t_2 \in T_s$, $s \in S$.*

**Proof.** Immediate from lemma 2.2.30, with $P = S$. □

## 2.3 Ordered Algebras

This section consists of the basic definitions and results concerning ordered algebras that will be needed in the sequel. We begin by considering posets, cpo's, continuous functions and inductive pre-orderings. Ordered algebras, complete ordered algebras and inductive subalgebras are then defined, followed by two results concerning the derived operations of ordered algebras, and the definitions of the ordered term algebra and free ordered algebras. Generated inductive subalgebras and inductive reachability are then considered, followed by two lemmas relating substitutivity and unary-substitutivity for complete ordered algebras. The section concludes with two lemmas concerning the pre-orderings over the terms algebra that are induced by inductive pre-orderings over complete ordered algebras.

**Definition 2.3.1** A *pre-ordered set* (*preset*) $P$ is a set $P$, together with a pre-ordering $\sqsubseteq_P$ over $P$. If $p \in P$ and $P' \subseteq P$ then $p$ is an *upper bound* (*ub*) of $P'$ iff $p' \sqsubseteq_P p$, for all $p' \in P'$, and $p$ is a *least upper bound* (*lub*) of $P'$ iff $p$ is an ub of $P'$ and $p \sqsubseteq_P p''$, for all ub's $p''$ of $P'$. We write $P' \sqsubseteq_P p$, for $p$ is an ub of $P'$. A subset $D \subseteq P$ is *directed* iff it is nonempty and every pair of elements of $D$ has an ub in $D$. If $P'' \subseteq P' \subseteq P$ then $P''$ is *cofinal* in $P'$ iff for all $p' \in P'$, there exists a $p'' \in P''$ such that $p' \sqsubseteq_P p''$. A subset $P' \subseteq P$ is *downward-closed* iff for all $p' \in P'$ and $p \in P$, if $p \sqsubseteq_P p'$ then $p \in P'$. We write $down_P(P')$ for $\{ p \in P \mid p \sqsubseteq_P p', \text{for some } p' \in P' \}$, the *downward-closure* of $P'$.

We often drop the $P$ from $\sqsubseteq_P$ and $down_P(P')$ when it is clear from the context.

Equivalently, $D \subseteq P$ is directed iff all finite subsets of $D$ have ub's in $D$. Note that lub's in presets are not necessarily unique.

**Definition 2.3.2** A *partially ordered set* (*poset*) $P$ is a preset such that $\sqsubseteq_P$ is a partial ordering. Such a $P$ is *pointed* iff it contains a least element, $\perp_P$. A pointed poset $P$ is *flat* iff for all $p_1, p_2 \in P$, $p_1 \sqsubseteq_P p_2$ iff $p_1 = \perp_P$ or $p_1 = p_2$. A *complete partial order* (*cpo*) $P$ is a pointed poset with the property that every directed set $D$ of P has a lub $\bigsqcup_P D$ in $P$.

We often drop the $P$ from $\perp_P$ and $\bigsqcup_P$ when it is clear from the context.

Note that all flat pointed posets are cpo's.

**Definition 2.3.3** A function $f: P \to Q$ over posets is *monotonic* iff $f\,p \sqsubseteq_Q f\,p'$ if $p \sqsubseteq_P p'$, an *order-embedding* iff $f\,p \sqsubseteq_Q f\,p'$ iff $p \sqsubseteq_P p'$, and an *order-isomorphism* iff $f$ is a surjective order-embedding. Two posets are *order-isomorphic* iff there is an order-isomorphism from one to the other. A function $f: P \to Q$ over pointed posets is *strict* iff $f \perp_P = \perp_Q$. A function $f: P \to Q$ over cpo's is *continuous* iff it is monotonic and $f \bigsqcup_P D = \bigsqcup_Q f\,D$, for all directed sets $D \subseteq P$.

Note that order-isomorphism coincides with isomorphism in the category of posets and monotonic functions, and that order-isomorphisms over cpo's are continuous.

We could just as well have worked with the larger category of $\omega$-complete partial orders and $\omega$-continuous functions in this monograph. On the other hand, some of our constructions, e.g., the quotienting constructions of section 2.4, do not preserve $\omega$-algebraicity and consistent completeness, and so we cannot work in the smaller category of cpo's with these additional properties.

**Definition 2.3.4** A *pre-ordering* over a poset $\langle P, \sqsubseteq_P \rangle$ is simply a pre-ordering over the set $P$. A pre-ordering $\leq$ over a cpo $\langle P, \sqsubseteq_P \rangle$ is *inductive* iff $\sqsubseteq_P \subseteq \leq$ and whenever $D$ is a directed set in $\langle P, \sqsubseteq_P \rangle$ and $D \leq d$, $\bigsqcup D \leq d$.

Note the requirement that $\leq$ respect the ordering $\sqsubseteq_P$ of $P$.

**Definition 2.3.5** The *product* $P_1 \times \cdots \times P_n$ of posets $P_i$, $1 \leq i \leq n$, $n \geq 0$, is the product of their underlying sets $P_i$, ordered componentwise:

$$\langle p_1, \ldots, p_n \rangle \sqsubseteq \langle p'_1, \ldots, p'_n \rangle \text{ iff } p_i \sqsubseteq p'_i, 1 \leq i \leq n.$$

The projection functions $\pi_i: P_1 \times \cdots \times P_n \to P_i$ are monotonic. A directed set $D \subseteq P_1 \times \cdots \times P_n$ has a lub iff the directed sets $\pi_i\,D$, $1 \leq i \leq n$, have lub's, and $\langle \bigsqcup \pi_1\,D, \ldots, \bigsqcup \pi_n\,D \rangle$ is the lub of $D$, when it exists. Thus, if all of the $P_i$'s are cpo's then so is $P_1 \times \cdots \times P_n$, and the projection functions are continuous. If $D_i \subseteq P_i$, $1 \le i \le n$, are directed sets then so is $D_1 \times \cdots \times D_n$. Finally, if $f\colon P_1 \times \cdots \times P_n \to Q$ is a monotonic function, for cpo's $P_i$, $1 \le i \le n$, and $Q$, then $f$ is continuous iff for all directed sets $D_i \subseteq P_i$, $1 \le i \le n$,

$$f\langle \bigsqcup D_1, \ldots, \bigsqcup D_n \rangle = \bigsqcup f(D_1 \times \cdots \times D_n).$$

**Definition 2.3.6** If $P$ and $Q$ are cpo's then $[P \to Q]$ is the cpo of *continuous functions* from $P$ to $Q$, with the pointwise ordering:

$$f \sqsubseteq g \text{ iff for all } p \in P, f\,p \sqsubseteq g\,p.$$

The constantly $\bot$ function is the least element of $[P \to Q]$ and if $F \subseteq [P \to Q]$ is a directed set then $(\bigsqcup F)p = \bigsqcup \{ f\,p \mid f \in F \}$, for all $p \in P$.

**Definition 2.3.7** An *ordered* $\Sigma$*-algebra* $\mathcal{A}$ is an $S$-indexed family of pointed posets $A$ (the *carrier* of $\mathcal{A}$), together with a monotonic *operation* $\sigma_{\mathcal{A}}\colon A_{s_1} \times \cdots \times A_{s_n} \to A_{s'}$, for each $\sigma \in \Sigma$ of type $s_1 \times \cdots \times s_n \to s'$, and such that $\Omega_{s\mathcal{A}}\langle\rangle$ is the least element of $A_s$, for all $s \in S$. Such an $\mathcal{A}$ is *complete* iff each $A_s$ is a cpo and each $\sigma_{\mathcal{A}}$ is continuous.

We write $\sqsubseteq_A$ for the family of posets $\sqsubseteq_{(A_s)}$, $s \in S$, so that $\sqsubseteq_A$ is a partial ordering over $A$. We often write $\sqsubseteq_s$ instead of $\sqsubseteq_{A_s}$. As usual, if $\Phi(-)$ is an operation on ordered algebras then we write $\Phi(A)$ for the carrier of $\Phi(\mathcal{A})$.

Ordered algebras can be viewed as algebras by forgetting the partial orderings, and we will often do so without explicit comment. Thus, for an ordered algebra $\mathcal{A}$, $A$ will stand for both the carrier of $\mathcal{A}$ (a family of posets) and for the carrier of the underlying algebra (a family of sets). For example, we call an ordered algebra *reachable* iff its underlying algebra is reachable (cf., inductively reachable complete ordered algebras, definition 2.3.30).

Note that a homomorphism $h\colon \mathcal{A} \to \mathcal{B}$ over ordered algebras (i.e., a homomorphism over the underlying algebras) is strict, since for all $s \in S$,

$$h_s \bot_{A_s} = h_s \Omega_{s\mathcal{A}} = \Omega_{s\mathcal{B}} = \bot_{B_s}.$$

**Definition 2.3.8** For complete ordered algebras $\mathcal{A}$ and $\mathcal{B}$, $\mathcal{A}$ is an *inductive subalgebra* of $\mathcal{B}$ iff $\mathcal{A}$ is a subalgebra of $\mathcal{B}$, and for all $s \in S$, $\sqsubseteq_{A_s}$ is the restriction of $\sqsubseteq_{B_s}$ to $A_s$ and $\bigsqcup_{A_s} D = \bigsqcup_{B_s} D$, whenever $D \subseteq A_s$ is a directed set. If $\mathcal{A}$ is a complete ordered algebra and $B \subseteq A$ then by $B$ is an *inductive subalgebra* of $\mathcal{A}$ we mean that $B$ is a subalgebra of $\mathcal{A}$ and $\bigsqcup_{A_s} D \in B_s$, whenever $D \subseteq B_s$ is a directed set in $A_s$. This is sensible since if $B$ is an inductive subalgebra of $\mathcal{A}$ then the complete ordered algebra $\mathcal{B}$ consisting of $B$, together with the restrictions of the operations and partial orderings of $\mathcal{A}$ to $B$, is indeed an inductive subalgebra of $\mathcal{A}$. We write $\mathcal{A} \preceq \mathcal{B}$ for $\mathcal{A}$ is an inductive subalgebra of $\mathcal{B}$.

Note that the relation $\preceq$ over the class of complete ordered algebras is a partial ordering.

**Definition 2.3.9** An *order-embedding* $h: \mathcal{A} \to \mathcal{B}$ over ordered algebras is a homomorphism such that $h: A \to B$ is an order-embedding. An *order-isomorphism* over ordered algebras is a surjective order-embedding. Two ordered algebras are order-isomorphic iff there is an order-isomorphism from one to the other.

Note that order-isomorphism coincides with isomorphism in the category of ordered algebras and monotonic homomorphisms. Furthermore, if $h: \mathcal{A} \to \mathcal{B}$ is an order-isomorphism over complete ordered algebras then $h$ is continuous. A consequence of the above definitions is that for complete ordered algebras $\mathcal{A}$ and $\mathcal{B}$, $\mathcal{A}$ is an inductive subalgebra of $\mathcal{B}$ iff $A \subseteq B$ and the inclusion from $A$ to $B$ is a continuous order-embedding from $\mathcal{A}$ to $\mathcal{B}$.

**Definition 2.3.10** For an ordered algebra $\mathcal{A}$, the *$\Omega$-least substitutive pre-ordering over $\mathcal{T}$ induced by $\mathcal{A}$, $\preceq_{\mathcal{A}}$*, is defined by:

$$t_1 \preceq_{\mathcal{A}s} t_2 \text{ iff } M_s\, t_1 \sqsubseteq_s M_s\, t_2.$$

Note that for any ordered algebra $\mathcal{A}$, $\approx_{\mathcal{A}} = (\preceq_{\mathcal{A}} \cap \succeq_{\mathcal{A}})$, and that if $\mathcal{A}$ and $\mathcal{B}$ are complete ordered algebras and $\mathcal{A} \preceq \mathcal{B}$ then $\preceq_{\mathcal{A}} = \preceq_{\mathcal{B}}$.

**Definition 2.3.11** If $f: P \to Q$ is a monotonic function over posets then the *pre-ordering over $P$ induced by $f$, $\leq_f$*, is defined by:

$$p_1 \leq_f p_2 \text{ iff } f\, p_1 \sqsubseteq_Q f\, p_2.$$

Clearly $\leq_f$ respects the ordering of $P$, and if $f$ is a continuous function over cpo's then $\leq_f$ is inductive. Furthermore, if $h: \mathcal{A} \to \mathcal{B}$ is a monotonic homomorphism over ordered algebras then $\leq_h$ is a substitutive pre-ordering over $\mathcal{A}$.

**Lemma 2.3.12** *If $\mathcal{A}$ is an inductive subalgebra of $\mathcal{B}$ and $\leq$ is a substitutive (respectively, unary-substitutive) inductive pre-ordering over $\mathcal{B}$ then the restriction of $\leq$ to $A$ is a substitutive (respectively, unary-substitutive) inductive pre-ordering over $\mathcal{A}$.*

**Proof.** Immediate from the definitions and lemma 2.2.22. $\square$

Two results concerning derived operations of ordered algebras now follow.

**Lemma 2.3.13** *Derived operations of ordered algebras are monotonic and derived operations of complete ordered algebras are continuous.*

**Proof.** Both parts are easy and standard structural inductions over $T(X)$, for appropriate $X$'s. $\square$

**Lemma 2.3.14** *If $\mathcal{A}$ is a complete ordered algebra and $\leq$ is an inductive pre-ordering over $A|P$, for $P \subseteq S$, then $\leq^c$ is a unary-substitutive inductive pre-ordering over $\mathcal{A}$.*

**Proof.** By lemma 2.2.25, it is sufficient to show that $\leq^c$ is inductive. We begin by showing that $\sqsubseteq_A \subseteq \leq^c$. Suppose $a \sqsubseteq_s a'$. If $c[v]$ is a derived operator of type $s \to p$, $p \in P$, then $c\langle a\rangle \sqsubseteq_p c\langle a'\rangle$, by lemma 2.3.13, and thus $c\langle a\rangle \leq_p c\langle a'\rangle$, since $\leq$ is inductive. Thus $a \leq^c_s a'$, as required. Now, suppose $D \subseteq A_s$ is a directed set, $a \in A_s$ and $D \leq^c_s a$. If $c[v]$ is a derived operator of type $s \to p$, $p \in P$, then

$$c\langle \bigsqcup D\rangle = \bigsqcup\{\, c\langle d\rangle \mid d \in D\,\} \leq_p c\langle a\rangle,$$

by lemma 2.3.13, and since $D \leq^c_s a$ and $\leq$ is inductive. Thus $\bigsqcup D \leq^c_s a$, as required. $\square$

We now give a definition and two lemmas in preparation for the definition of the ordered term algebra.

**Definition 2.3.15** Let $\preceq^\Omega$ be the least $\Omega$-least substitutive pre-ordering over $\mathcal{T}$.

The next lemma shows that one term is less than another in $\preceq^\Omega$ iff the second can be formed by replacing occurrences of $\Omega$ in the first by terms.

**Lemma 2.3.16** *For all $s \in S$ and $t, t' \in T_s$, $t \preceq^\Omega_s t'$ iff (†) $t = \Omega_s$ or there is a $\sigma \in \Sigma$ of type $s_1 \times \cdots \times s_n \to s$ and $t_i, t'_i \in T_{s_i}$, $1 \leq i \leq n$, such that $t = \sigma\langle t_1, \ldots, t_n\rangle$, $t' = \sigma\langle t'_1, \ldots, t'_n\rangle$ and $t_i \preceq^\Omega_{s_i} t'_i$, $1 \leq i \leq n$.*

**Proof.** Define a relation $R$ over $T$ by: $t\,R_s\,t'$ iff (†) holds. It is sufficient to show that $\preceq^{\Omega} = R$. Clearly $R \subseteq \preceq^{\Omega}$. Furthermore, it is easy to see that $R$ is an $\Omega$-least substitutive pre-ordering over $\mathcal{T}$. Thus, by the leastness of $\preceq^{\Omega}$, $\preceq^{\Omega} \subseteq R$. □

**Lemma 2.3.17** *The relation $\preceq^{\Omega}$ is a partial ordering.*

**Proof.** An easy structural induction over $t$, using lemma 2.3.16, shows that for all $t \in T_s$, $t' \in T_s$, $s \in S$, if $t \preceq^{\Omega}_s t'$ and $t' \preceq^{\Omega}_s t$ then $t = t'$. □

**Definition 2.3.18** The ordered algebra $\mathcal{OT}_{\Sigma}$ (or simply $\mathcal{OT}$) consists of $\mathcal{T}$ ordered by $\preceq^{\Omega}$.

If $\mathcal{A}$ is an ordered algebra then $M_{\mathcal{A}}: \mathcal{OT} \rightarrow \mathcal{A}$ is monotonic, since if $t \preceq^{\Omega}_s t'$ then $t \preceq_{\mathcal{A}s} t'$, by the leastness of $\preceq^{\Omega}$, and so $M_{\mathcal{A}s}\, t \sqsubseteq_s M_{\mathcal{A}s}\, t'$, by the definition of $\preceq_{\mathcal{A}}$. Thus we have the following lemma.

**Lemma 2.3.19** *The ordered algebra $\mathcal{OT}$ is initial in the category of ordered algebras and monotonic homomorphisms.* □

We can now generalize from the initial ordered algebra to free ordered algebras.

**Definition 2.3.20** If $X$ is an $S$-indexed family of disjoint sets of context variables not occurring in $\Sigma$ then $\mathcal{OT}_{\Sigma}(X)$ (or simply $\mathcal{OT}(X)$) is the restriction of $\mathcal{OT}_{\Sigma(X)}$ to an ordered $\Sigma$-algebra.

The standard result that $\mathcal{OT}(X)$ is the *free ordered algebra generated by $X$* now easily follows.

**Lemma 2.3.21** *Define $f: X \rightarrow OT(X)$ by $f_s\, x = x$. If $\mathcal{A}$ is an ordered algebra and $g: X \rightarrow A$ then there exists a unique monotonic homomorphism $h: \mathcal{OT}(X) \rightarrow \mathcal{A}$ such that $g = h \circ f$:*

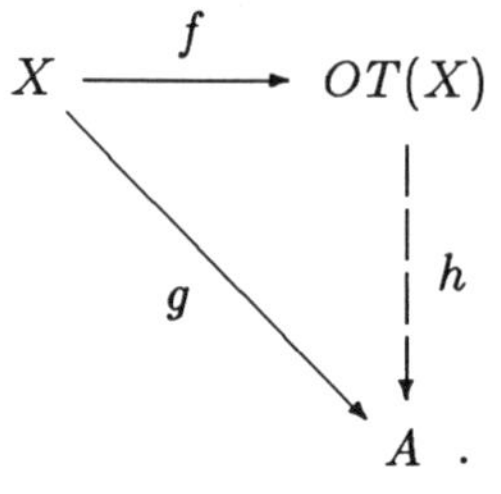


□

The next lemma shows that we could have defined derived operations over ordered algebras via free ordered algebras, instead of free algebras.

**Lemma 2.3.22** *If $\mathcal{A}$ is an ordered algebra and $c[v_1, \ldots, v_n]$ is a derived operator of type $s_1 \times \cdots \times s_n \to s'$ then for all $a_i \in A_{s_i}$, $1 \le i \le n$,*

$$c_{\mathcal{A}}\langle a_1, \ldots, a_n \rangle = h_{s'}\, c,$$

*where $h: \mathcal{OT}(\{v_1, \ldots, v_n\}) \to \mathcal{A}$ is defined via lemma 2.3.21, by taking $\{v_1, \ldots, v_n\}$ for $X$ and defining $g$ by $g_{s_i}\, v_i = a_i$, $1 \le i \le n$.*

**Proof.** Simply note that $h$ is a homomorphism from $\mathcal{T}(\{v_1, \ldots, v_n\})$ to the algebra $\mathcal{A}$ such that $g = h \circ f$. □

**Lemma 2.3.23** *If $\mathcal{A}$ is an ordered algebra and $c_1[v_1, \ldots, v_n]$ and $c_2[v_1, \ldots, v_n]$ are derived operators of type $s_1 \times \cdots \times s_n \to s'$ such that*

$$c_1 \sqsubseteq_{OT(\{v_1,\ldots,v_n\})_{s'}} c_2$$

*then for all $a_i \in A_{s_i}$, $1 \le i \le n$,*

$$c_{1\mathcal{A}}\langle a_1, \ldots, a_n \rangle \sqsubseteq_{s'} c_{2\mathcal{A}}\langle a_1, \ldots, a_n \rangle.$$

**Proof.** Immediate from lemma 2.3.22. □

We now consider the inductive subalgebras of complete ordered algebras that are generated by ordinary subalgebras. This notion is then specialized to reachable inductive subalgebras.

**Definition 2.3.24** If $\mathcal{A}$ is a complete ordered algebra and $\mathcal{B}$ is a subalgebra of $\mathcal{A}$ ($\mathcal{B}$ is an ordinary algebra) then $[B]$, the *subset of $A$ generated by $B$*, is the least subset of $A$ such that for all $s \in S$, $B_s \subseteq [B]_s$ and $\bigsqcup D \in [B]_s$, whenever $D \subseteq [B]_s$ is a directed set in $A_s$.

The next lemma shows that $[B]$ is a subalgebra of $\mathcal{A}$ and thus, since $[B]$ is closed under $A$-lub's, that $[B]$ is an inductive subalgebra of $\mathcal{A}$.

**Lemma 2.3.25** *If $\mathcal{A}$ is a complete ordered algebra and $\mathcal{B}$ is a subalgebra of $\mathcal{A}$ then $[B]$ is a subalgebra of $\mathcal{A}$.*

**Proof.** Let $\sigma \in \Sigma$ have type $s_1 \times \cdots \times s_n \to s'$. We must show that

$$\sigma_{\mathcal{A}}([B]_{s_1} \times \cdots \times [B]_{s_n}) \subseteq [B]_{s'}.$$

By the definition of subalgebra,

$$\sigma_{\mathcal{A}}(B_{s_1} \times \cdots \times B_{s_n}) \subseteq B_{s'} \subseteq [B]_{s'}.$$

If $n = 0$ then

$$\sigma_{\mathcal{A}}([B]_{s_1} \times \cdots \times [B]_{s_n}) = \sigma_{\mathcal{A}}(\{\langle\rangle\}) = \sigma_{\mathcal{A}}(B_{s_1} \times \cdots \times B_{s_n});$$

so, assume $n \geq 1$. It is sufficient to show that the following chain of implications holds:

$$\begin{aligned}
& \sigma_{\mathcal{A}}(B_{s_1} \times \cdots \times B_{s_n}) \subseteq [B]_{s'} \\
\Rightarrow\ & \sigma_{\mathcal{A}}([B]_{s_1} \times B_{s_2} \times \cdots \times B_{s_n}) \subseteq [B]_{s'} \\
\Rightarrow\ & \sigma_{\mathcal{A}}([B]_{s_1} \times [B]_{s_2} \times B_{s_3} \times \cdots \times B_{s_n}) \subseteq [B]_{s'} \\
\vdots\ & \\
\Rightarrow\ & \sigma_{\mathcal{A}}([B]_{s_1} \times \cdots \times [B]_{s_n}) \subseteq [B]_{s'}.
\end{aligned}$$

We show a representative step

$$\begin{aligned}
& \sigma([B]_{s_1} \times \cdots \times [B]_{s_{i-1}} \times B_{s_i} \times B_{s_{i+1}} \times \cdots \times B_{s_n}) \subseteq [B]_{s'} \\
\Rightarrow\ & \sigma([B]_{s_1} \times \cdots \times [B]_{s_{i-1}} \times [B]_{s_i} \times B_{s_{i+1}} \times \cdots \times B_{s_n}) \subseteq [B]_{s'},
\end{aligned}$$

by induction on $[B]_{s_i}$. Let $C$ be the set of all $b_i \in [B]_{s_i}$ such that $\sigma\langle b_1, \ldots, b_n\rangle \in [B]_{s'}$, for all $b_1 \in [B]_{s_1}$, $\ldots$, $b_{i-1} \in [B]_{s_{i-1}}$, $b_{i+1} \in B_{s_{i+1}}$, $\ldots$, $b_n \in B_{s_n}$. By assumption, $B_{s_i} \subseteq C$. Let $D \subseteq C$ be a directed set in $A_{s_i}$; we must show that $\bigsqcup D \in C$. Let $b_1 \in [B]_{s_1}$, $\ldots$, $b_{i-1} \in [B]_{s_{i-1}}$, $b_{i+1} \in B_{s_{i+1}}$, $\ldots$, $b_n \in B_{s_n}$. Then,

$$\begin{aligned}
& \sigma\langle b_1, \ldots, b_{i-1}, \textstyle\bigsqcup D, b_{i+1}, \ldots, b_n\rangle \\
&= \textstyle\bigsqcup \sigma(\{b_1\} \times \cdots \times \{b_{i-1}\} \times D \times \{b_{i+1}\} \times \cdots \times \{b_n\}) \\
&\in [B]_{s'},
\end{aligned}$$

since

$$\sigma(\{b_1\} \times \cdots \times \{b_{i-1}\} \times D \times \{b_{i+1}\} \times \cdots \times \{b_n\}) \subseteq [B]_{s'}$$

is a directed set in $A_{s'}$. □

**Definition 2.3.26** For a complete ordered algebra $\mathcal{A}$ and a subalgebra $\mathcal{B}$ of $\mathcal{A}$, $[\mathcal{B}]$, the *inductive subalgebra of $\mathcal{A}$ generated by $\mathcal{B}$*, is $[B]$, together with the restrictions of the operations and partial orderings of $\mathcal{A}$ to $[B]$.

**Lemma 2.3.27** *If $\mathcal{A}$ is a complete ordered algebra and $\mathcal{B}$ is a subalgebra of $\mathcal{A}$ then $[\mathcal{B}]$ is the $\preceq$-least inductive subalgebra of $\mathcal{A}$ that contains $B$.*

**Proof.** If $\mathcal{C}$ is an inductive subalgebra of $\mathcal{A}$ that contains $B$ then $C$ is closed under the defining conditions of $[B]$, and so $[B] \subseteq C$. Then, since $[\mathcal{B}]$ and $\mathcal{C}$ are both inductive subalgebras of $\mathcal{A}$, it follows that $[\mathcal{B}] \preceq \mathcal{C}$. □

**Definition 2.3.28** For a complete ordered algebra $\mathcal{A}$, define $R(\mathcal{A})$, the *reachable inductive subalgebra* of $\mathcal{A}$, to be $[M_{\mathcal{A}}\,\mathcal{T}]$.

The following lemma is an immediate consequence of lemma 2.3.27.

**Lemma 2.3.29** *If $\mathcal{A}$ is a complete ordered algebra then $R(\mathcal{A})$ is the $\preceq$-least inductive subalgebra of $\mathcal{A}$.* □

**Definition 2.3.30** A complete ordered algebra $\mathcal{A}$ is *inductively reachable* iff $\mathcal{A} = R(\mathcal{A})$.

It is easy to see that $R(\mathcal{A})$ itself is inductively reachable (clearly $R(R(\mathcal{A})) \preceq R(\mathcal{A})$, and $R(\mathcal{A}) \preceq R(R(\mathcal{A}))$ since $R(R(\mathcal{A}))$ is an inductive subalgebra of $\mathcal{A}$ and $R(\mathcal{A})$ is the $\preceq$-least such inductive subalgebra), and that a complete ordered algebra is inductively reachable iff it has no proper inductive subalgebras. We can carry out proofs by induction over inductively reachable complete ordered algebras $\mathcal{A}$: if $B \subseteq A_s$ contains $M_s T_s$, and $\bigsqcup D \in B$, whenever $D \subseteq B$ is a directed set, then $B = A_s$.

A sufficient—but not necessary—condition for a complete ordered algebra to be inductively reachable is that its carrier is $\omega$-algebraic and all of its finite elements are denotable.

Three useful lemmas concerning inductive reachability now follow.

**Lemma 2.3.31** *There is at most one continuous homomorphism from an inductively reachable complete ordered algebra to a complete ordered algebra.*

**Proof.** Suppose $f$ and $g$ are continuous homomorphisms from an inductively reachable complete ordered algebra $\mathcal{A}$ to a complete ordered algebra $\mathcal{B}$, and let $s \in S$. We prove that $f_s\, a = g_s\, a$, for all $a \in A_s$, by induction over $A_s$. Let $A' = \{\, a \in A_s \mid f_s\, a = g_s\, a \,\}$. Firstly, $M_s\, T_s \subseteq A'$, since, by the initiality of $\mathcal{T}$,

$$f_s(M_{\mathcal{A}_s}\, t) = M_{\mathcal{B}_s}\, t = g_s(M_{\mathcal{A}_s}\, t),$$

for all $t \in T_s$. Secondly, if $D \subseteq A'$ is a directed set then

$$f_s \bigsqcup D = \bigsqcup f_s\, D = \bigsqcup g_s\, D = g_s \bigsqcup D,$$

and thus $\bigsqcup D \in A'$. □

**Lemma 2.3.32** *If $\mathcal{A}$ and $\mathcal{B}$ are complete ordered algebras, $\mathcal{A}$ is inductively reachable and $f\colon \mathcal{A} \to \mathcal{B}$ is a continuous homomorphism then $f$ is also a continuous homomorphism from $\mathcal{A}$ to $R(\mathcal{B})$.*

**Proof.** It is sufficient to show that $f_s\, a \in R(B)_s$, for all $a \in A_s$, $s \in S$, and this follows by induction over $A_s$. □

The next lemma shows that inductive reachability is preserved by order-isomorphisms.

**Lemma 2.3.33** *If $\mathcal{A}$ and $\mathcal{B}$ are order-isomorphic complete ordered algebras and, in addition, $\mathcal{A}$ is inductively reachable then $\mathcal{B}$ is also inductively reachable.*

**Proof.** Since $\mathcal{A}$ and $\mathcal{B}$ are order-isomorphic, there is a continuous, surjective order-embedding $f\colon \mathcal{A} \to \mathcal{B}$. By lemma 2.3.32, it follows that $f\, A \subseteq R(B)$. Then, since $f$ is surjective, it follows that $B = R(B)$, and thus that $\mathcal{B} = R(\mathcal{B})$. □

We now consider the relationship between substitutive and unary-substitutive inductive pre-orderings over complete ordered algebras. The following two lemmas show that the situation is similar to that for unary-substitutive and substitutive pre-orderings over ordinary algebras: there exist unary-substitutive inductive pre-orderings that are not substitutive, and unary-substitutive inductive pre-orderings over inductively reachable complete ordered algebras are substitutive.

**Lemma 2.3.34** *There is a signature $\Sigma$, a complete ordered algebra $\mathcal{A}$ and a unary-substitutive inductive pre-ordering $\leq$ over $\mathcal{A}$ such that:*

(i) *$\leq$ is not substitutive;*

(ii) *The unary-substitutive equivalence relation $\equiv\, = \,\leq \cap \geq$ is not substitutive; and*

(iii) *There does not exist a congruence* $\equiv'$ *over* $\mathcal{A}$ *such that*

$$M_s\, t_1 \equiv_s M_s\, t_2 \textit{ iff } M_s\, t_1 \equiv'_s M_s\, t_2,$$

*for all* $t_1, t_2 \in T_s$, $s \in S$.

**Proof.** Consider the $\Sigma$, $\mathcal{A}$ and $\leq$ from the proof of lemma 2.2.27. Order each $A_s$ by $a_1 \sqsubseteq_s a_2$ iff $a_1 = \Omega_s$ or $a_1 = a_2$. Then $\mathcal{A}$ is an ordered algebra and $\sqsubseteq_A \subseteq \leq$. Since $A$ is finite, it then follows that $\mathcal{A}$ is complete and $\leq$ is inductive. The rest of the lemma follows by lemma 2.2.27. □

**Lemma 2.3.35** *Unary-substitutive inductive pre-orderings over inductively reachable complete ordered algebras are substitutive.*

**Proof.** Let $\leq$ be a unary-substitutive inductive pre-ordering over an inductively reachable complete ordered algebra $\mathcal{A}$. We make use of the characterization of substitutivity given by lemma 2.2.28. It is sufficient to show that for all derived operators $c[v, v_1, \ldots, v_n]$ of type $s \times s_1 \times \cdots \times s_n \rightarrow s'$ and $a, a' \in A_s$, if $a \leq_s a'$ then

$$c\langle a, a_1, \ldots, a_n\rangle \leq_{s'} c\langle a', a_1, \ldots, a_n\rangle, \text{ for all } a_i \in A_{s_i}, 1 \leq i \leq n;$$

we prove this by induction on $n$. The case $n = 0$ follows from the unary-substitutivity of $\leq$. For the induction step, suppose that $c[v, v_1, \ldots, v_{n+1}]$ is a derived operator of type $s \times s_1 \times \cdots \times s_{n+1} \rightarrow s'$ and that $a \leq_s a'$. We show by induction over $A_{s_{n+1}}$ that for all $a_{n+1} \in A_{s_{n+1}}$,

$$c\langle a, a_1, \ldots, a_{n+1}\rangle \leq_{s'} c\langle a', a_1, \ldots, a_{n+1}\rangle, \text{ for all } a_i \in A_{s_i}, 1 \leq i \leq n. \qquad (2.1)$$

Let $A'$ be the set of all $a_{n+1} \in A_{s_{n+1}}$ such that (2.1). Suppose $t \in T_{s_{n+1}}$; we must show that $M_{s_{n+1}}\, t \in A'$. Then,

$$(c\langle v, v_1, \ldots, v_n, t\rangle)[v, v_1, \ldots, v_n]$$

is a derived operator of type $s \times s_1 \times \cdots \times s_n \rightarrow s'$, and, by the inductive hypothesis on $n$,

$$\begin{aligned} c\langle a, a_1, \ldots, a_n, M_{s_{n+1}}\, t\rangle &= (c\langle v, v_1, \ldots, v_n, t\rangle)\langle a, a_1, \ldots, a_n\rangle \\ &\leq_{s'} (c\langle v, v_1, \ldots, v_n, t\rangle)\langle a', a_1, \ldots, a_n\rangle \\ &= c\langle a', a_1, \ldots, a_n, M_{s_{n+1}}\, t\rangle, \end{aligned}$$

for all $a_i \in A_{s_i}$, $1 \leq i \leq n$. Now, suppose $D \subseteq A'$ is a directed set; we must show that $\bigsqcup D \in A'$. Suppose $a_i \in A_{s_i}$, $1 \leq i \leq n$. Then,

$$\begin{aligned} c\langle a, a_1, \ldots, a_n, \bigsqcup D\rangle &= \bigsqcup c(\{a\} \times \{a_1\} \times \cdots \times \{a_n\} \times D) \\ &\leq_{s'} \bigsqcup c(\{a'\} \times \{a_1\} \times \cdots \times \{a_n\} \times D) \\ &= c\langle a', a_1, \ldots, a_n, \bigsqcup D\rangle, \end{aligned}$$

since $\mathcal{A}$ is complete and $\leq$ is inductive. □

A consequence of lemmas 2.2.25, 2.3.14 and 2.3.35 is that if $P \subseteq S$, $\mathcal{A}$ is an inductively reachable complete ordered algebra, and $\leq$ is an inductive pre-ordering over $A|P$ then $\leq^c$ is the greatest substitutive inductive pre-ordering over $\mathcal{A}$ whose restriction to $P$ is included in $\leq$.

This section concludes with two lemmas concerning the pre-orderings over $T$ that are induced by inductive pre-orderings over the carriers of complete ordered algebras.

**Lemma 2.3.36** *Suppose $P \subseteq S$, $\mathcal{A}$ is a complete ordered algebra, $\leq$ is an inductive pre-ordering over $A|P$, and $\preceq$ is the pre-ordering over $T|P$ defined by*

$$t_1 \preceq_p t_2 \text{ iff } M_p\, t_1 \leq_p M_p\, t_2.$$

*Then $\leq^c$ is a unary-substitutive inductive pre-ordering over $\mathcal{A}$, $\preceq^c$ is an $\Omega$-least substitutive pre-ordering over $\mathcal{T}$, and*

$$t_1 \preceq^c_s t_2 \text{ iff } M_s\, t_1 \leq^c_s M_s\, t_2,$$

*for all $t_1, t_2 \in T_s$, $s \in S$.*

**Proof.** All that remains after applying lemma 2.2.30 is to show that $\leq^c$ is inductive and $\preceq^c$ is $\Omega$-least. The former fact follows from lemma 2.3.14. For the second, if $t \in T_s$, $s \in S$, then

$$M_s\, \Omega_s = \bot \leq^c_s M_s\, t,$$

since $\sqsubseteq_A \subseteq \leq^c$, and thus $\Omega_s \preceq^c_s t$. □

**Lemma 2.3.37** *Suppose $\mathcal{A}$ is a complete ordered algebra, $\leq$ is an inductive pre-ordering over $A$, and $\preceq$ is the pre-ordering over $T$ defined by*

$$t_1 \preceq_s t_2 \text{ iff } M_s\, t_1 \leq_s M_s\, t_2.$$

(i) *If* $\leq$ *is unary-substitutive then* $\preceq$ *is* $\Omega$*-least and substitutive.*

(ii) *If* $\preceq$ *is substitutive then*

$$t_1 \preceq_s t_2 \textit{ iff } M_s\, t_1 \leq^c_s M_s\, t_2,$$

*for all* $t_1, t_2 \in T_s$, $s \in S$.

**Proof.** Immediate from lemma 2.3.36, with $P = S$. □

## 2.4 Completion and Quotienting Theorems

In this section, we present a completion theorem and two quotienting theorems for ordered algebras, which will be employed in chapters 5 and 7. The main result is theorem 2.4.2, a completion construction in which ordered algebras are embedded into complete ordered algebras in such a way that *certain* existing lub's are preserved. Because the operations of complete ordered algebras are required to be continuous, it is impossible, in general, to preserve arbitrary sets of existing lub's. Thus, to begin with, we need a way to specify suitably consistent sets of lub's of ordered algebras. This we do via *families of subsets.*

**Definition 2.4.1** A *family of subsets* $\Gamma$ for a pointed poset $P$ is a set of directed subsets of $P$. Such a $P$ is $\Gamma$*-complete* iff for all $D \in \Gamma$, $D$ has a lub in $P$. A function $f$ from a $\Gamma$-complete pointed poset $P$ to a cpo $Q$ is $\Gamma$*-continuous* iff it is monotonic and for all $D \in \Gamma$, $f \bigsqcup D = \bigsqcup f\, D$.

A *family of subsets* $\Gamma$ for an ordered algebra $\mathcal{A}$ is an $S$-indexed family of sets such that:

(i) $\Gamma_s$ is a family of subsets of $A_s$, for all $s \in S$;

(ii) $\{a\} \in \Gamma_s$, for all $a \in A_s$, $s \in S$; and

(iii) if $\sigma \in \Sigma$ has type $s_1 \times \cdots \times s_n \rightarrow s'$ and $D_i \in \Gamma_{s_i}$, $1 \leq i \leq n$, then $\sigma(D_1 \times \cdots \times D_n) \in \Gamma_{s'}$.

Such an $\mathcal{A}$ is $\Gamma$*-complete* iff $A_s$ is $\Gamma_s$-complete, for all $s \in S$, and if $\sigma \in \Sigma$ has type $s_1 \times \cdots \times s_n \rightarrow s'$ and $D_i \in \Gamma_{s_i}$, $1 \leq i \leq n$, then

$$\sigma\langle \bigsqcup D_1, \ldots, \bigsqcup D_n \rangle = \bigsqcup \sigma(D_1 \times \cdots \times D_n).$$

A homomorphism $f$ from a $\Gamma$-complete ordered algebra $\mathcal{A}$ to a complete ordered algebra $\mathcal{B}$ is $\Gamma$*-continuous* iff $f_s\colon A_s \rightarrow B_s$ is $\Gamma_s$-continuous, for all $s \in S$.

In contrast to [CouRao] and [ADJ2], we associate families of subsets with individual ordered algebras—i.e., we deal with non-uniform families of subsets. As a consequence, we must explicitly include the singleton directed sets in our families of subsets. See the proof of lemma 2.4.13 to see why this is necessary.

Next, we state our completion theorem, which is a variation of Theorem 1 of [CouRao].

**Theorem 2.4.2** *If $\mathcal{A}$ is a $\Gamma$-complete ordered algebra then there is a complete ordered algebra $\mathcal{C}$, together with a $\Gamma$-continuous order-embedding $f: \mathcal{A} \to \mathcal{C}$, such that if $\mathcal{D}$ is a complete ordered algebra and $g: \mathcal{A} \to \mathcal{D}$ is a $\Gamma$-continuous homomorphism then there exists a unique continuous homomorphism $h: \mathcal{C} \to \mathcal{D}$ such that $g = h \circ f$:*

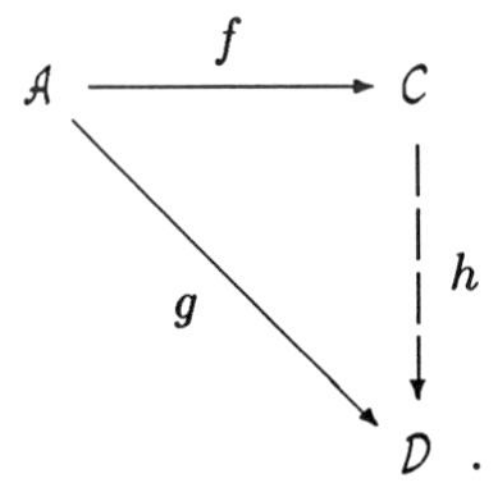


Before giving the proof of theorem 2.4.2, we give two definitions and a series of lemmas, some of which are motivated by sections 5 and 6 of [Mar]. Until lemma 2.4.13, below, let $P$ be a $\Gamma$-complete pointed poset.

**Definition 2.4.3** A subset $P'$ of $P$ is *closed* iff the following conditions hold:

(i) $\bot_P \in P'$;

(ii) If $p \sqsubseteq p'$ and $p' \in P'$ then $p \in P'$; and

(iii) If $D \subseteq P'$ and $D \in \Gamma$ then $\bigsqcup D \in P'$.

For a subset $P'$ of $P$, $cl(P')$, the *closure* of $P'$, is the least closed set containing $P'$.

A set $P'$ is closed iff it is nonempty, downward-closed and closed under $\Gamma$-lub's. Thus, if $P'$ is nonempty then $cl(P')$ is simply the least set containing $P'$ that is downward-closed and closed under $\Gamma$-lub's. Since $cl(P')$ is inductively defined, we can give proofs by induction over it.

**Lemma 2.4.4** *For all $X, Y \subseteq P$:*

(i) *$X \subseteq cl(X)$;*

(ii) *$cl(X) = cl(cl(X))$; and*

(iii) *if $X \subseteq Y$ then $cl(X) \subseteq cl(Y)$.*

**Proof.** (i) and (ii) are obvious from the definition. For (iii), suppose $X \subseteq Y$. Then, by (i), $X \subseteq Y \subseteq cl(Y)$, and so $cl(Y)$ is a closed set containing $X$. Thus, by the leastness of $cl(X)$, $cl(X) \subseteq cl(Y)$. □

**Lemma 2.4.5** *If $P'$ is a nonempty, finite subset of $P$ then $cl(P') = down(P')$.*

**Proof.** It is sufficient to show that $down(P')$ is closed under $\Gamma$-lub's. Let $D \subseteq down(P')$ and $D \in \Gamma$. Suppose, toward a contradiction, that $\bigsqcup D \notin down(P')$. Then for all $p' \in P'$, there exists a $d_{p'} \in D$ such that $d_{p'} \not\sqsubseteq p'$, and thus, since $D$ is directed, there exists an ub $d$ of $\{\, d_{p'} \mid p' \in P' \,\}$ in $D$. But then $d_{p'} \sqsubseteq d \sqsubseteq p'$, for some $p' \in P'$—a contradiction. □

**Lemma 2.4.6** *If $D \in \Gamma$ then $cl(\{\bigsqcup D\}) = cl(D)$.*

**Proof.** First, $\{\bigsqcup D\} \subseteq cl(D)$, and thus $cl(\{\bigsqcup D\}) \subseteq cl(D)$. Second, $D \subseteq cl(\{\bigsqcup D\})$, since $cl(\{\bigsqcup D\})$ is downward-closed, and thus $cl(D) \subseteq cl(\{\bigsqcup D\})$. □

**Lemma 2.4.7** *If $X$ is a set of subsets of $P$ then $cl(\bigcup X) = cl(\bigcup_{P' \in X} cl(P'))$.*

**Proof.** First, $\bigcup X \subseteq \bigcup_{P' \in X} cl(P')$, and so $cl(\bigcup X) \subseteq cl(\bigcup_{P' \in X} cl(P'))$. Second, for all $P' \in X$, $cl(P') \subseteq cl(\bigcup X)$, and thus $cl(\bigcup_{P' \in X} cl(P')) \subseteq cl(\bigcup X)$. □

**Lemma 2.4.8** *If $P'$ is a nonempty subset of $P$ and $g$ is a $\Gamma$-continuous function from $P$ to a cpo $Q$ then $g\,P'$ has a lub iff $g\,cl(P')$ has a lub, and they are equal if they exist.*

**Proof.** It is sufficient to show that for $q \in Q$, $q$ is an ub of $g\,P'$ iff $q$ is an ub of $g\,cl(P')$. The "if" direction is trivial, since $P' \subseteq cl(P')$. For the "only if" direction, suppose $q$ is an ub of $g\,P'$. Let $P''$ be $\{\, p'' \in cl(P') \mid g\,p'' \sqsubseteq q \,\}$. Clearly $P' \subseteq P''$. Suppose $p'' \in P''$ and $p \sqsubseteq p''$, for some $p \in P$. Then $g\,p \sqsubseteq g\,p'' \sqsubseteq q$, showing that $p \in P''$. Suppose $D \subseteq P''$ and $D \in \Gamma$. Then $g \bigsqcup D = \bigsqcup g\,D \sqsubseteq q$, since $g$ is $\Gamma$-continuous, showing that $\bigsqcup D \in P''$. Thus $P'' = cl(P')$, and so $q$ is an ub of $g\,cl(P')$. □

**Definition 2.4.9** A subset $P'$ of $P$ is *continuously directed* iff for all $\Gamma$-continuous functions $g\colon P \to Q$, for cpo's $Q$, $g\,P'$ has a lub in $Q$.

Clearly, directed sets are continuously directed. To see that the converse is false, let $P$ be the poset

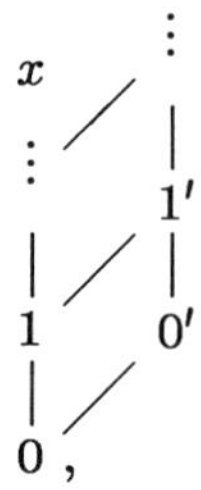


so that $x = \bigsqcup \omega$ and $\omega' = \{ n' \mid n \in \omega \}$ has no lub, and let $\Gamma = \{\omega\}$. Then $P$ itself is continuously directed, by lemma 2.4.8, but is obviously not directed.

Returning to the general case, we can now give our completion construction for posets.

**Lemma 2.4.10** *Let $C$ be the least set of closed subsets of $P$ such that*

(i) *$cl(\{p\}) \in C$, if $p \in P$; and*

(ii) *$cl(\bigcup X) \in C$, if $X$ is a directed subset of $C$, ordered by inclusion.*

*Define $f : P \to C$ by $f\,p = cl(\{p\})$. Then $C$, ordered by inclusion, is a cpo, $f$ is a $\Gamma$-continuous order-embedding, all elements of $C$ are continuously directed, and for all $\Gamma$-continuous $g : P \to Q$, for cpo's $Q$, the function $P' \mapsto \bigsqcup g\,P'$ is the unique continuous $h : C \to Q$ such that $h \circ f = g$.*

**Proof.** Clearly $cl(\{\bot_P\}) = \{\bot_P\}$ is the least element of $C$, and $cl(\bigcup X)$ is the lub of any directed $X \subseteq C$. Since $cl(\{p\}) = down(\{p\})$, by lemma 2.4.5, it is easy to see that $f$ is an order-embedding. If $D \in \Gamma$ then

$$
\begin{aligned}
f \bigsqcup D &= cl(\{\bigsqcup D\}) \\
&= cl(D) \qquad \text{(lemma 2.4.6)} \\
&= cl(\bigcup_{d \in D} \{d\}) \\
&= cl(\bigcup_{d \in D} cl(\{d\})) \qquad \text{(lemma 2.4.7)} \\
&= \bigsqcup f\,D,
\end{aligned}
$$

showing that $f$ is $\Gamma$-continuous.

Next, we show that all elements of $C$ are continuously directed. Suppose $g : P \to Q$ is $\Gamma$-continuous, for a cpo $Q$. We show, by induction over $C$, that $g\,P'$ has a lub in $Q$, for all $P' \in C$. Let $C' = \{ P' \in C \mid \bigsqcup g\,P' \text{ exists} \}$. Clearly $cl(\{p\}) \in C'$, for all $p \in P$, since $g\,p$ is the lub of $g\,\{p\}$, and thus, by lemma 2.4.8, is also the lub of $g\,cl(\{p\})$. If $X \subseteq C'$ is directed then $\{ \bigsqcup g\,P' \mid P' \in X \}$ is directed, and thus has a lub $q$ in $Q$. Furthermore,

$\{\bigsqcup g\,P' \mid P' \in X\}$ and $g\,(\bigcup X)$ share the same ub's, and thus $q$ is the lub of $g\,(\bigcup X)$. Finally, by lemma 2.4.8, $q$ is also the lub of $g\,cl(\bigcup X)$, showing that $cl(\bigcup X) \in C'$.

For the universal property, suppose $g: P \to Q$ is $\Gamma$-continuous, for a cpo $Q$. Define $h: C \to Q$ by $h\,P' = \bigsqcup g\,P'$. Clearly $h$ is monotonic, and

$$\begin{aligned} h(f\,p) &= \bigsqcup g\,cl(\{p\}) \\ &= \bigsqcup g\,\{p\} \qquad \text{(lemma 2.4.8)} \\ &= g\,p, \end{aligned}$$

for all $p \in P$. For continuity, if $X \subseteq C$ is directed then

$$\begin{aligned} h \bigsqcup X &= h\,cl(\bigcup X) \\ &= \bigsqcup g\,cl(\bigcup X) \\ &= \bigsqcup \{\bigsqcup g\,P' \mid P' \in X\} \\ &= \bigsqcup h\,X. \end{aligned}$$

Finally, suppose $h': C \to Q$ is continuous and $h' \circ f = g$. We show by induction over $C$ that $h\,P' = h'\,P'$, for all $P' \in C$. Let $C' = \{\,P' \in C \mid h\,P' = h'\,P'\,\}$. First, for all $p \in P$,

$$h\,cl(\{p\}) = h(f\,p) = g\,p = h'(f\,p) = h'\,cl(\{p\}),$$

showing that $cl(\{p\}) \in C'$. Second, if $X \subseteq C'$ is directed then

$$h\,cl(\bigcup X) = h \bigsqcup X = \bigsqcup h\,X = \bigsqcup h'\,X = h' \bigsqcup X = h'\,cl(\bigcup X),$$

showing that $cl(\bigcup X) \in C'$. □

If $\Gamma$ is empty (or contains only singletons) then the $C$ of lemma 2.4.10 consists of all of the downward-closed, directed subsets of $P$, and is thus the usual ideal completion. In general, however, the elements of $C$ need not be directed sets, as can been seen from the above example, in which the non-directed poset $P$ is an element of its own completion. It would be nice to give a direct characterization of $C$, in the general case, and I cannot resist making the following conjecture.

**Conjecture 2.4.11** *The cpo $C$ of lemma* 2.4.10 *consists of the set of all closed, continuously directed subsets of $P$.*

The following lemma, concerning the internal structure of the completion $C$ of $P$, will not be used until chapter 7, but is included here for convenience.

**Lemma 2.4.12** *Let $C$ be the cpo defined in the statement of lemma 2.4.10. If $cl(P') \in C$, for a nonempty, finite subset $P'$ of $P$, then there exists a $p' \in P'$ such that $cl(P') = cl(\{p'\})$.*

**Proof.** By lemma 2.4.5, $cl(P') = down(P')$, and thus $cl(P') = down(P'')$, where $P''$ is the set of maximal elements of $P'$. It is thus sufficient to show that $|P''| = 1$. Make $P''$ into a cpo, $Q$, by adding a lower bound, $\bot$, and two incomparable ub's, $x$ and $y$. Formally, let $Q$ be $P'' \cup \{\bot, x, y\}$, ordered by $q_1 \sqsubseteq q_2$ iff

(i) $q_1 = \bot$; or

(ii) $q_2 = x$ and $q_1 \neq y$; or

(iii) $q_2 = y$ and $q_1 \neq x$; or

(iv) $q_1, q_2 \in P''$ and $q_1 = q_2$.

For $p \in P$, let $\delta_p = \{\, p'' \in P'' \mid p \sqsubseteq p'' \,\}$. Define $f: P \to Q$ by:

$$f\,p = \begin{cases} x & \text{if } \delta_p = \emptyset; \\ p'' & \text{if } \delta_p = \{p''\}; \\ \bot & \text{if } |\delta_p| \geq 2. \end{cases}$$

Thus $y \notin f\,P$. It is easy to see that $f$ is monotonic. For $\Gamma$-continuity, suppose $D \in \Gamma$. If $D \not\subseteq down(P'')$ then $f \bigsqcup D = x = \bigsqcup f\,D$; so, suppose $D \subseteq down(P'')$. Since $down(P'')$ is closed, $\bigsqcup D \in down(P'')$, and thus $\delta_{\bigsqcup D} \neq \emptyset$. If $|\delta_{\bigsqcup D}| \geq 2$ then $f \bigsqcup D = \bot = \bigsqcup f\,D$; so, assume $\delta_{\bigsqcup D} = \{p''\}$, for some $p'' \in P''$. If there is a $d \in D$ such that $|\delta_d| = 1$ then $f \bigsqcup D = p'' = \bigsqcup f\,D$; so, suppose, toward a contradiction, that $|\delta_d| \geq 2$, for all $d \in D$. Then $Z = (\bigcup_{d \in D} \delta_d) - \{p''\}$ is a nonempty subset of $P''$, and for all $z \in Z$, there exists a $d_z \in D$ such that $d_z \not\sqsubseteq z$. But, since $D$ is directed, there exists an ub $d$ of $\{\, d_z \mid z \in Z \,\}$ in $D$, and thus $d_z \sqsubseteq d \sqsubseteq z$, for some $z \in Z$—a contradiction. Thus $f$ is indeed $\Gamma$-continuous, and, by lemma 2.4.10, $f\,down(P'')$ has a lub in $Q$. But $P'' \subseteq f\,down(P'')$ and $x \notin f\,down(P'')$, and thus $|P''| = 1$, as required. □

**Lemma 2.4.13** *Suppose $\mathcal{A}$ is a $\Gamma$-complete ordered algebra. If $\sigma \in \Sigma$ has type $s_1 \times \cdots \times s_n \to s'$ and $A'_i \subseteq A_{s_i}$, $1 \leq i \leq n$, are nonempty then*

$$cl(\sigma(cl(A'_1) \times \cdots \times cl(A'_n))) = cl(\sigma(A'_1 \times \cdots \times A'_n)).$$

**Proof.** Showing that the rhs is a subset of the lhs is trivial by lemma 2.4.4. For the other direction, it is sufficient to show that

$$\sigma(cl(A'_1) \times \cdots \times cl(A'_n)) \subseteq cl(\sigma(A'_1 \times \cdots \times A'_n)).$$

If $n = 0$ then $\sigma\{\langle\rangle\} \subseteq cl(\sigma\{\langle\rangle\})$; so, assume $n \geq 1$. Clearly,

$$\sigma(A'_1 \times \cdots \times A'_n) \subseteq cl(\sigma(A'_1 \times \cdots \times A'_n)),$$

and thus it is sufficient to show that the following chain of implications holds:

$$\begin{aligned}
& \sigma(A'_1 \times \cdots \times A'_n) \subseteq cl(\sigma(A'_1 \times \cdots \times A'_n)) \\
\Rightarrow\ & \sigma(cl(A'_1) \times A'_2 \times \cdots \times A'_n) \subseteq cl(\sigma(A'_1 \times \cdots \times A'_n)) \\
\Rightarrow\ & \sigma(cl(A'_1) \times cl(A'_2) \times A'_3 \times \cdots \times A'_n) \subseteq cl(\sigma(A'_1 \times \cdots \times A'_n)) \\
\vdots\ & \\
\Rightarrow\ & \sigma(cl(A'_1) \times \cdots \times cl(A'_n)) \subseteq cl(\sigma(A'_1 \times \cdots \times A'_n)).
\end{aligned}$$

We show a representative step

$$\sigma(cl(A'_1) \times \cdots \times cl(A'_{i-1}) \times A'_i \times A'_{i+1} \times \cdots \times A'_n) \subseteq cl(\sigma(A'_1 \times \cdots \times A'_n))$$
$$\Downarrow$$
$$\sigma(cl(A'_1) \times \cdots \times cl(A'_{i-1}) \times cl(A'_i) \times A'_{i+1} \times \cdots \times A'_n) \subseteq cl(\sigma(A'_1 \times \cdots \times A'_n)),$$

by induction over $cl(A'_i)$. Let $B$ be the set of all $a_i \in cl(A'_i)$ such that

$$\sigma\langle a_1, \ldots, a_n\rangle \in cl(\sigma(A'_1 \times \cdots \times A'_n)),$$

for all $a_1 \in cl(A'_1)$, ..., $a_{i-1} \in cl(A'_{i-1})$, $a_{i+1} \in A'_{i+1}$, ..., $a_n \in A'_n$. By assumption, $A'_i \subseteq B$. Furthermore, $B$ is downward-closed, since $\sigma$ is monotonic and $cl(\sigma(A'_1 \times \cdots \times A'_n))$ is downward-closed. Since $A'_i$ is nonempty, it only remains to show that $B$ is closed under $\Gamma$-lub's. Suppose $D \subseteq B$ and $D \in \Gamma_{s_i}$; we must show that $\bigsqcup D \in B$. Let $a_1 \in cl(A'_1)$, ..., $a_{i-1} \in cl(A'_{i-1})$, $a_{i+1} \in A'_{i+1}$, ..., $a_n \in A'_n$. Then,

$$\begin{aligned}
& \sigma\langle a_1, \ldots, a_{i-1}, \textstyle\bigsqcup D, a_{i+1}, \ldots, a_n\rangle \\
= & \textstyle\bigsqcup \sigma(\{a_1\} \times \cdots \times \{a_{i-1}\} \times D \times \{a_{i+1}\} \times \cdots \times \{a_n\}) \\
\in & cl(\sigma(A'_1 \times \cdots \times A'_n)),
\end{aligned}$$

since $\mathcal{A}$ is $\Gamma$-complete and

$$\sigma(\{a_1\} \times \cdots \times \{a_{i-1}\} \times D \times \{a_{i+1}\} \times \cdots \times \{a_n\})$$

is a subset of $cl(\sigma(A'_1 \times \cdots \times A'_n))$ and an element of $\Gamma_{s'}$. (Here, it is essential that $\Gamma$ contain all singleton sets.) □

**Proof of theorem 2.4.2.** We begin by defining a complete ordered algebra $\mathcal{B}$, together with a homomorphism $f: \mathcal{A} \to \mathcal{B}$. For $s \in S$, $B_s$ is the set of all closed subsets of $A_s$, ordered by inclusion, and for $\sigma \in \Sigma$ of type $s_1 \times \cdots \times s_n \to s'$ and $A'_i \in B_{s_i}$, $1 \leq i \leq n$,

$$\sigma_{\mathcal{B}}\langle A'_1, \ldots, A'_n\rangle = cl(\sigma_{\mathcal{A}}(A'_1 \times \cdots \times A'_n)).$$

Then, for $s \in S$,

$$\Omega_{s\mathcal{B}}\langle\rangle = cl(\Omega_{s\mathcal{A}}\{\langle\rangle\}) = cl(\{\perp_{A_s}\}) = \{\perp_{A_s}\}$$

is the least element of $B_s$. The monotonicity of the operations follows from lemma 2.4.4. Thus $\mathcal{B}$ is an ordered algebra.

If $B' \subseteq B_s$, $s \in S$, then $cl(\bigcup B')$ is the lub of $B'$, and so $B$ is a cpo (actually, a complete lattice). Suppose $\sigma \in \Sigma$ has type $s_1 \times \cdots \times s_n \to s'$ and $B'_i \subseteq B_{s_i}$, $1 \leq i \leq n$, are nonempty. Then,

$$\begin{aligned}
\sigma_{\mathcal{B}}\langle \bigsqcup B'_1, \ldots, \bigsqcup B'_n\rangle &= \sigma_{\mathcal{B}}\langle cl(\bigcup B'_1), \ldots, cl(\bigcup B'_n)\rangle \\
&= cl(\sigma_{\mathcal{A}}(cl(\bigcup B'_1) \times \cdots \times cl(\bigcup B'_n))) \\
&= cl(\sigma_{\mathcal{A}}(\bigcup B'_1 \times \cdots \times \bigcup B'_n)) \qquad \text{(lemma 2.4.13)} \\
&= cl(\bigcup\{\, \sigma_{\mathcal{A}}(A'_1 \times \cdots \times A'_n) \mid A'_i \in B'_i\,\}) \\
&= cl(\bigcup\{\, cl(\sigma_{\mathcal{A}}(A'_1 \times \cdots \times A'_n)) \mid A'_i \in B'_i\,\}) \qquad \text{(lemma 2.4.7)} \\
&= \bigsqcup\{\, cl(\sigma_{\mathcal{A}}(A'_1 \times \cdots \times A'_n)) \mid A'_i \in B'_i\,\} \\
&= \bigsqcup\{\, \sigma_{\mathcal{B}}\langle A'_1, \ldots, A'_n\rangle \mid A'_i \in B'_i\,\} \\
&= \bigsqcup \sigma_{\mathcal{B}}\langle B'_1, \ldots, B'_n\rangle,
\end{aligned}$$

and thus $\mathcal{B}$ is complete.

Define $f: A \to B$ by $f_s\, a = cl(\{a\})$, for $a \in A_s$, $s \in S$. Then, $f$ is a homomorphism from $\mathcal{A}$ to $\mathcal{B}$, since if $\sigma \in \Sigma$ has type $s_1 \times \cdots \times s_n \to s'$ and $a_i \in A_{s_i}$, $1 \leq i \leq n$, then

$$\begin{aligned}
f_s\, \sigma_{\mathcal{A}}\langle a_1, \ldots, a_n\rangle &= cl(\{\sigma_{\mathcal{A}}\langle a_1, \ldots, a_n\rangle\}) \\
&= cl(\sigma_{\mathcal{A}}(\{a_1\} \times \cdots \times \{a_n\})) \\
&= cl(\sigma_{\mathcal{A}}(cl(\{a_1\}) \times \cdots \times cl(\{a_n\}))) \qquad \text{(lemma 2.4.13)} \\
&= \sigma_{\mathcal{B}}\langle cl(\{a_1\}), \ldots, cl(\{a_n\})\rangle \\
&= \sigma_{\mathcal{B}}\langle f_{s_1}\, a_1, \ldots, f_{s_n}\, a_n\rangle.
\end{aligned}$$

$\mathcal{B}$ has lub's of too many sets, in general, and thus we take the $\preceq$-least inductive subalgebra of $\mathcal{B}$ containing $f\, A$ as our candidate for $\mathcal{C}$, i.e., we define $\mathcal{C}$ to be $[f\, \mathcal{A}]$ (see definition 2.3.26). Since $\mathcal{C}$ is a subalgebra of $\mathcal{B}$, $f$ is also a homomorphism from $\mathcal{A}$ to $\mathcal{C}$. For all $s \in S$, $C_s$ is the least subset of $B_s$ such that

(i) $f_s\, a = cl(\{a\}) \in C_s$, if $a \in A_s$; and

(ii) $\bigsqcup X = cl(\bigcup X) \in C_s$, if $X \subseteq C_s$ is directed.

Thus we can apply lemma 2.4.10 and conclude that $f$ is a $\Gamma$-continuous order-embedding from $\mathcal{A}$ to $\mathcal{C}$.

It remains to show the universal property of $(f, \mathcal{C})$. Suppose $g: \mathcal{A} \rightarrow \mathcal{D}$ is a $\Gamma$-continuous homomorphism, for a complete ordered algebra $\mathcal{D}$. By lemma 2.4.10, we can define a continuous function $h: C \rightarrow D$ by $h_s\, A' = \bigsqcup g_s A'$, for $A' \in C_s$, $s \in S$, and, furthermore, $h \circ f = g$.

Next, we show that $h$ is a homomorphism from $\mathcal{C}$ to $\mathcal{D}$. Let $\sigma \in \Sigma$ have type $s_1 \times \cdots \times s_n \rightarrow s'$. For $C'_i \subseteq C_{s_i}$, $1 \leq i \leq n$, let $\Phi(C'_1, \ldots, C'_n)$ abbreviate the assertion that for all $c_i \in C'_i$, $1 \leq i \leq n$,

$$h_{s'}\, \sigma_{\mathcal{C}}\langle c_1, \ldots, c_n\rangle = \sigma_{\mathcal{D}}\langle h_{s_1}\, c_1, \ldots, h_{s_n}\, c_n\rangle.$$

If $a_i \in A_{s_i}$, $1 \leq i \leq n$, then

$$\begin{aligned}
h_{s'}\, \sigma_{\mathcal{C}}\langle f_{s_1}\, a_1, \ldots, f_{s_n}\, a_n\rangle &= h_{s'}\, cl(\sigma_{\mathcal{A}}(cl(\{a_1\}) \times \cdots \times cl(\{a_n\}))) \\
&= h_{s'}\, cl(\sigma_{\mathcal{A}}(\{a_1\} \times \cdots \times \{a_n\})) \qquad \text{(lemma 2.4.13)} \\
&= h_{s'}\, cl(\{\sigma_{\mathcal{A}}\langle a_1, \ldots, a_n\rangle\}) \\
&= h_{s'}(f_{s'}\, \sigma_{\mathcal{A}}\langle a_1, \ldots, a_n\rangle) \\
&= g_{s'}\, \sigma_{\mathcal{A}}\langle a_1, \ldots, a_n\rangle \\
&= \sigma_{\mathcal{D}}\langle g_{s_1}\, a_1, \ldots, g_{s_n}\, a_n\rangle \\
&= \sigma_{\mathcal{D}}\langle h_{s_1}(f_{s_1}\, a_1), \ldots, h_{s_n}(f_{s_n}\, a_n)\rangle,
\end{aligned}$$

showing that $\Phi(f_{s_1}\, A_{s_1}, \ldots, f_{s_n}\, A_{s_n})$ holds. If $n = 0$ then $h_{s'}\, \sigma_{\mathcal{C}}\langle\rangle = \sigma_{\mathcal{D}}\langle\rangle$; so, assume $n \geq 1$. It is sufficient to show that the following chain of implications holds:

$$\begin{aligned}
\Phi(f_{s_1}\, A_{s_1}, \ldots, f_{s_n}\, A_{s_n}) &\Rightarrow \Phi(C_{s_1}, f_{s_2}\, A_{s_2}, \ldots, f_{s_n}\, A_{s_n}) \\
&\Rightarrow \Phi(C_{s_1}, C_{s_2}, f_{s_3}\, A_{s_3}, \ldots, f_{s_n}\, A_{s_n}) \\
&\;\;\vdots \\
&\Rightarrow \Phi(C_{s_1}, \ldots, C_{s_n}).
\end{aligned}$$

We show a representative step

$$\begin{aligned}
&\Phi(C_{s_1}, \ldots, C_{s_{i-1}}, f_{s_i}\, A_{s_i}, f_{s_{i+1}}\, A_{s_{i+1}}, \ldots, f_{s_n}\, A_{s_n}) \\
\Rightarrow\;& \Phi(C_{s_1}, \ldots, C_{s_{i-1}}, C_{s_i}, f_{s_{i+1}}\, A_{s_{i+1}}, \ldots, f_{s_n}\, A_{s_n})
\end{aligned}$$

by induction over $C_{s_i}$. Let $C'$ be the set of all $c_i \in C_{s_i}$ such that

$$h_{s'}\,\sigma_C\langle c_1,\ldots,c_n\rangle = \sigma_D\langle h_{s_1}\,c_1,\ldots,h_{s_n}\,c_n\rangle,$$

for all $c_1 \in C_{s_1}$, ..., $c_{i-1} \in C_{s_{i-1}}$, $c_{i+1} \in f_{s_{i+1}}\,A_{s_{i+1}}$, ..., $c_n \in f_{s_n}\,A_{s_n}$. Then $f_{s_i}\,A_{s_i} \subseteq C'$, and $C'$ is closed under lub's of directed sets, since $h$ is continuous and $\mathcal{C}$ and $\mathcal{D}$ are complete. Thus we have shown that $h\colon \mathcal{C} \to \mathcal{D}$ is a homomorphism.

Finally, we can apply lemma 2.4.10 once again to show that $h$ is the unique continuous homomorphism from $\mathcal{C}$ to $\mathcal{D}$ such that $h \circ f = g$. This completes the proof of theorem 2.4.2. □

We now introduce some notation that is based upon theorem 2.4.2.

**Definition 2.4.14** Let $\mathcal{A}$ be a $\Gamma$-complete ordered algebra. We write $\mathcal{A}^\Gamma$ (the $\Gamma$-*completion* of $\mathcal{A}$) and *em* for the complete ordered algebra $\mathcal{C}$ and the $\Gamma$-continuous order-embedding $f$, respectively, that are given by the proof of theorem 2.4.2. If $g\colon \mathcal{A} \to \mathcal{D}$ is a $\Gamma$-continuous homomorphism, for a complete ordered algebra $\mathcal{D}$, then we write $g^\Gamma$ for the unique continuous homomorphism from $\mathcal{A}^\Gamma$ to $\mathcal{D}$ such that $g = g^\Gamma \circ em$.

In the remainder of this section, we present two quotienting constructions: one for ordered algebras and substitutive pre-orderings, and the other for complete ordered algebras and substitutive inductive pre-orderings.

**Theorem 2.4.15 (Courcelle and Nivat)** *Let $\mathcal{A}$ be an ordered algebra and $\leq$ a substitutive pre-ordering over $\mathcal{A}$ that respects the ordering of $\mathcal{A}$, i.e., $\sqsubseteq_A \subseteq \leq$. There is an ordered algebra $\mathcal{B}$, together with a surjective monotonic homomorphism $f\colon \mathcal{A} \to \mathcal{B}$ with the property that $\leq = \leq_f$, such that if $\mathcal{C}$ is an ordered algebra and $g\colon \mathcal{A} \to \mathcal{C}$ is a monotonic homomorphism with the property that $\leq \subseteq \leq_g$ then there is a unique monotonic homomorphism $h\colon \mathcal{B} \to \mathcal{C}$ such that $g = h \circ f$:*

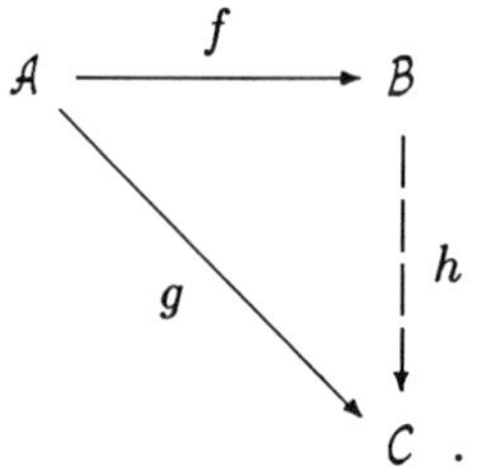

**Proof.** Let $\equiv$ be the congruence over $\mathcal{A}$ induced by $\leq$, i.e., $\equiv\, = \,\leq \cap \geq$. We define an ordered algebra $\mathcal{B}$ as follows. For $s \in S$, $B_s = A_s/{\equiv_s}$, and $\sqsubseteq_{B_s}$ is defined by

$$[a_1]\equiv_s \sqsubseteq_s [a_n]\equiv_s \text{ iff } a_1 \leq_s a_2.$$

If $\sigma \in \Sigma$ has type $s_1 \times \cdots \times s_n \to s'$ then the operation $\sigma_{\mathcal{B}}$ is defined by

$$\sigma_{\mathcal{B}}\langle [a_1]\equiv_{s_1}, \ldots, [a_n]\equiv_{s_n}\rangle = [\sigma_{\mathcal{A}}\langle a_1, \ldots, a_n\rangle]\equiv_{s'}.$$

It is easy to see that $\sqsubseteq_{\mathcal{B}}$ is well-defined on the equivalence classes and is a partial ordering, that the operations are well-defined and monotonic, and that

$$\Omega_{s\mathcal{B}} = [\Omega_{s\mathcal{A}}]\equiv_s = [\bot_{A_s}]\equiv_s = \bot_{B_s},$$

for all $s \in S$.

Next, we define a surjective homomorphism $f: \mathcal{A} \to \mathcal{B}$ by $f_s\, a = [a]\equiv_s$. Then $f$ is monotonic, since $\sqsubseteq_A \subseteq \leq$, and $\leq\, = \,\leq_f$, since

$$a_1 \leq_s a_2 \text{ iff } [a_1]\equiv_s \sqsubseteq_s [a_2]\equiv_s \text{ iff } f_s\, a_1 \sqsubseteq_s f_s\, a_2,$$

for all $a_1, a_2 \in A_s$, $s \in S$.

It remains to show the universal property of $(f, \mathcal{B})$. Let $\mathcal{C}$ and $g$ be as in the statement of the theorem. Define a monotonic homomorphism $h: \mathcal{B} \to \mathcal{C}$ by $h_s\, [a]\equiv_s = g_s\, a$. Clearly, $h$ is well-defined on the equivalence classes and monotonic, since $\leq\, \subseteq\, \leq_g$. Suppose $\sigma \in \Sigma$ has type $s_1 \times \cdots \times s_n \to s'$ and $a_i \in A_{s_i}$, $1 \leq i \leq n$. Then,

$$\begin{aligned} h_{s'}\, \sigma_{\mathcal{B}}\langle [a_1]\equiv_{s_1}, \ldots, [a_n]\equiv_{s_n}\rangle &= h_{s'}\, [\sigma_{\mathcal{A}}\langle a_1, \ldots, a_n\rangle]\equiv_{s'} \\ &= g_{s'}\, \sigma_{\mathcal{A}}\langle a_1, \ldots, a_n\rangle \\ &= \sigma_{\mathcal{C}}\langle g_{s_1}\, a_1, \ldots, g_{s_n}\, a_n\rangle \\ &= \sigma_{\mathcal{C}}\langle h_{s_1}\, [a_1]\equiv_{s_1}, \ldots, h_{s_n}\, [a_n]\equiv_{s_n}\rangle. \end{aligned}$$

Thus $h$ is, indeed, a homomorphism. From the definitions of $h$ and $f$, it follows immediately that $g = h \circ f$. For the uniqueness of $h$, let $h': \mathcal{B} \to \mathcal{C}$ be a monotonic homomorphism such that $g = h' \circ f$. Then,

$$h_s\, [a]\equiv_s = h_s(f_s\, a) = g_s\, a = h'_s(f_s\, a) = h'_s\, [a]\equiv_s,$$

for all $a \in A_s$, $s \in S$, showing that $h = h'$. □

We now give some notation that is based upon theorem 2.4.15.

**Definition 2.4.16** Let $\mathcal{A}$ be an ordered algebra and $\leq$ a substitutive pre-ordering over $\mathcal{A}$ such that $\sqsubseteq_A \subseteq \leq$. We write $\mathcal{A}/\!\leq$ (the *quotient* of $\mathcal{A}$ *by* $\leq$) and $qt_{\leq}$ for the ordered algebra $\mathcal{B}$ and the surjective monotonic homomorphism $f$, respectively, that are given by the proof of theorem 2.4.15. If $g: \mathcal{A} \to \mathcal{C}$ is a monotonic homomorphism with the property that $\leq \subseteq \leq_g$ then we write $g/\!\leq$ for the unique monotonic homomorphism from $\mathcal{A}/\!\leq$ to $\mathcal{C}$ such that $g = (g/\!\leq) \circ qt_{\leq}$. We often drop the subscript $\leq$ from $qt_{\leq}$ when it is clear from the context.

Note that if $\preceq$ is an $\Omega$-least substitutive pre-ordering over $\mathcal{T}$ then $\sqsubseteq_{OT} = \preceq^{\Omega} \subseteq \preceq$, and so $\mathcal{OT}/\!\preceq$ is well defined. Clearly, such an $\mathcal{OT}/\!\preceq$ is reachable.

We now present two simple corollaries of theorem 2.4.15, followed by the second of our quotienting theorems, theorem 2.4.19.

**Corollary 2.4.17** *Let $\mathcal{A}$ be an ordered algebra and $\leq$ a substitutive pre-ordering over $\mathcal{A}$ such that $\sqsubseteq_A \subseteq \leq$. Let $A' \subseteq A_s$ and $a \in A_s$, $s \in S$. Then, $a$ is a lub of $A'$ in $\langle A_s, \leq_s\rangle$ iff $qt_s\, a$ is the lub of $qt_s\, A'$ in $(A/\!\leq)_s$.*

**Proof.** Follows easily from the surjectivity of $qt$ and the fact that $a_1 \leq_s a_2$ iff $qt_s\, a_1 \sqsubseteq_s qt_s\, a_2$, for $a_1, a_2 \in A_s$, $s \in S$. □

**Corollary 2.4.18** *If $\mathcal{A}$ is a reachable ordered algebra then $\mathcal{A}$ is order-isomorphic to $\mathcal{OT}/\!\preceq_{\mathcal{A}}$.*

**Proof.** By theorem 2.4.15, the following diagram commutes:

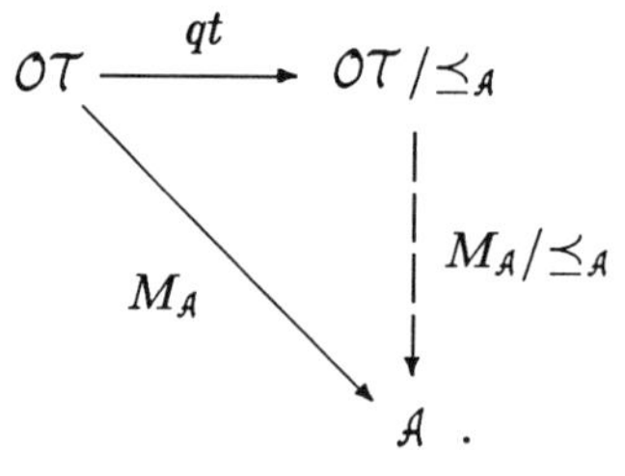


It is sufficient to show that $M_{\mathcal{A}}/\!\preceq_{\mathcal{A}}$ is a surjective order-embedding. The surjectivity of $M_{\mathcal{A}}/\!\preceq_{\mathcal{A}}$ follows from the surjectivity of $M_{\mathcal{A}}$, and $M_{\mathcal{A}}/\!\preceq_{\mathcal{A}}$ is an order-embedding since $qt$ is surjective and $\leq_{qt} = \preceq_{\mathcal{A}}$. □

**Theorem 2.4.19 (Courcelle and Raoult)** *Let $\mathcal{A}$ be a complete ordered algebra and $\leq$ a substitutive inductive pre-ordering over $\mathcal{A}$. There is a complete ordered algebra $\mathcal{B}$,* *together with a continuous homomorphism* $f\colon \mathcal{A} \to \mathcal{B}$ *with the property that* $\leq\, = \,\leq_f$*, such that if* $\mathcal{C}$ *is a complete ordered algebra and* $g\colon \mathcal{A} \to \mathcal{C}$ *is a continuous homomorphism with the property that* $\leq\, \subseteq\, \leq_g$ *then there is a unique continuous homomorphism* $h\colon \mathcal{B} \to \mathcal{C}$ *such that* $g = h \circ f$*:*

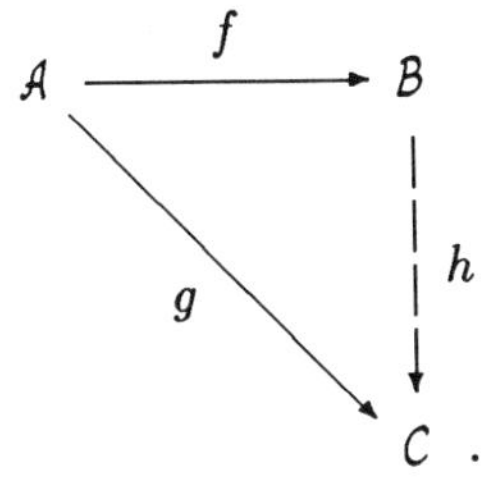


**Proof.** By theorem 2.4.15, we know that $qt\colon \mathcal{A} \to \mathcal{A}/\leq$ is a surjective monotonic homomorphism ($\sqsubseteq_A \subseteq \leq$ since $\leq$ is inductive). Define a family of subsets $\Gamma$ of $\mathcal{A}/\leq$ by

$$\Gamma_s = \{\, qt_s\, D \mid D \subseteq A_s \text{ is a directed set}\,\}.$$

If $a \in A_s$, $s \in S$, then $\{qt_s\, a\} = qt_s\{a\} \in \Gamma_s$. If $\sigma \in \Sigma$ has type $s_1 \times \cdots \times s_n \to s'$ and $D_i \subseteq A_{s_i}$, $1 \leq i \leq n$, are directed sets then

$$\sigma((qt_{s_1} D_1) \times \cdots \times (qt_{s_n} D_n)) = qt_{s'}\, \sigma(D_1 \times \cdots \times D_n) \in \Gamma_{s'}.$$

Thus $\Gamma$ is well-defined. Next, we show that $\mathcal{A}/\leq$ is $\Gamma$-complete. Suppose $D \subseteq A_s$, $s \in S$, is a directed set; we show that $qt_s \bigsqcup D = \bigsqcup qt_s\, D$. Clearly $qt_s \bigsqcup D$ is an ub of $qt_s\, D$. Suppose $qt_s\, a$ is an ub of $qt_s\, D$. Then $D \leq_s a$ and, since $\leq$ is inductive, $\bigsqcup D \leq_s a$. Thus $qt_s \bigsqcup D \sqsubseteq_s qt_s\, a$, as required. Suppose $\sigma \in \Sigma$ has type $s_1 \times \cdots \times s_n \to s'$ and $D_i \subseteq A_{s_i}$, $1 \leq i \leq n$, are directed sets. Then,

$$\begin{aligned}
\sigma\langle \bigsqcup qt_{s_1} D_1, \ldots, \bigsqcup qt_{s_n} D_n\rangle &= \sigma\langle qt_{s_1} \bigsqcup D_1, \ldots, qt_{s_n} \bigsqcup D_n\rangle \\
&= qt_{s'}\, \sigma\langle \bigsqcup D_1, \ldots, \bigsqcup D_n\rangle \\
&= qt_{s'} \bigsqcup \sigma(D_1 \times \cdots \times D_n) \\
&= \bigsqcup qt_{s'}\, \sigma(D_1 \times \cdots \times D_n) \\
&= \bigsqcup \sigma((qt_{s_1} D_1) \times \cdots \times (qt_{s_n} D_n)).
\end{aligned}$$

By theorem 2.4.2, we know that $em\colon \mathcal{A}/\leq \to (\mathcal{A}/\leq)^\Gamma$ is a $\Gamma$-continuous order-embedding into a complete ordered algebra. We take $(\mathcal{A}/\leq)^\Gamma$ as our candidate for $\mathcal{B}$ and $em \circ qt$ as our candidate for $f$. Clearly $f$ is a monotonic homomorphism. For continuity, let $D \subseteq A_s$, $s \in S$, be a directed set. Then,

$$em_s(qt_s \bigsqcup D) = em_s \bigsqcup qt_s\, D = \bigsqcup em_s(qt_s\, D),$$

since $qt_s D \in \Gamma_s$. To show that $\leq \; = \; \leq_f$, let $a_1, a_2 \in A_s$, $s \in S$. Then,

$$a_1 \leq_s a_2 \text{ iff } qt_s\, a_1 \sqsubseteq_s qt_s\, a_2 \text{ iff } em_s(qt_s\, a_1) \sqsubseteq_s em_s(qt_s\, a_2),$$

since $em$ is an order-embedding.

It remains to show the universal property of $(f, \mathcal{B})$. Let $\mathcal{C}$ and $g$ be as in the statement of the theorem.

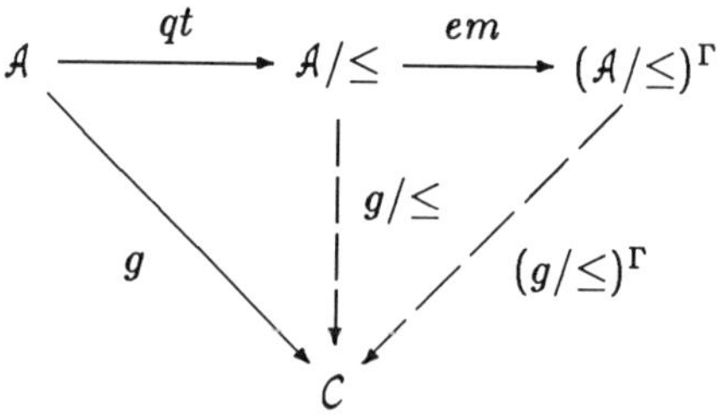


By theorem 2.4.15, we know that (†) $g/\leq$ is the unique monotonic homomorphism from $\mathcal{A}/\leq$ to $\mathcal{C}$ such that $g = (g/\leq) \circ qt$. To see that $g/\leq$ is $\Gamma$-continuous, let $D \subseteq A_s$, $s \in S$, be a directed set. Then,

$$\begin{aligned}(g/\leq)_s \bigsqcup qt_s\, D &= (g/\leq)_s(qt_s \bigsqcup D) \\ &= g_s \bigsqcup D \\ &= \bigsqcup g_s\, D \\ &= \bigsqcup (g/\leq)_s(qt_s\, D),\end{aligned}$$

since $g$ is continuous. Thus, by theorem 2.4.2, we know that (‡) $(g/\leq)^\Gamma$ is the unique continuous homomorphism from $(\mathcal{A}/\leq)^\Gamma$ to $\mathcal{C}$ such that $g/\leq \; = (g/\leq)^\Gamma \circ em$. We take $(g/\leq)^\Gamma$ as our candidate for $h\colon \mathcal{B} \to \mathcal{C}$. Clearly $g = h \circ f$, i.e., $g = (g/\leq)^\Gamma \circ em \circ qt$. For uniqueness, suppose $h'\colon \mathcal{B} \to \mathcal{C}$ is a continuous homomorphism such that $g = h' \circ f$, i.e., $g = h' \circ em \circ qt$. Then $g/\leq \; = h' \circ em$, by (†), and thus $h' = h$, by (‡) and the continuity of $h'$. □

We now give some notation that is based upon theorem 2.4.19.

**Definition 2.4.20** Let $\mathcal{A}$ be a complete ordered algebra and $\leq$ a substitutive inductive pre-ordering over $\mathcal{A}$. We write $\mathcal{A}/\!/\leq$ (the *inductive quotient* of $\mathcal{A}$ *by* $\leq$) and $qt_{\leq}$ for the complete ordered algebra $\mathcal{B}$ and the continuous homomorphism $f$, respectively, that are given by the proof of theorem 2.4.19. If $g\colon \mathcal{A} \to \mathcal{C}$ is a continuous homomorphism with the property that $\leq \; \subseteq \; \leq_g$ then we write $g/\!/\leq$ for the unique continuous homomorphism from $\mathcal{A}/\!/\leq$ to $\mathcal{C}$ such that $g = (g/\!/\leq) \circ qt_{\leq}$.

The section concludes with the lemma that inductive quotients of inductively reachable complete ordered algebras are themselves inductively reachable.

**Lemma 2.4.21** *If $\mathcal{A}$ is an inductively reachable complete ordered algebra and $\leq$ is a substitutive inductive pre-ordering over $\mathcal{A}$ then $\mathcal{A}//\leq$ is also inductively reachable.*

**Proof.** By lemma 2.3.33, it is sufficient to show that $\mathcal{A}//\leq$ and $R(\mathcal{A}//\leq)$ are order-isomorphic. Let $i$ be the inclusion from $R(A//\leq)$ to $A//\leq$, so that $i$ is a continuous homomorphism from $R(\mathcal{A}//\leq)$ to $\mathcal{A}//\leq$. By lemma 2.3.32, $qt\colon \mathcal{A} \to \mathcal{A}//\leq$ is also a continuous homomorphism from $\mathcal{A}$ to $R(\mathcal{A}//\leq)$, and if $a_1 \leq_s a_2$, for $a_1, a_2 \in A_s$, $s \in S$, then $qt_s\, a_1 \sqsubseteq_{(A//\leq)_s} qt_s\, a_2$, and thus $qt_s\, a_1 \sqsubseteq_{R(A//\leq)_s} qt_s\, a_2$. Then, by theorem 2.4.19, we may let $h\colon \mathcal{A}//\leq \to R(\mathcal{A}//\leq)$ be the unique continuous homomorphism such that $qt = h \circ qt$.

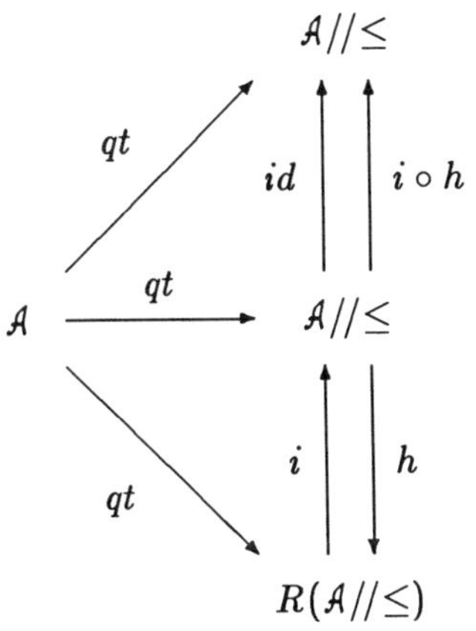


By lemma 2.3.31, $h \circ i = id_{R(\mathcal{A}//\leq)}$. Also by lemma 2.3.31, it follows that $(i \circ h) \circ qt = qt$, and thus $i \circ h = id_{(\mathcal{A}//\leq)}$, since, by theorem 2.4.19, $id_{(\mathcal{A}//\leq)}$ is the unique continuous homomorphism over $\mathcal{A}//\leq$ such that $qt = id_{(\mathcal{A}//\leq)} \circ qt$. $\square$

# 3 Full Abstraction and Least Fixed Point Models

This chapter is devoted to the definitions and elementary results concerning full abstraction and least fixed point models. This material is based upon the universal algebra of the previous chapter, and the combination of these two chapters forms the foundation upon which the remainder of the monograph is built.

Although we will apply this material to several programming languages in subsequent chapters, it is convenient to have an example programming language available in this chapter, in order to motivate the various definitions and results. For this purpose, we consider an imperative programming language skeleton with null, sequencing, conditional and iteration statements. Formally, consider a signature $\Sigma$ over a single sort, $\star$, that contains the following operators, where *Exp* is some unspecified set of boolean expressions:

(i) $\Omega_\star$ and *skip* of type $\star$;

(ii) *while E do−od* of type $\star \to \star$, for all $E \in Exp$; and

(iii) ; and *if E then−else−fi* of type $\star \times \star \to \star$, for all $E \in Exp$.

Since there is only one sort, we drop the sort subscripts from carriers, relations, etc., when considering this language below.

## 3.1 Full Abstraction

In this section, we formalize what it means for an algebra or ordered algebra to be correct or fully abstract. We actually consider three kinds of correctness and full abstraction: equational, inequational and contextual. The first and third are relations between algebras and congruences over $\mathcal{T}$, whereas the second is a relation between ordered algebras and $\Omega$-least substitutive pre-orderings over $\mathcal{T}$. As usual, we think of these congruences and pre-orderings over the term algebra as notions of program equivalence and ordering, respectively.

**Definition 3.1.1** Let $\approx$ be a congruence over $\mathcal{T}$ and $\mathcal{A}$ be an algebra. Then $\mathcal{A}$ is $\approx$-*equationally correct* (or simply $\approx$-*correct*) iff $\approx_{\mathcal{A}} \subseteq \approx$, and $\approx$-*equationally fully abstract* (or simply $\approx$-*fully abstract*) iff $\approx_{\mathcal{A}} = \approx$.

**Definition 3.1.2** Let $\preceq$ be an $\Omega$-least substitutive pre-ordering over $\mathcal{T}$ and $\mathcal{A}$ be an ordered algebra. Then $\mathcal{A}$ is ***$\preceq$-inequationally correct*** iff $\preceq_{\mathcal{A}} \subseteq \preceq$, and ***$\preceq$-inequationally fully abstract*** iff $\preceq_{\mathcal{A}} = \preceq$.

It is easy to see that equational (respectively, inequational) full abstraction implies equational (respectively, inequational) correctness, but that the converse, in general, fails. Note that if $\preceq$ is an $\Omega$-least substitutive pre-ordering over $\mathcal{T}$ and $\mathcal{A}$ is a $\preceq$-inequationally fully abstract (respectively, $\preceq$-inequationally correct) ordered algebra then $\mathcal{A}$ is $\approx$-fully abstract (respectively, $\approx$-correct), where $\approx$ is the congruence over $\mathcal{T}$ induced by $\preceq$: $\approx \, = \, \preceq \cap \succeq$.

Suppose that we are given a notion of program equivalence $\approx$ for our example programming language, i.e., a congruence over $\mathcal{T}$, with the expected property that

$$\textit{while } E \textit{ do } t \textit{ od} \approx \textit{if } E \textit{ then } t; \textit{while } E \textit{ do } t \textit{ od else skip fi},$$

for all boolean expressions $E \in \mathit{Exp}$ and terms $t \in T$. Then every while-loop will have the same meaning as its expansion in any $\approx$-fully abstract algebra $\mathcal{A}$, and thus for all $E \in \mathit{Exp}$, the equation

$$\textit{while } E \textit{ do } a \textit{ od} = \textit{if } E \textit{ then } a; \textit{while } E \textit{ do } a \textit{ od else skip fi}$$

will hold for all elements of $A$ that are denotable. But it is also reasonable to ask that this equation hold for all $a \in A$, i.e., that the unary derived operations

$$\textit{while } E \textit{ do } v \textit{ od}[v]$$

and

$$\textit{if } E \textit{ then } v; \textit{while } E \textit{ do } v \textit{ od else skip fi}[v]$$

be equal, for all $E \in \mathit{Exp}$. This suggests that we consider the following generalization of equational full abstraction from terms to contexts, or, more precisely, to derived operators.

**Definition 3.1.3** Let $\approx$ be a congruence over $\mathcal{T}$ and $\mathcal{A}$ be an algebra. Then $\mathcal{A}$ is ***$\approx$-contextually correct*** iff for all derived operators $c_1[v_1, \ldots, v_n]$ and $c_2[v_1, \ldots, v_n]$ of type $s_1 \times \cdots \times s_n \rightarrow s'$,

$$\text{if } c_{1\mathcal{A}} = c_{2\mathcal{A}} \text{ then for all } t_i \in T_{s_i}, 1 \leq i \leq n,\ c_1\langle t_1, \ldots, t_n \rangle \approx_{s'} c_2\langle t_1, \ldots, t_n \rangle,$$

and $\mathcal{A}$ is ***$\approx$-contextually fully abstract*** iff for all derived operators $c_1[v_1, \ldots, v_n]$ and $c_2[v_1, \ldots, v_n]$ of type $s_1 \times \cdots \times s_n \rightarrow s'$,

$$c_{1\mathcal{A}} = c_{2\mathcal{A}} \text{ iff for all } t_i \in T_{s_i}, 1 \leq i \leq n,\ c_1\langle t_1, \ldots, t_n \rangle \approx_{s'} c_2\langle t_1, \ldots, t_n \rangle.$$

Thus an algebra $\mathcal{A}$ is equationally fully abstract with reference to a congruence $\approx$ iff ground equations (equations with no free variables) hold in $\mathcal{A}$ exactly when they hold in $\approx$, and contextually fully abstract iff universally quantified equations hold in $\mathcal{A}$ exactly when they hold in $\approx$.

Note that we could also define the notions of inequational contextual full abstraction and correctness, in the obvious way.

It is easy to see that contextual full abstraction implies contextual correctness but that the converse, in general, fails. Furthermore, contextual full abstraction (respectively, contextual correctness) implies full abstraction (respectively, correctness), since for every term $t$ of sort $s$, $t[\,]$ is a constant derived operator of type $s$. The next two theorems show that full abstraction does not, in general, imply contextual full abstraction, but that correctness does imply contextual correctness.

**Theorem 3.1.4** *There is a signature $\Sigma$, a congruence $\approx$ over $\mathcal{T}$, and a $\approx$-fully abstract, complete ordered algebra that is not $\approx$-contextually fully abstract.*

**Proof.** Let $\Sigma$ over $S = \{\star\}$ have the following operators:

(i) $\Omega_\star$ of type $\star$; and

(ii) $f$ and $g$ of type $\star \to \star$.

Since there is only one sort, we drop the sort subscripts from carriers, relations, etc., below. Let $\approx$ be the greatest congruence over $\mathcal{T}$ (all terms are congruent). Define a complete ordered algebra $\mathcal{A}$ as follows. It's domain $A$ is the two-point cpo $\{\bot, \top\}$, where $\bot \sqsubseteq \top$. It's operations are defined by:

$$\Omega = \bot;$$

$$f\,a = \bot;$$

$$g\,a = \begin{cases} \bot & \text{if } a = \bot, \\ \top & \text{if } a = \top. \end{cases}$$

It is easy to see that $M\,t = \bot$, for all $t \in T$, and thus that $\mathcal{A}$ is $\approx$-fully abstract. If $v \in V$, $(f\langle v\rangle)[v]$ and $(g\langle v\rangle)[v]$ are unary derived operators, and

$$(f\langle v\rangle)\langle t\rangle \approx (g\langle v\rangle)\langle t\rangle,$$

for all $t \in T$, but

$$(f\langle v\rangle)_{\mathcal{A}} = f \neq g = (g\langle v\rangle)_{\mathcal{A}},$$

showing that $\mathcal{A}$ is not contextually fully abstract. □

Note that the complete ordered algebra $\mathcal{A}$ in the previous proof is not inductively reachable. In chapter 5, we will see that inductive reachability is a sufficient condition for full abstraction and contextual full abstraction to coincide.

**Theorem 3.1.5** *Let $\approx$ be a congruence over $\mathcal{T}$. An algebra is $\approx$-correct iff it is $\approx$-contextually correct.*

**Proof.** Let $\mathcal{A}$ be an algebra. The "if" direction is trivial. For the "only if" direction, suppose $c_1[v_1, \ldots, v_n]$ and $c_2[v_1, \ldots, v_n]$ are derived operators of type $s_1 \times \cdots \times s_n \to s'$, and that $c_{1\mathcal{A}} = c_{2\mathcal{A}}$. Then, for all $t_i \in T_{s_i}$, $1 \leq i \leq n$,

$$\begin{aligned} M_{s'}\, c_1\langle t_1, \ldots, t_n\rangle &= c_1\langle M_{s_1}\, t_1, \ldots, M_{s_n}\, t_n\rangle \\ &= c_2\langle M_{s_1}\, t_1, \ldots, M_{s_n}\, t_n\rangle \\ &= M_{s'}\, c_2\langle t_1, \ldots, t_n\rangle, \end{aligned}$$

and thus

$$c_1\langle t_1, \ldots, t_n\rangle \approx_{s'} c_2\langle t_1, \ldots, t_n\rangle,$$

since $\mathcal{A}$ is $\approx$-correct. □

Mulmuley has constructed a fully abstract model of the combinatory logic version of PCF that fails to satisfy the usual equational axiom for the $K$ combinator [Mul]. This equation does hold, however, in the notion of program equivalence for PCF, and thus Mulmuley's model is not contextually fully abstract. It would be interesting to find other examples of fully abstract models that fail to be contextually fully abstract.

## 3.2 Least Fixed Point Models

In this section, we say what it means for a complete ordered algebra to be a least fixed point model. This is not an intrinsic property of complete ordered algebras, but is expressed via the satisfaction of families of least fixed point constraints. We consider two kinds of least fixed point models: ordinary and contextual. The latter is the natural generalization of the former from terms to contexts, or, more precisely, to derived operators. We also consider the satisfaction of families of least fixed point constraints by $\Omega$-least substitutive pre-orderings over the term algebra.

We begin by considering our example imperative programming language again. Conventionally, a model $\mathcal{A}$ of this language, i.e., a complete ordered algebra, should assign a while-loop *while E do t od* the meaning $\bigsqcup_{n\in\omega} w^n(E,t)$, where $w^n(E,t)$ is the $\omega$-chain in $A$ defined by

$$\begin{aligned} w^0(E,t) &= \bot, \\ w^{n+1}(E,t) &= \textit{if } E \textit{ then } (M\,t); w^n(E,t) \textit{ else skip fi}. \end{aligned}$$

This requirement can be expressed syntactically, as follows. Define an $\omega$-chain $W^n(E,t)$ in the ordered term algebra by

$$\begin{aligned} W^0(E,t) &= \Omega, \\ W^{n+1}(E,t) &= \textit{if } E \textit{ then } t; W^n(E,t) \textit{ else skip fi}, \end{aligned}$$

so that $w^n(E,t) = M\,W^n(E,t)$, for all $n \subset \omega$. Then we require that

$$M \textit{ while } E \textit{ do } t \textit{ od} = \bigsqcup_{n\in\omega} M\,W^n(E,t).$$

This situation is quite general, and we are led to the following definitions.

**Definition 3.2.1** A *family of least fixed point constraints* $\Phi$ is an $S$-indexed family of sets such that for all $s \in S$, $\Phi_s \subseteq T_s \times \mathcal{P}T_s$, and for all $\langle t, T'\rangle \in \Phi_s$, $T'$ is a directed set in $OT_s$. We write $t \equiv \bigsqcup T'$ instead of $\langle t, T'\rangle$ for elements of $\Phi_s$.

**Definition 3.2.2** Let $\Phi$ be a family of least fixed point constraints and $\mathcal{A}$ be a complete ordered algebra. Then $\mathcal{A}$ is a *$\Phi$-least fixed point model* (or *$\mathcal{A}$ satisfies $\Phi$*) iff for all $t \equiv \bigsqcup T' \in \Phi_s$, $s \in S$, $M_s\,t = \bigsqcup M_s\,T'$.

Note that if $T' \subseteq OT_s$ is a directed set and $\mathcal{A}$ is an ordered algebra then $M_s\,T' \subseteq A_s$ is also a directed set.

The family of least fixed point constraints $\Phi$ for our example language would be

$$\{\, \textit{while } E \textit{ do } t \textit{ od} \equiv \bigsqcup\{\, W^n(E,t) \mid n \in \omega \,\} \mid E \in \textit{Exp}, t \in T \,\}.$$

Next, we introduce a natural notion of closure, under the operations of the term algebra, for families of least fixed point constraints.

**Definition 3.2.3** A family of least fixed point constraints $\Phi$ is *closed* iff for all $\sigma \in \Sigma$ of type $s_1 \times \cdots \times s_n \to s'$, if $t_i \equiv \bigsqcup T'_i \in \Phi_{s_i}$, $1 \leq i \leq n$, and $T''$ is a cofinal subset of $\sigma(T'_1 \times \cdots \times T'_n)$ then $\sigma\langle t_1, \ldots, t_n\rangle \equiv \bigsqcup T'' \in \Phi_{s'}$.

We write $\overline{\Phi}$ for the *closure* of $\Phi$, i.e., the least closed family of least fixed point constraints containing $\Phi$.

This closure operation is well-defined, because cofinal subsets of directed sets are themselves directed. Since $\overline{\Phi}$ is defined inductively, we can give proofs by induction over $\overline{\Phi}$. The next lemma shows that $\overline{\Phi}$ has the usual closure properties.

**Lemma 3.2.4** (i) $\Phi \subseteq \overline{\Phi}$
(ii) $\overline{\Phi} = \overline{\overline{\Phi}}$
(iii) *if* $\Phi_1 \subseteq \Phi_2$ *then* $\overline{\Phi_1} \subseteq \overline{\Phi_2}$

**Proof.** (i) and (ii) are immediate from the definition. For (iii), suppose $\Phi_1 \subseteq \Phi_2$. Then $\Phi_1 \subseteq \overline{\Phi_2}$, by (i), and so $\overline{\Phi_2}$ is a closed family that contains $\Phi_1$. But $\overline{\Phi_1}$ is the least such family, and thus $\overline{\Phi_1} \subseteq \overline{\Phi_2}$. $\square$

Three lemmas concerning closed families of least fixed point constraints now follow. The first two concern "singleton" constraints of the form $t \equiv \bigsqcup\{t\}$, and the third shows that if a complete ordered algebra satisfies a family of least fixed point constraints then it also satisfies the closure of that family of constraints.

**Lemma 3.2.5** *If* $\Phi$ *is a closed family of least fixed point constraints then* $t \equiv \bigsqcup\{t\} \in \Phi_s$, *for all* $t \in T_s$, $s \in S$.

**Proof.** By structural induction over $T$. Define $T' \subseteq T$ by $T'_s = \{\, t \in T_s \mid t \equiv \bigsqcup\{t\} \in \Phi_s \,\}$. Suppose $\sigma \in \Sigma$ has type $s_1 \times \cdots \times s_n \rightarrow s'$, and $t_i \in T'_{s_i}$, $1 \leq i \leq n$. Then $t_i \equiv \bigsqcup\{t_i\} \in \Phi_{s_i}$, $1 \leq i \leq n$, and, since $\Phi$ is closed,

$$\begin{aligned}\sigma\langle t_1, \ldots, t_n\rangle \equiv \bigsqcup\{\sigma\langle t_1, \ldots, t_n\rangle\} &= \sigma\langle t_1, \ldots, t_n\rangle \equiv \bigsqcup \sigma(\{t_1\} \times \cdots \times \{t_n\}) \\ &\in \Phi_{s'}.\end{aligned}$$

Thus $\sigma\langle t_1, \ldots, t_n\rangle \in T'_{s'}$, as required. $\square$

**Lemma 3.2.6** *The family of least fixed point constraints* $\Phi$ *defined by*

$$\Phi_s = \{\, t \equiv \bigsqcup\{t\} \mid t \in T_s \,\}$$

*is the least closed family of least fixed point constraints, i.e.,* $\Phi = \overline{\emptyset}$.

**Proof.** By lemma 3.2.5 it is sufficient to show that $\Phi$ is closed. Suppose $\sigma \in \Sigma$ has type $s_1 \times \cdots \times s_n \rightarrow s'$, and $t_i \equiv \bigsqcup\{t_i\} \in \Phi_{s_i}$, $1 \leq i \leq n$. Then,

$$\sigma(\{t_1\} \times \cdots \times \{t_n\}) = \{\sigma\langle t_1, \ldots, t_n\rangle\}$$

is the only cofinal subset of itself, and $\sigma\langle t_1, \ldots, t_n\rangle \equiv \bigsqcup\{\sigma\langle t_1, \ldots, t_n\rangle\} \in \Phi_{s'}$. $\square$

**Lemma 3.2.7** *Let $\Phi$ be a family of least fixed point constraints and $\mathcal{A}$ be a complete ordered algebra. If $\mathcal{A}$ satisfies $\Phi$ then $\mathcal{A}$ satisfies $\overline{\Phi}$.*

**Proof.** By induction over $\overline{\Phi}$. Define $\Phi' \subseteq \overline{\Phi}$ by

$$\Phi'_s = \{\, t \equiv \bigsqcup T' \in \overline{\Phi}_s \mid M_s\, t = \bigsqcup M_s\, T' \,\};$$

we must show that $\Phi'$ is closed (clearly it contains $\Phi$). Suppose $\sigma \in \Sigma$ has type $s_1 \times \cdots \times s_n \to s'$, $t_i \equiv \bigsqcup T'_i \in \Phi'_{s_i}$, $1 \leq i \leq n$, and $T''$ is a cofinal subset of $\sigma(T'_1 \times \cdots \times T'_n)$. Then,

$$\begin{aligned} M_{s'}\, \sigma\langle t_1, \ldots, t_n\rangle &= \sigma\langle M_{s_1}\, t_1, \ldots, M_{s_n}\, t_n\rangle \\ &= \sigma\langle \bigsqcup M_{s_1}\, T'_1, \ldots, \bigsqcup M_{s_n}\, T'_n\rangle \\ &= \bigsqcup \sigma((M_{s_1}\, T'_1) \times \cdots \times (M_{s_n}\, T'_n)) \\ &= \bigsqcup M_{s'}\, \sigma(T'_1 \times \cdots \times T'_n) \\ &= \bigsqcup M_{s'}\, T'', \end{aligned}$$

since $M_{s'}\, T''$ is a cofinal subset of $M_{s'}\, \sigma(T'_1 \times \cdots \times T'_n)$. Thus $\sigma\langle t_1, \ldots, t_n\rangle \equiv \bigsqcup T'' \in \Phi'_{s'}$, as required. $\square$

Considering our example language again, we have, e.g., that

$$(\textit{while } E \textit{ do } t \textit{ od}; (\textit{skip}; \textit{while } E \textit{ do } t \textit{ od})) \equiv \bigsqcup\{\, W^n(E,t); (\textit{skip}; W^n(E,t)) \mid n \in \omega \,\}$$

is an element of $\overline{\Phi}$.

Next, we consider the generalization of least fixed point models from terms to contexts, or, more precisely, to derived operators.

**Definition 3.2.8** A *family of contextual least fixed point constraints* $\Delta$ is an $S$-indexed family of sets such that for all $s \in S$, $\Delta_s$ consists of a set of triples

$$\langle\langle v_1, \ldots, v_n\rangle, c, C'\rangle,$$

where the $v_i \in V_{s'_i}$ are distinct context variables, $c \in T(\{v_1, \ldots, v_n\})_s$, and $C' \subseteq OT(\{v_1, \ldots, v_n\})_s$ is a directed set. We write $c \equiv_{v_1,\ldots,v_n} \bigsqcup C'$ instead of $\langle\langle v_1, \ldots, v_n\rangle, c, C'\rangle$ for elements of $\Delta_s$. Sometimes we write $c \equiv \bigsqcup C'$ instead of $c \equiv_{v_1,\ldots,v_n} \bigsqcup C'$, when the variables are clear from the context.

**Definition 3.2.9** Let $\Delta$ be a family of contextual least fixed point constraints and $\mathcal{A}$ be a complete ordered algebra. Then $\mathcal{A}$ is a $\Delta$-*contextually least fixed point model* (or $\mathcal{A}$ satisfies $\Delta$) iff for all $c \equiv_{v_1,\ldots,v_n} \bigsqcup C' \in \Delta_s$, where $v_i \in V_{s'_i}$, $1 \leq i \leq n$, $c_{\mathcal{A}}[v_1, \ldots, v_n]$ is the lub of $\{ c'_{\mathcal{A}}[v_1, \ldots, v_n] \mid c' \in C' \}$ in $[A_{s'_1} \times \cdots \times A_{s'_n} \to A_s]$.

Note that $\{ c'_{\mathcal{A}}[v_1, \ldots, v_n] \mid c' \in C' \}$ is a directed set, by lemma 2.3.23.

A suitable family of contextual least fixed point constraints $\Delta$ for our example imperative language is

$$\{ \textit{while } E \textit{ do } v \textit{ od} \equiv \bigsqcup \{ W^n(E, v) \mid n \in \omega \} \mid E \in \textit{Exp} \},$$

where $v \in V$ is an arbitrary context variable, and $W^n(E, v)$ is the $\omega$-chain in $OT(\{v\})$ defined by

$$\begin{aligned} W^0(E, v) &= \Omega, \\ W^{n+1}(E, v) &= \textit{if } E \textit{ then } v; W^n(E, v) \textit{ else skip fi}. \end{aligned}$$

Let $\mathcal{A}$ be a complete ordered algebra, and define an $\omega$-chain $w^n(E, a)$ in $A$, for $E \in \textit{Exp}$ and $a \in A$, by

$$\begin{aligned} w^0(E, a) &= \bot, \\ w^{n+1}(E, a) &= \textit{if } E \textit{ then } a; w^n(E, a) \textit{ else skip fi}, \end{aligned}$$

so that $w^n(E, a) = W^n(E, v)_{\mathcal{A}}\langle a \rangle$, for all $n \in \omega$. Thus for all $E \in \textit{Exp}$,

$$\begin{aligned} & \textit{while } E \textit{ do } v \textit{ od}_{\mathcal{A}} = \bigsqcup_{n \in \omega} W^n(E, v)_{\mathcal{A}} \\ \text{iff} \quad & \textit{while } E \textit{ do } a \textit{ od} = \bigsqcup_{n \in \omega} W^n(E, v)\langle a \rangle, \text{ for all } a \in A \\ \text{iff} \quad & \textit{while } E \textit{ do } a \textit{ od} = \bigsqcup_{n \in \omega} w^n(E, a), \text{ for all } a \in A, \end{aligned}$$

showing that $\mathcal{A}$ is a $\Delta$-contextually least fixed point model iff for all $E \in \textit{Exp}$ and $a \in A$, *while E do a od* is the lub of the $\omega$-chain $w^n(E, a)$. In contrast, $\mathcal{A}$ satisfies the family of least fixed point constraints $\Phi$ of our example language iff *while E do a od* is the lub of $w^n(E, a)$, for all denotable $a \in A$ and $E \in \textit{Exp}$.

Next, we consider the natural family of least fixed point constraints generated by a family of contextual least fixed point constraints.

**Definition 3.2.10** If $\Delta$ is a family of contextual least fixed point constraints then $\Delta^\star$, the *family of least fixed point constraints generated by* $\Delta$, is defined by: $\Delta^\star_s$ is the set of all

$$c\langle t_1,\ldots,t_n\rangle \equiv \bigsqcup\{\, c'\langle t_1,\ldots,t_n\rangle \mid c' \in C'\,\}$$

such that $c \equiv_{v_1,\ldots,v_n} \bigsqcup C' \in \Delta_s$, $v_i \in V_{s'_i}$, $1 \leq i \leq n$, and $t_i \in T_{s'_i}$, $1 \leq i \leq n$.

Lemma 2.3.23 shows that $\Delta^\star$ is well-defined. It is easy to see that the families $\Phi$ of least fixed point constraints and $\Delta$ of contextual least fixed point constraints that we have defined for our example language are related by $\Phi = \Delta^\star$.

**Lemma 3.2.11** *If $\Delta$ is a family of contextual least fixed point constraints and $\mathcal{A}$ is a complete ordered algebra that satisfies $\Delta$ then $\mathcal{A}$ also satisfies the family of least fixed point constraints $\Delta^\star$.*

**Proof.** Let $c \equiv_{v_1,\ldots,v_n} \bigsqcup C' \in \Delta_s$, $s \in S$, where $v_i \in V_{s'_i}$, $1 \leq i \leq n$, and $t_i \in T_{s'_i}$, $1 \leq i \leq n$. We must show that

$$M_s\, c\langle t_1,\ldots,t_n\rangle = \bigsqcup M_s\{\, c'\langle t_1,\ldots,t_n\rangle \mid c' \in C'\,\},$$

i.e.,

$$c\langle M_{s'_1}\, t_1,\ldots,M_{s'_n}\, t_n\rangle = \bigsqcup_{c'\in C'} c'\langle M_{s'_1}\, t_1,\ldots,M_{s'_n}\, t_n\rangle,$$

and this follows from the assumption that $\mathcal{A}$ satisfies $\Delta$. □

On the other hand, $\mathcal{A}$ may satisfy $\Delta^\star$ yet fail to satisfy $\Delta$. We omit the proof, which is similar to that of lemma 3.1.4. In chapter 5 we will see that if $\mathcal{A}$ is inductively reachable and satisfies $\Delta^\star$ then it also satisfies $\Delta$.

This section concludes with the definition of when an $\Omega$-least substitutive pre-ordering over $\mathcal{T}$ satisfies a family of least fixed point constraints. We will use this definition in chapter 5 when we give conditions for the existence of fully abstract, least fixed point models.

**Definition 3.2.12** Let $\Phi$ be a family of least fixed point constraints and $\preceq$ be an $\Omega$-least substitutive pre-ordering over $\mathcal{T}$. Then $\preceq$ *satisfies* $\Phi$ iff for all $t \equiv \bigsqcup T' \in \Phi_s$, $s \in S$, $t$ is a lub of $T'$ in $\langle T_s, \preceq_s\rangle$.

Note that if $T' \subseteq OT_s$ is a directed set and $\preceq$ is an $\Omega$-least substitutive pre-ordering over $\mathcal{T}$ then $T'$ is a directed set in $\langle T_s, \preceq_s \rangle$, since $OT_s = \langle T_s, \preceq_s^{\Omega} \rangle$ and $\preceq^{\Omega} \subseteq \preceq$. The following lemma shows that an $\Omega$-least substitutive pre-ordering may satisfy a family of least fixed point constraints without satisfying its closure.

**Lemma 3.2.13** *There is a signature $\Sigma$, an $\Omega$-least substitutive pre-ordering $\preceq$ over $\mathcal{T}$, and a family of least fixed point constraints $\Phi$ such that $\preceq$ satisfies $\Phi$ but does not satisfy $\overline{\Phi}$.*

**Proof.** Let $\Sigma$ over $S = \{\star\}$ have the following operators:

(i) $\Omega_\star$ and $x$ of type $\star$; and

(ii) $f$ of type $\star \rightarrow \star$.

Since there is only one sort, we drop the sort subscripts from relations, etc., below. Define $\preceq$ over $\mathcal{T}$ by

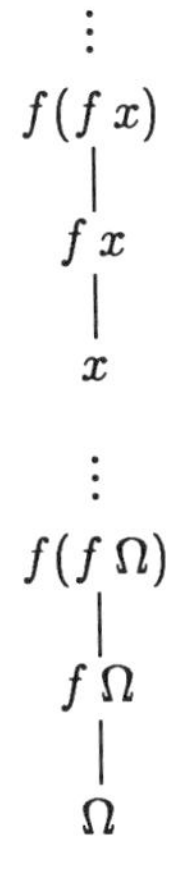


,

and let $x \equiv \bigsqcup\{\Omega, f\,\Omega, f(f\,\Omega), \ldots\}$ be the only element of $\Phi$. Clearly $\preceq$ satisfies $\Phi$. On the other hand, $(f\,x) \equiv \bigsqcup\{f\,\Omega, f(f\,\Omega), \ldots\}$ is an element of $\overline{\Phi}$, but $(f\,x)$ is not a lub of $\{f\,\Omega, f(f\,\Omega), \ldots\}$ in $\preceq$. $\square$

# 4 Example Correct Models

In this chapter, we study two programming languages within our framework. The first is PCF, and the second is TIE, an imperative language with explicit storage allocation and higher and recursive types. We give denotational semantics for both of these languages, define notions of program ordering and equivalence from these models in a uniform manner, and show that the models are inequationally correct with reference to these notions of program ordering. In contrast, the model of PCF is already known not to be fully abstract and we conjecture that neither is our model of the second language.

A comprehensive treatment of these languages would include the characterization of their notions of program ordering and equivalence in terms of operational semantics. This was done for PCF in [Plo1] and [BerCurLév], and appears to be feasible for our second language.

## 4.1 Defining Notions of Program Ordering

We begin by describing the technique for defining notions of program ordering and equivalence, as abstractions of models, that we use in sections 4.3 and 4.4, and that forms the basis for our positive results of chapter 7. Given a complete ordered algebra $\mathcal{A}$, an $\Omega$-least substitutive pre-ordering over $\mathcal{T}$ is defined as follows. First, a set of *program sorts* $P \subseteq S$ is selected, and the terms of sort $p \in P$ are designated as *programs.* Next, a notion of program behaviour is defined by giving a continuous function $h: A|P \to B$, for a $P$-indexed family of cpo's $B$ of *program behaviours*, and defining the *behaviour* of a program $t$ of sort $p$ to be $h_p(M_p\, t)$. Finally, one term is defined to be less than another iff the behaviour of the first is less than that of the second, in all program contexts. We then take the congruence over $\mathcal{T}$ that is induced by this substitutive pre-ordering as our notion of program equivalence, so that two terms are equivalent iff they have the same behaviour in all program contexts.

The following lemma formalizes this technique, using the contextualization operation $R^c$ of definition 2.2.24.

**Lemma 4.1.1** *Suppose $\mathcal{A}$ is a complete ordered algebra and $h: A|P \to B$ is a continuous function, for $P \subseteq S$ and $B$ a $P$-indexed family of cpo's. Define a pre-ordering $\leq$ over*

*$A|P$ by*

$$a_1 \leq_p a_2 \textit{ iff } h_p\, a_1 \sqsubseteq_p h_p\, a_2,$$

*and a pre-ordering $\preceq$ over $T|P$ by*

$$t_1 \preceq_p t_2 \textit{ iff } M_p\, t_1 \leq_p M_p\, t_2.$$

*Then $\preceq^c$ is an $\Omega$-least substitutive pre-ordering over $\mathcal{T}$, $\leq^c$ is a unary-substitutive inductive pre-ordering over $\mathcal{A}$, and*

$$t_1 \preceq_s^c t_2 \textit{ iff } M_s\, t_1 \leq_s^c M_s\, t_2,$$

*for all $t_1, t_2 \in T_s$, $s \in S$. Furthermore, $\mathcal{A}$ is $\preceq^c$-inequationally correct.*

**Proof.** Everything except the final claim follows from lemma 2.3.36, since $\leq = \leq_h$ is inductive. For the inequational correctness of $\mathcal{A}$, simply note that if $M_s\, t_1 \sqsubseteq_s M_s\, t_2$ then $M_s\, t_1 \leq_s^c M_s\, t_2$ (as $\leq^c$ is inductive), and thus $t_1 \preceq_s^c t_2$. □

The unary-substitutive inductive pre-ordering $\leq^c$ can be seen as the semantic analogue of $\preceq^c$, and its existence forms the basis for the positive results of chapter 7. Note that if $\approx$ is the equivalence relation over $T|P$ that is induced by $\preceq$ then $\approx^c$ is the congruence over $\mathcal{T}$ induced by $\preceq^c$, and thus $\mathcal{A}$ is also $\approx^c$-correct.

## 4.2 A Metalanguage for Denotational Semantics

In sections 4.3 and 4.4, we make use of a mostly standard metalanguage for defining cpo's and their elements that is taken from [Plo3], with minor variations. The following brief description is mainly intended to fix notation.

If $P_1$ and $P_2$ are cpo's then $P_1 \to P_2$ is the cpo of continuous functions from $P_1$ to $P_2$ (i.e., $[P_1 \to P_2]$). If $x$ is a variable of type $P_1$ and $E$ is an expression of type $P_2$ then $\lambda x{:}\, P_1.\, E$ is the usual lambda abstraction of type $P_1 \to P_2$. If $E_1$ has type $P_1 \to P_2$ and $E_2$ has type $P_1$ then $E_1\, E_2$ is the application of $E_1$ to $E_2$ of type $P_2$. Function space formation associates to the right and function application associates to the left.

If $P_1, \ldots, P_n$, $n \geq 0$, are cpo's then $P_1 \times \cdots \times P_n$ is their product (see definition 2.3.5) and $P_1 + \cdots + P_n$ is their *separated* sum (the least elements are not identified). We use tupling notation $\langle E_1, \ldots, E_n \rangle$ and the projection functions $\pi_i$ to construct and select, respectively, elements of $P_1 \times \cdots \times P_n$. In addition, for an expression $E$ of type $P_1 \times \cdots \times P_n$, we write

$$\textit{let } x_1{:}\, P_1, \ldots, x_n{:}\, P_n \textit{ be } E \textit{ in } E'$$

as an abbreviation for

$$(\lambda x_1{:}\, P_1.\ \cdots\ \lambda x_n{:}\, P_n.\, E')(\pi_1\, E)\cdots(\pi_n\, E).$$

As usual, $in_i{:}\, P_i \to P_1 + \cdots + P_n$ is the $i$'th (nonstrict) injection function, and if $f_i{:}\, P_i \to P'$, $1 \le i \le n$, are continuous functions then $[f_1, \ldots, f_n]{:}\, P_1 + \cdots + P_n \to P'$ is the strict continuous function such that $[f_1, \ldots, f_n](in_i\, p) = f_i\, p$, for all $1 \le i \le n$ and $p \in P_i$. For an expression $E$ of type $P_1 + \cdots + P_n$ and expressions $E'_i$ of type $P'$, $1 \le i \le n$,

$$case\ E\ in\ x_1{:}\, P_1.\, E'_1, \ldots, x_n{:}\, P_n.\, E'_n$$

is an abbreviation for

$$[\lambda x_1{:}\, P_1.\, E'_1, \ldots, \lambda x_n{:}\, P_n.\, E'_n]\, E.$$

We also consider the product $\prod_{x \in X} P_x$ of arbitrary $X$-indexed families of cpo's $P$, which consists of the product of the underlying sets, ordered componentwise. Such products are manipulated using the projection ($\rho[x]$) and updating ($\rho[p/x]$) operations that were defined in section 2.1.

For a set $S$, $S_\perp$ is the flat cpo $S \cup \{\perp\}$, for some $\perp \notin S$. For an operation $f{:}\, S_1 \times \cdots \times S_n \to S'$ over sets, we also write $f$ for the unique extension of $f$ to $S_{1\perp} \times \cdots \times S_{n\perp} \to S'_\perp$ that is strict in each argument, individually. In particular, we make use of the bistrict extensions of addition, $+{:}\, N \times N \to N$, and the equality operation over the natural numbers, $={:}\, N \times N \to Tr$. Define a predecessor function $pred{:}\, N_\perp \to N_\perp$ by

$$pred\ x = \begin{cases} x - 1 & \text{if } x \in (N - \{0\}), \\ \perp & \text{if } x = \perp \text{ or } x = 0. \end{cases}$$

We can use the theory developed in [SmyPlo] (and also [Plo3]) in order to solve recursive domain equations involving $\to$, $\times$, $+$ and $\Pi$, up to order-isomorphism.

For any cpo $P$,

$$if - then - else -{:}\ Tr_\perp \times P \times P \to P$$

is the usual conditional function (strict in its first argument), and for cpo's $P_1$ and $P_2$,

$$ifdef - then -{:}\ P_1 \times P_2 \to P_2$$

is defined by

$$ifdef\ p_1\ then\ p_2 = \begin{cases} \perp & \text{if } p_1 = \perp, \\ p_2 & \text{otherwise.} \end{cases}$$

Finally, $\mu x{:}\, P.\, E$ is an abbreviation for $(fix\ \lambda x{:}\, P.\, E)$, where $fix{:}\, (P \to P) \to P$ is the usual least fixed point operation, and $let\ x{:}\, P\ be\ E\ in\ E'$ is an abbreviation for $((\lambda x{:}\, P.\, E')\, E)$.

## 4.3 The Programming Language PCF

In this section, we study the programming language PCF within our framework. Two major variants of PCF are considered in the literature: the first is based upon the typed lambda calculus, and studied in [Plo1] and [BerCurLév], and the second is based upon typed combinatory logic, and studied in [Mil2] and [Mul]. The combinatory form lacks the intuitive appeal of the lambda calculus version, but is technically easier to work with, since it avoids the complexities of bound variables. Because our theory gives no formal status to bound variables and their scopes, it is more effective for us to work with the combinatory form of PCF. An indication of how we could have treated the lambda calculus version—with less success—can be found in the following section, which considers an imperative language that is based upon the typed lambda calculus.

We begin by defining the syntax of PCF, i.e., its signature. The sorts of this signature consist of PCF's types.

**Definition 4.3.1** The set of *sorts* $S$ is least such that:

(i) $nat \in S$,

(ii) $bool \in S$, and

(iii) $s_1 \to s_2 \in S$ if $s_1 \in S$ and $s_2 \in S$.

The set of *program sorts* $P \subseteq S$ is $\{nat, bool\}$. We let the sort constructor $\to$ associate to the right.

Note that every sort is of the form $s_1 \to \cdots \to s_n \to p$, for $n \geq 0$, $s_i \in S$, $1 \leq i \leq n$, and $p \in P$.

**Definition 4.3.2** The signature $\Sigma$ over $S$ has the following operators:

(i) $\Omega_s$ of type $s$,

(ii) $\cdot_{s_1,s_2}$ of type $(s_1 \to s_2) \times s_1 \to s_2$,

(iii) $K_{s_1,s_2}$ of type $(s_1 \to s_2 \to s_1)$,

(iv) $S_{s_1,s_2,s_3}$ of type $((s_1 \to s_2 \to s_3) \to (s_1 \to s_2) \to s_1 \to s_3)$,

(v) $Y_s$ of type $((s \to s) \to s)$,

(vi) *tt* and *ff* of type *bool*,

(vii) $n$ of type *nat*, for $n \in \omega$,

(viii) *succ* and *pred* of type $(nat \to nat)$,

(ix) *zero?* of type $(nat \to bool)$,

(x) $if_{nat}$ of type $(bool \to nat \to nat \to nat)$, and

(xi) $if_{bool}$ of type $(bool \to bool \to bool \to bool)$,

for all $s, s_i \in S$, where the compound sorts are parenthesized in order to avoid confusion. Thus $\cdot$ is a binary operator, and all of the other operators are nullary. We drop the sort suffixes from the operators when they are clear from the context, and let $\cdot$ associate to the left.

**Definition 4.3.3** Let $I$ be an $S$-indexed family of disjoint countably-infinite sets of *identifiers*. We confuse the family $I$ with the set of all identifiers $\bigcup_{s \in S} I_s$. For an identifier $x \in I$, we write $sort(x)$ for the unique $s \in S$ such that $x \in I_s$.

Form a signature $\Sigma^+$ by adding nullary operators $x$ of type $s$, for all $x \in I_s$, $s \in S$, to $\Sigma$. The set of identifiers that occur in an term $t$ of $T_{\Sigma^+}$ is denoted by $ID(t)$. We write $\mathcal{T}^+$ and $T^+$ for $\mathcal{T}_{\Sigma^+}$ and $T_{\Sigma^+}$, respectively.

Note that for all $t \in T_s^+$, $ID(t) = \emptyset$ iff $t \in T_s$.

**Definition 4.3.4** For $x \in I_{s_1}$ and $t \in T_{s_2}^+$, the *abstraction operation* $[x]t \in T_{s_1 \to s_2}^+$ is defined by structural recursion:

(i) $[x]x = S_{s,s \to s,s} \cdot K_{s,s \to s} \cdot K_{s,s}$, for $x \in I_s$;

(ii) $[x]t = K_{s_2,s_1} \cdot t$, if $x \notin ID(t)$, for $x \in I_{s_1}$, and $t \in T_{s_2}^+$; and

(iii) $[x](t_1 \cdot t_2) = S_{s_1,s_3,s_2} \cdot [x]t_1 \cdot [x]t_2$, if $x \in ID(t_1 \cdot t_2)$, for $x \in I_{s_1}$, $t_1 \in T_{s_3 \to s_2}^+$ and $t_2 \in T_{s_3}^+$.

In the literature $[x]t$ is sometimes written $\lambda^* x.\, t$, or even $\lambda x.\, t$. The reader should remember that identifier abstraction is not a formal part of our language, and cannot be treated as a derived operator. In fact, $t$ is not a subterm of $[x]t$, whenever $x \in ID(t)$. It is easy to see that $ID([x]t) = ID(t) - \{x\}$, for all terms $t$ of $T^+$.

Next, we present the natural continuous function model $\mathcal{E}$ of PCF.

**Definition 4.3.5** Let $\mathcal{E}$ be the complete ordered algebra whose carrier is defined by

$$
\begin{aligned}
E_{nat} &= N_\perp, \\
E_{bool} &= Tr_\perp, \\
E_{s_1 \to s_2} &= E_{s_1} \to E_{s_2},
\end{aligned}
$$

and whose operations are defined by

$$
\begin{aligned}
\Omega_s &= \perp_{E_s} \\
e_1 \cdot_{s_1,s_2} e_2 &= e_1\, e_2
\end{aligned}
$$

$$
\begin{aligned}
K_{s_1,s_2} &= \lambda e_1{:}\, E_{s_1}.\, \lambda e_2{:}\, E_{s_2}.\, e_1 \\
S_{s_1,s_2,s_3} &= \lambda e_1{:}\, E_{s_1\to s_2\to s_3}.\, \lambda e_2{:}\, E_{s_1\to s_2}.\, \lambda e_3{:}\, E_{s_1}.\, e_1\, e_3\, (e_2\, e_3) \\
Y_s &= \lambda e{:}\, E_{s\to s}.\, \mu e'{:}\, E_s.\, e\, e' \\
tt &= tt \\
f\!f &= f\!f \\
n &= n \\
succ &= \lambda n{:}\, N_\perp.\, n{+}1 \\
pred &= pred \\
zero? &= \lambda n{:}\, N_\perp.\, n{=}0 \\
if_{nat} &= \lambda b{:}\, Tr_\perp.\, \lambda n_1{:}\, N_\perp.\, \lambda n_2{:}\, N_\perp.\, if\; b\; then\; n_1\; else\; n_2 \\
if_{bool} &= \lambda b{:}\, Tr_\perp.\, \lambda b_1{:}\, Tr_\perp.\, \lambda b_2{:}\, Tr_\perp.\, if\; b\; then\; b_1\; else\; b_2.
\end{aligned}
$$

**Definition 4.3.6** An algebra $\mathcal{A}$ is *combinatorial* (or is a *combinatory algebra*) iff

(i) $K_{s_1,s_2} \cdot a_1 \cdot a_2 = a_1$, for all $a_1 \in A_{s_1}$ and $a_2 \in A_{s_2}$; and

(ii) $S_{s_1,s_2,s_3} \cdot a_1 \cdot a_2 \cdot a_3 = a_1 \cdot a_3 \cdot (a_2 \cdot a_3)$, for all $a_1 \in A_{s_1\to s_2\to s_3}$, $a_2 \in A_{s_1\to s_2}$ and $a_3 \in A_{s_1}$.

**Definition 4.3.7** An algebra $\mathcal{A}$ is *extensional* iff for all $a_1, a_2 \in A_{s_1\to s_2}$, if $a_1 \cdot a' = a_2 \cdot a'$, for all $a' \in A_{s_1}$, then $a_1 = a_2$. An ordered algebra $\mathcal{A}$ is *order-extensional* iff for all $a_1, a_2 \in A_{s_1\to s_2}$, if $a_1 \cdot a' \sqsubseteq_{s_2} a_2 \cdot a'$, for all $a' \in A_{s_1}$, then $a_1 \sqsubseteq_{s_1\to s_2} a_2$.

Clearly, any order-extensional ordered algebra is also extensional.

**Definition 4.3.8** An ordered algebra $\mathcal{A}$ is *standard* iff

(i) $\Omega_{bool\,\mathcal{A}}$, $tt_{\mathcal{A}}$ and $f\!f_{\mathcal{A}}$ are distinct and form all of $A_{bool}$, and $a_1 \sqsubseteq_{bool} a_2$ iff $a_1 = \Omega_{bool}$ or $a_1 = a_2$;

(ii) $\Omega_{nat\,\mathcal{A}}$ and $n_{\mathcal{A}}$, $n \in \omega$, are distinct and form all of $A_{nat}$, and $a_1 \sqsubseteq_{nat} a_2$ iff $a_1 = \Omega_{nat}$ or $a_1 = a_2$; and

(iii) for all $n \in \omega$, the following equations (equalities between derived operations of $\mathcal{A}$) hold:

$$
\begin{aligned}
succ \cdot \Omega_{nat} &= \Omega_{nat} \\
succ \cdot n &= n + 1 \\
pred \cdot \Omega_{nat} &= \Omega_{nat} \\
pred \cdot (n+1) &= n
\end{aligned}
$$

$$pred \cdot 0 = \Omega_{nat}$$

$$zero? \cdot \Omega_{nat} = \Omega_{bool}$$

$$zero? \cdot 0 = tt$$

$$zero? \cdot (n+1) = ff$$

$$if_{nat} \cdot \Omega_{bool} \cdot v_1 \cdot v_2 = \Omega_{nat}$$

$$if_{nat} \cdot tt \cdot v_1 \cdot v_2 = v_1$$

$$if_{nat} \cdot ff \cdot v_1 \cdot v_2 = v_2$$

$$if_{bool} \cdot \Omega_{bool} \cdot v_1' \cdot v_2' = \Omega_{bool}$$

$$if_{bool} \cdot tt \cdot v_1' \cdot v_2' = v_1'$$

$$if_{bool} \cdot ff \cdot v_1' \cdot v_2' = v_2'.$$

Note that $n$ is not a context variable in the above equations. It is easy to see that $\mathcal{E}$ is a standard, order-extensional, combinatory algebra.

Next, we develop tools for evaluating terms that are constructed by the identifier abstraction operation.

**Definition 4.3.9** Given a $\Sigma$-algebra $\mathcal{A}$, define a $\Sigma^+$-algebra $\mathcal{A}^+$, as follows. Its carrier is defined by

$$A_s^+ = Env_A \to A_s,$$

where the set $Env_A$ of *environments* is $\prod_{x \in I} A_{sort(x)}$. For all nullary operations $\sigma \in \Sigma$, define

$$\sigma\, \rho = \sigma,$$

for all $\rho \in Env_A$. For identifiers $x \in I_s$, $s \in S$, define

$$x\, \rho = \rho[x],$$

for all $\rho \in Env_A$. For $a_1 \in A^+_{s_1 \to s_2}$, $a_2 \in A^+_{s_1}$ and $\rho \in Env_A$, define

$$(a_1 \cdot a_2)\rho = (a_1\, \rho) \cdot (a_2\, \rho).$$

We write $M^+$ for $M_{\mathcal{A}^+}\colon \mathcal{T}^+ \to \mathcal{A}^+$.

**Lemma 4.3.10** *Let $\mathcal{A}$ be an algebra.*

(i) *For all $t \in T_s$ and $\rho \in Env_A$, $M_s\, t = M_s^+\, t\, \rho$.*

(ii) *For all $t \in T_s^+$ and $\rho_1, \rho_2 \in Env_A$, if $\rho_1[x] = \rho_2[x]$, for all $x \in ID(t)$, then $M_s^+\, t\, \rho_1 = M_s^+\, t\, \rho_2$.*

**Proof.** Both parts are standard structural inductions. □

**Lemma 4.3.11** *Let $\mathcal{A}$ be a combinatory algebra. For all $x \in I_{s_1}$, $t \in T^+_{s_2}$, $\rho \in Env_A$ and $a \in A_{s_1}$,*

$$(M^+_{s_1 \to s_2}[x]t\,\rho) \cdot a = M^+_{s_2}\,t\,\rho[a/x].$$

**Proof.** A standard structural induction, using lemma 4.3.10 (ii). □

Now, we define a family of contextual least fixed point constraints $\Delta$ for PCF, and prove that a complete ordered algebra satisfies $\Delta$ iff the constant $Y$ is the usual least fixed point operation. An immediate consequence is that $\mathcal{E}$ is a $\Delta$-contextually least fixed point model.

**Definition 4.3.12** The family of contextual least fixed point constraints $\Delta$ is defined by

$$\Delta_s = \{(Y \cdot v) \equiv \bigsqcup \{ Y^n \mid n \in \omega \}\},$$

for some $v \in V_{s \to s}$, where the $\omega$-chain $Y^n$ in $OT(\{v\})_s$ is defined by

$$\begin{aligned} Y^0 &= \Omega, \\ Y^{n+1} &= v \cdot Y^n. \end{aligned}$$

**Lemma 4.3.13** *A complete ordered algebra $\mathcal{A}$ is a $\Delta$-contextually least fixed point model iff for all $a \in A_{s \to s}$,*

$$Y \cdot a = \bigsqcup_{n \in \omega} a^n(\perp),$$

*where the $\omega$-chain $a^n(\perp)$ in $A_s$ is defined by*

$$\begin{aligned} a^0(\perp) &= \perp, \\ a^{n+1}(\perp) &= a \cdot a^n(\perp). \end{aligned}$$

**Proof.** A simple induction on $n$ shows that for all $n \in \omega$, $Y^n\langle a \rangle = a^n(\perp)$, for all $a \in A_{s \to s}$. Thus,

$$\begin{aligned} (Y \cdot v)_{\mathcal{A}} = \bigsqcup_{n \in \omega} Y^n{}_{\mathcal{A}} \text{ iff } & (Y \cdot a) = \bigsqcup_{n \in \omega} Y^n\langle a \rangle, \text{ for all } a \in A_{s \to s} \\ \text{iff } & (Y \cdot a) = \bigsqcup_{n \in \omega} a^n(\perp), \text{ for all } a \in A_{s \to s}, \end{aligned}$$

as required. □

Note that $\mathcal{E}$ also satisfies the family of least fixed point constraints $\Delta^*$, by lemma 3.2.11.

Next, we define notions of program ordering and equivalence for PCF. We take the terms of program sort as *programs*, $E|P$ as the cpo of *program behaviours*, and define the *behaviour* of a program to be its meaning.

**Definition 4.3.14** Define a pre-ordering $\leq$ over $E|P$ by

$$e_1 \leq_p e_2 \text{ iff } e_1 \sqsubseteq_p e_2,$$

and a pre-ordering $\preceq$ over $T|P$ by

$$t_1 \preceq_p t_2 \text{ iff } M_p\, t_1 \leq_p M_p\, t_2.$$

Let $\approx$ be the equivalence relation over $T|P$ that is induced by $\preceq$.

By lemma 4.1.1, $\preceq^c$ is an $\Omega$-least substitutive pre-ordering over $\mathcal{T}$, $\leq^c$ is a unary-substitutive inductive pre-ordering over $\mathcal{E}$,

$$t_1 \preceq^c_s t_2 \text{ iff } M_s\, t_1 \leq^c_s M_s\, t_2,$$

for all $t_1, t_2 \in T_s$, $s \in S$, and $\mathcal{E}$ is $\preceq^c$-inequationally correct. Furthermore, $\approx^c$ is the congruence over $\mathcal{T}$ induced by $\preceq^c$, and $\mathcal{E}$ is $\approx^c$-correct.

We now recall Plotkin's theorem that $\mathcal{E}$ is not $\approx^c$-fully abstract, and thus is not $\preceq^c$-inequationally fully abstract, since the "parallel or" (por) function is not definable in PCF.

**Definition 4.3.15** Let $bbb$ be the sort $bool \rightarrow bool \rightarrow bool$. Define terms $portest_i \in T_{bbb \rightarrow nat}$, for $i = 1, 2$, by

$$\begin{aligned}
portest_i = [x](&if_{nat} \cdot (x \cdot tt \cdot \Omega_{bool}) \\
&\cdot (if_{nat} \cdot (x \cdot \Omega_{bool} \cdot tt) \\
&\qquad \cdot (if_{nat} \cdot (x \cdot ff \cdot ff) \\
&\qquad\qquad \cdot \Omega_{nat} \\
&\qquad\qquad \cdot i) \\
&\qquad \cdot \Omega_{nat}) \\
&\cdot \Omega_{nat}).
\end{aligned}$$

Let $por \in E_{bbb}$ be unique such that $por\ tt\ \bot = tt$, $por\ \bot\ tt = tt$ and $por\ ff\ ff = ff$.

It easy to see that for all $i \in \{1,2\}$ and $e \in E_{bbb}$, $(M_{bbb\to nat}\, portest_i) \cdot e$ is equal to $i$ iff $e = por$, and is equal to $\perp$ iff $e \neq por$.

**Lemma 4.3.16** (i) $\preceq_{\mathcal{E}}|P = \preceq^c|P$

(ii) $\approx_{\mathcal{E}}|P = \approx^c|P$

**Proof.** (i) Since $\preceq_{\mathcal{E}} \subseteq \preceq^c$, it is sufficient to show that $\preceq^c_p \subseteq \preceq_{\mathcal{E}\,p}$, for all $p \in P$. If $t_1 \preceq^c_p t_2$ then $t_1 \preceq_p t_2$, because of the existence of projection derived operators $v[v]$ of type $p \to p$, and thus $M_p\, t_1 \sqsubseteq_p M_p\, t_2$, i.e., $t_1 \preceq_{\mathcal{E}\,p} t_2$.

(ii) Immediate from (i). □

**Theorem 4.3.17** (i) *For all* $t_1, t_2 \in T_{s_1 \to s_2}$, *if* $t_1 \cdot t' \preceq^c_{s_2} t_2 \cdot t'$, *for all* $t' \in T_{s_1}$, *then* $t_1 \preceq^c_{s_1 \to s_2} t_2$.

(ii) *For all* $t_1, t_2 \in T_{s_1 \to s_2}$, *if* $t_1 \cdot t' \approx^c_{s_2} t_2 \cdot t'$, *for all* $t' \in T_{s_1}$, *then* $t_1 \approx^c_{s_1 \to s_2} t_2$.

**Proof.** (i) follows from the adaptation of theorem 3.5.9 of [Ber1] (proposition 4.1.3 of [Ber2]) to our version of PCF, and (ii) follows immediately from (i). □

**Lemma 4.3.18** *por is not denotable.*

**Proof.** Follows from the adaptation of the stability theorem (2.8.8) of [Ber1] (theorem 3.6.5 of [BerCurLév]) to our version of PCF. □

From lemma 4.3.18 and the fact that $E_{bbb}$ is finite, and thus has no nontrivial directed subsets, we can conclude that $\mathcal{E}$ is not inductively reachable.

**Lemma 4.3.19** $portest_1 \approx^c_{bbb\to nat} portest_2$

**Proof.** By lemma 4.3.18, *por* is not denotable, and thus

$$M_{\mathcal{E}\,nat}(portest_1 \cdot t) = \perp = M_{\mathcal{E}\,nat}(portest_2 \cdot t),$$

for all $t \in T_{bbb}$. Then, by lemma 4.3.16,

$$portest_1 \cdot t \approx^c_{nat} portest_2 \cdot t,$$

for all $t \in T_{bbb}$, and the result follows by theorem 4.3.17. □

**Theorem 4.3.20** $\mathcal{E}$ *is not* $\approx^c$*-fully abstract.*

**Proof.** The terms $portest_1$ and $portest_2$ are distinguished by $\approx_{\mathcal{E}}$, since they yield different values when applied to *por*, but are identified by $\approx^c$, by lemma 4.3.19. □

## 4.4 TIE: A Typed Imperative Programming Language

In this section, we study a programming language called TIE, for Typed Imperative Expressions. TIE is strongly typed, expression-oriented and imperative: every term in the language is an expression of a fixed type, (potentially) yielding a value of that type, but expressions can have side effects, and thus are evaluated in a fixed order. The language has higher and recursive types, as well as reference types and explicit storage allocation. Procedures, i.e., values of higher type, can be returned as the results of other procedures, as well as stored in storage locations of appropriate type. Thus an implementation of TIE cannot follow a simple stack discipline, in the sense of [HalMeyTra], but must retain scopes in a heap. With the exception of not including nondeterminism, our language is thus a good deal more general and uniform than the typed imperative language of [HalMeyTra].

We begin by defining TIE's syntax, i.e., its signature. The sorts of this signature consist of TIE's types.

**Definition 4.4.1** Let *SVar* be a countably infinite set of *sort variables.* The set *SExp* of *sort expressions* is least such that:

(i) $\mathbf{1} \in \mathit{SExp}$,

(ii) $\nu \in \mathit{SExp}$ if $\nu \in \mathit{SVar}$,

(iii) $\mathit{ref}\ s \in \mathit{SExp}$ if $s \in \mathit{SExp}$,

(iv) $s_1 \times s_2, s_1 + s_2, s_1 \rightarrow s_2 \in \mathit{SExp}$ if $s_1, s_2 \in \mathit{SExp}$, and

(v) $\mu\nu.\, s \in \mathit{SExp}$ if $\nu \in \mathit{SVar}$ and $s \in \mathit{SExp}$.

Here $\mu$ is a variable binding operator, and we have the usual notions of free and bound occurrences of variables in expressions, as well as open and closed expressions. We write $[s_1/\nu]s_2$ for the substitution of $s_1$ for all of the free occurrences of $\nu$ in $s_2$, where bound variables are renamed, as necessary, to avoid capturing. In the following, we identify sort expressions up to the renaming of bound variables, in the usual way.

The set of *sorts* $S$ consists of the closed sort expressions, and the set of *program sorts* $P \subseteq S$ consists of the sorts that do not involve the sort constructors *ref* and $\rightarrow$, i.e., the ones built up from $\mathbf{1}$, $\times$, $+$ and recursion.

**Definition 4.4.2** Let $I$ be an $S$-indexed family of disjoint countably infinite sets of *identifiers.* We confuse the family $I$ with the set of all identifiers $\bigcup_{s \in S} I_s$. For an identifier $x \in I$, we write $\mathit{sort}(x)$ for the $s \in S$ such that $x \in I_s$.

Define a signature $\Sigma$ over $S$ with the following operators:

(i) $\Omega_s$ of type $s$,

(ii) $x$ of type $s$, for $x \in I_s$,

(iii) $\star$ of type $\mathbf{1}$,

(iv) $new_s$ of type $s \to (ref\ s)$,

(v) $:=_s$ of type $(ref\ s) \times s \to s$,

(vi) $cont_s$ of type $(ref\ s) \to s$,

(vii) $\equiv_s$ of type $(ref\ s) \times (ref\ s) \to (\mathbf{1} + \mathbf{1})$,

(viii) $pair_{s_1,s_2}$ of type $s_1 \times s_2 \to (s_1 \times s_2)$,

(ix) $first_{s_1,s_2}$ of type $(s_1 \times s_2) \to s_1$,

(x) $second_{s_1,s_2}$ of type $(s_1 \times s_2) \to s_2$,

(xi) $infirst_{s_1,s_2}$ of type $s_1 \to (s_1 + s_2)$,

(xii) $insecond_{s_1,s_2}$ of type $s_2 \to (s_1 + s_2)$,

(xiii) $case{-}first_x{-}second_y{-}esac_{s_3}$ of type $(s_1 + s_2) \times s_3 \times s_3 \to s_3$, for $x \in I_{s_1}$ and $y \in I_{s_2}$,

(xiv) $\lambda_{x,s_2}$ of type $s_2 \to (s_1 \to s_2)$, for $x \in I_{s_1}$,

(xv) $\cdot_{s_1,s_2}$ of type $(s_1 \to s_2) \times s_1 \to s_2$,

(xvi) $in_{\mu\nu.\,s}$ of type $([\mu\nu.\,s/\nu]s) \to (\mu\nu.\,s)$, for $\mu\nu.\,s \in S$,

(xvii) $out_{\mu\nu.\,s}$ of type $(\mu\nu.\,s) \to ([\mu\nu.\,s/\nu]s)$, for $\mu\nu.\,s \in S$,

(xviii) $;_{s_1,s_2}$ of type $s_1 \times s_2 \to s_2$, and

(xix) $rec_x$ of type $s \to s$, for $x \in I_s$,

for all $s, s_i \in S$, where compound sorts are parenthesized in order to avoid confusion. Thus, e.g., *first* and $\lambda$ are unary operators, whereas *pair* and $\cdot$ are binary operators. We drop the sort subscripts from the operators when no confusion can occur, and let $\cdot$ and ; associate to the left and right, respectively.

The operators *case*, $\lambda$ and *rec* bind identifiers:

$$case\ t_1\ first_x\ t_2\ second_y\ t_3\ esac$$

binds $x$ in $t_2$ and $y$ in $t_3$, and $\lambda_x t$ and $rec_x t$ bind $x$ in $t$. We have the usual notions of bound and free occurrences of identifiers in terms, and of open and closed terms. We write $[t_1/x]t_2$ for the substitution of $t_1$ for all of the free occurrences of $x$ in $t_2$, where bound variables are renamed, when necessary, to avoid capturing.

The sort $\mathbf{1}$ is intended to contain a single element, $\star$. Elements of reference sorts, *ref s*, are pointers to storage locations, which are created (and initialized) by *new*, modified by assignment (:=), and accessed by *cont* (contents). The product ($\times$), sum

(+) and function ($\rightarrow$) sorts have their usual meanings and associated operators, where function application ($\cdot$) is intended to be by-name, instead of by-value. The sort $bool = \mathbf{1}+\mathbf{1}$ can be seen as the booleans; $\equiv_s$ of type $(ref\ s) \times (ref\ s) \rightarrow bool$ is a test for equality between pointers to storage locations. Recursive sorts are defined via $\mu$, and, e.g., $nat = \mu\nu.(\mathbf{1}+\nu)$ is the *natural numbers.* The *in* and *out* operators are used to package and unpackage elements of recursive sorts. The sequencing operator (;) evaluates its first argument, discards its value (but not its side effects) and yields the result of evaluating its second argument. Finally, the operator *rec* is used to give recursive definitions in the usual way. For example, $rec_x\, x$ and $\Omega$ are intended to be equivalent. With the exception of the the *case*, $\lambda$ and $\cdot$ operators, the arguments of operators are evaluated from left to right. Only one of the second and third arguments of the *case* operator is evaluated, depending upon the value of the first, and neither the only argument of $\lambda$ nor the second argument of $\cdot$ is ever evaluated (the latter, since application is by-name).

The usual operators over the derived sorts *bool* and *nat* can be defined as derived operators in TIE. For example, *infirst* $\star$ and *insecond* $\star$ are the nullary derived operators of type *bool* that stand for *true* and *false*, respectively, and for any $s \in S$, a derived operator

$$if-then-else-fi[v_1, v_2, v_3]$$

of type $bool \times s \times s \rightarrow s$ can be defined by

$$(\lambda_w(\lambda_x(\lambda_y\, case\ w\ first_z\, x\ second_z\, y\ esac))) \cdot v_1 \cdot v_2 \cdot v_3,$$

for arbitrary identifiers $w \in I_{bool}$, $x, y \in I_s$ and $z \in I_{\mathbf{1}}$. The case expression must be abstracted and then applied to the context variables in order to prevent the capture of any occurrences of the identifier $z$ in the second and third arguments of the derived conditional. The suitability of this definition is thus dependent upon application being by-name instead of by-value.

Derived operators for strict (call-by-value) lambda abstraction and variable declaration can be defined, as follows. For $s_1, s_2 \in S$ and $x \in I_{s_1}$, let $\overline{\lambda}_x[v]$ of type $s_2 \rightarrow (s_1 \rightarrow s_2)$ be

$$\lambda_x\, case\ (infirst\ x)\ first_x\, v\ second_y\, \Omega\ esac,$$

for some $y \in I_{\mathbf{1}}$. For $s_1, s_2 \in S$ and $x \in I_{ref\ s_1}$, let

$$letvar\ x\ be-in-ni[v_1, v_2]$$

of type $s_1 \times s_2 \rightarrow s_2$ be

$$(\overline{\lambda}_x\, v_2) \cdot (new\ v_1).$$

It is essential that strict lambda abstraction be used when defining *letvar*.

Next, we define a model $\mathcal{L}$ of TIE, beginning with its semantic domains.

**Definition 4.4.3** The $S$-indexed family of cpo's *Val* of *values*, together with the $S$-indexed family of order-isomorphisms $\alpha$, is the initial solution, in the sense of [SmyPlo], of the infinite system of simultaneous isomorphism equations

$$\begin{aligned}
\alpha_{\mathbf{1}}\colon Val_{\mathbf{1}} &\cong \{\star\}_\perp,\\
\alpha_{ref\, s}\colon Val_{ref\, s} &\cong N_\perp,\\
\alpha_{s_1\times s_2}\colon Val_{s_1\times s_2} &\cong Val_{s_1}\times Val_{s_2},\\
\alpha_{s_1+s_2}\colon Val_{s_1+s_2} &\cong Val_{s_1}+Val_{s_2},\\
\alpha_{s_1\to s_2}\colon Val_{s_1\to s_2} &\cong Comp_{s_1}\to Comp_{s_2},\\
\alpha_{\mu\nu.\,s}\colon Val_{\mu\nu.\,s} &\cong Val_{[\mu\nu.\,s/\nu]s},
\end{aligned}$$

for all $s, s_i \in S$, where $Comp_s$, for *computation*, is

$$Sto \to (Val_s \times Sto),$$

and *Sto*, for *store*, is

$$\prod_{s\in S}[(N_\perp \to Val_s)\times N_\perp].$$

Define the cpo *Env* of *environments* to be

$$\prod_{x\in I} Comp_{sort(x)}.$$

The names of storage locations are, simply, natural numbers. A store $\sigma \in Sto$ consists, for each $s \in S$, of a pair $\langle f, n\rangle$, where $f\colon N_\perp \to Val_s$ and $n \in N_\perp$. In the semantics given below, we follow the convention that $n$ is the least available location in $f$. We write *empty* for the store with no locations allocated:

$$empty[s] = \langle \perp, 0\rangle, \text{ for all } s \in S.$$

**Definition 4.4.4** The complete ordered algebra $\mathcal{L}$ is defined as follows. Its carrier $L$ is defined by

$$L_s = Env \to Comp_s = Env \to Sto \to (Val_s \times Sto),$$

for all $s \in S$. Thus a term $t \in T_s$, when evaluated in an environment $\rho \in Env$ and a store $\sigma \in Sto$, produces a value $v \in Val_s$ and a new store $\sigma' \in Sto$. Divergence (nontermination) is indicated by $\sigma'$ being $\perp$; the value $v$ is only meaningful when $\sigma' \neq \perp$.

The operations of $\mathcal{L}$ are now defined below:

$\Omega_s = \perp_{L_s}$,

$x = \lambda\rho\colon Env.\, \rho[x]$
$\quad (x \in I_s)$,

$\star = \lambda\rho\colon Env.\, \lambda\sigma\colon Sto.\, \langle \alpha_{\mathbf{1}}^{-1} \star, \sigma \rangle$,

$$
\begin{aligned}
new_s\, l = {} & \lambda\rho\colon Env.\, \lambda\sigma\colon Sto. \\
& \quad let\ v\colon Val_s, \sigma'\colon Sto\ be\ (l\, \rho\, \sigma) \\
& \quad in\ ifdef\ \sigma' \\
& \quad\quad then\ let\ f\colon N_\perp \to Val_s, n\colon N_\perp\ be\ \sigma'[s] \\
& \quad\quad\quad in\ \langle \alpha_{(ref\ s)}^{-1}\, n, \\
& \quad\quad\quad\quad \sigma'[\langle \lambda n'\colon N_\perp.\, if\ n'{=}n\ then\ v\ else\ (f\, n'), \\
& \quad\quad\quad\quad\quad n+1 \rangle / s] \rangle,
\end{aligned}
$$

$$
\begin{aligned}
l_1 :=_s l_2 = {} & \lambda\rho\colon Env.\, \lambda\sigma\colon Sto. \\
& \quad let\ v_1\colon Val_{ref\ s}, \sigma'\colon Sto\ be\ (l_1\, \rho\, \sigma) \\
& \quad in\ let\ v_2\colon Val_s, \sigma''\colon Sto\ be\ (l_2\, \rho\, \sigma') \\
& \quad\quad in\ ifdef\ \sigma'' \\
& \quad\quad\quad then\ let\ f\colon N_\perp \to Val_s, n\colon N_\perp\ be\ \sigma''[s] \\
& \quad\quad\quad\quad in\ \langle v_2, \\
& \quad\quad\quad\quad\quad \sigma''[\langle \lambda n'\colon N_\perp.\, if\ n' = (\alpha_{ref\ s}\, v_1)\ then\ v_2\ else\ (f\, n'), \\
& \quad\quad\quad\quad\quad\quad n \rangle / s] \rangle,
\end{aligned}
$$

$$
\begin{aligned}
cont_s\, l = {} & \lambda\rho\colon Env.\, \lambda\sigma\colon Sto. \\
& \quad let\ v\colon Val_{ref\ s}, \sigma'\colon Sto\ be\ (l\, \rho\, \sigma) \\
& \quad in\ let\ f\colon N_\perp \to Val_s, n\colon N_\perp\ be\ \sigma'[s] \\
& \quad\quad in\ \langle (f\ (\alpha_{ref\ s}\, v)), \sigma' \rangle,
\end{aligned}
$$

$$
\begin{aligned}
l_1 \equiv_s l_2 = {} & \lambda\rho\colon Env.\, \lambda\sigma\colon Sto. \\
& \quad let\ v_1\colon Val_{ref\ s}, \sigma'\colon Sto\ be\ (l_1\, \rho\, \sigma) \\
& \quad in\ let\ v_2\colon Val_{ref\ s}, \sigma''\colon Sto\ be\ (l_2\, \rho\, \sigma') \\
& \quad\quad in\ \langle \alpha_{\mathbf{1+1}}^{-1}\, (if\ (\alpha_{ref\ s}\, v_1) = (\alpha_{ref\ s}\, v_2) \\
& \quad\quad\quad\quad then\ in_1(\alpha_{\mathbf{1}}^{-1} \star) \\
& \quad\quad\quad\quad else\ in_2(\alpha_{\mathbf{1}}^{-1} \star)), \\
& \quad\quad\quad \sigma'' \rangle,
\end{aligned}
$$

$$
\begin{aligned}
l_1\ \mathit{pair}_{s_1,s_2}\ l_2 = {} & \lambda\rho\colon \mathit{Env}.\,\lambda\sigma\colon \mathit{Sto}.\\
& \quad \mathit{let}\ v_1\colon \mathit{Val}_{s_1}, \sigma'\colon \mathit{Sto}\ \mathit{be}\ (l_1\,\rho\,\sigma)\\
& \quad \mathit{in}\ \mathit{let}\ v_2\colon \mathit{Val}_{s_2}, \sigma''\colon \mathit{Sto}\ \mathit{be}\ (l_2\,\rho\,\sigma')\\
& \quad\quad \mathit{in}\ \langle \alpha^{-1}_{s_1\times s_2}\,\langle v_1, v_2\rangle, \sigma''\rangle,
\end{aligned}
$$

$$
\begin{aligned}
\mathit{first}_{s_1,s_2}\ l = {} & \lambda\rho\colon \mathit{Env}.\,\lambda\sigma\colon \mathit{Sto}.\\
& \mathit{let}\ v\colon \mathit{Val}_{s_1\times s_2}, \sigma'\colon \mathit{Sto}\ \mathit{be}\ (l\,\rho\,\sigma)\\
& \mathit{in}\ \langle \pi_1(\alpha_{s_1\times s_2}\,v), \sigma'\rangle,
\end{aligned}
$$

$$
\begin{aligned}
\mathit{second}_{s_1,s_2}\ l = {} & \lambda\rho\colon \mathit{Env}.\,\lambda\sigma\colon \mathit{Sto}.\\
& \mathit{let}\ v\colon \mathit{Val}_{s_1\times s_2}, \sigma'\colon \mathit{Sto}\ \mathit{be}\ (l\,\rho\,\sigma)\\
& \mathit{in}\ \langle \pi_2(\alpha_{s_1\times s_2}\,v), \sigma'\rangle,
\end{aligned}
$$

$$
\begin{aligned}
\mathit{infirst}_{s_1,s_2}\ l = {} & \lambda\rho\colon \mathit{Env}.\,\lambda\sigma\colon \mathit{Sto}.\\
& \mathit{let}\ v\colon \mathit{Val}_{s_1}, \sigma'\colon \mathit{Sto}\ \mathit{be}\ (l\,\rho\,\sigma)\\
& \mathit{in}\ \langle \alpha^{-1}_{s_1+s_2}(\mathit{in}_1\,v), \sigma'\rangle,
\end{aligned}
$$

$$
\begin{aligned}
\mathit{insecond}_{s_1,s_2}\ l = {} & \lambda\rho\colon \mathit{Env}.\,\lambda\sigma\colon \mathit{Sto}.\\
& \mathit{let}\ v\colon \mathit{Val}_{s_2}, \sigma'\colon \mathit{Sto}\ \mathit{be}\ (l\,\rho\,\sigma)\\
& \mathit{in}\ \langle \alpha^{-1}_{s_1+s_2}(\mathit{in}_2\,v), \sigma'\rangle,
\end{aligned}
$$

$$
\begin{aligned}
& \mathit{case}\ l_1\ \mathit{first}_x\ l_2\ \mathit{second}_y\ l_3\ \mathit{esac}_{s_3} = \lambda\rho\colon \mathit{Env}.\,\lambda\sigma\colon \mathit{Sto}.\\
& \quad \mathit{let}\ v\colon \mathit{Val}_{s_1+s_2}, \sigma'\colon \mathit{Sto}\ \mathit{be}\ (l_1\,\rho\,\sigma)\\
& \quad \mathit{in}\ \mathit{case}\ (\alpha_{s_1+s_2}\,v)\\
& \quad\quad \mathit{in}\ v_1\colon \mathit{Val}_{s_1}.\,(l_2\,\rho[\lambda\sigma\colon \mathit{Sto}.\,\langle v_1, \sigma\rangle / x]\,\sigma'),\\
& \quad\quad\quad v_2\colon \mathit{Val}_{s_2}.\,(l_3\,\rho[\lambda\sigma\colon \mathit{Sto}.\,\langle v_2, \sigma\rangle / y]\,\sigma')\\
& \quad\quad\quad\quad (x \in I_{s_1}, y \in I_{s_2}),
\end{aligned}
$$

$$
\begin{aligned}
\lambda_{x,s_2}\ l = {} & \lambda\rho\colon \mathit{Env}.\,\lambda\sigma\colon \mathit{Sto}.\\
& \quad \langle \alpha^{-1}_{s_1\to s_2}(\lambda\kappa\colon \mathit{Comp}_{s_1}.\,(l\,\rho[\kappa/x])),\\
& \quad \sigma\rangle\\
& \quad\quad (x \in I_{s_1}),
\end{aligned}
$$

$$
\begin{aligned}
l_1 \cdot_{s_1,s_2} l_2 = {} & \lambda\rho\colon \mathit{Env}.\,\lambda\sigma\colon \mathit{Sto}.\\
& \mathit{let}\ v\colon \mathit{Val}_{s_1\to s_2}, \sigma'\colon \mathit{Sto}\ \mathit{be}\ (l_1\,\rho\,\sigma)\\
& \mathit{in}\ (\alpha_{s_1\to s_2}\,v\,(l_2\,\rho)\,\sigma'),
\end{aligned}
$$

$$in_{\mu\nu.\,s}\, l = \lambda\rho\colon Env.\, \lambda\sigma\colon Sto.$$
$$let\ v\colon Val_{[\mu\nu.\,s/\nu]s}, \sigma'\colon Sto\ be\ (l\,\rho\,\sigma)$$
$$in\ \langle \alpha^{-1}_{\mu\nu.\,s}\, v, \sigma' \rangle,$$

$$out_{\mu\nu.\,s}\, l = \lambda\rho\colon Env.\, \lambda\sigma\colon Sto.$$
$$let\ v\colon Val_{\mu\nu.\,s}, \sigma'\colon Sto\ be\ (l\,\rho\,\sigma)$$
$$in\ \langle \alpha_{\mu\nu.\,s}\, v, \sigma' \rangle,$$

$$l_1 \,;_{s_1,s_2}\, l_2 = \lambda\rho\colon Env.\, \lambda\sigma\colon Sto.$$
$$let\ v\colon Val_{s_1}, \sigma'\colon Sto\ be\ (l_1\,\rho\,\sigma)$$
$$in\ (l_2\,\rho\,\sigma'),$$

$$rec_x\, l = \mu l'\colon L_s.\, \lambda\rho\colon Env.\, (l\,\rho[(l'\,\rho)/x])$$
$$(x \in I_s).$$

As is usual for models of languages with block structure, terms are assigned meanings in $\mathcal{L}$ with the help of environments. It is important to remember that complete ordered algebras, in general, will not have environments as part of their formal structure. This is a significant limitation of our theory.

Note that for all $x \in I_s$, $s \in S$, the elements $\Omega_s$ and $rec_x\, x$ of $L_s$ are equal.

The obvious principle of extensionality under application is not valid in $\mathcal{L}$, as the following example shows. Let $x \in I_s$, $s \in S$, and consider the elements $\lambda_{x,s}\, \Omega_s$ and $\Omega_{s\to s}$ of $L_{s\to s}$. They are unequal, since for any $\rho \in Env$ and $\sigma \in Sto$, $\pi_2((\lambda_x\, \Omega)\,\rho\,\sigma) = \sigma$. One the other hand, for any $l \in L_s$, $\rho \in Env$ and $\sigma \in Sto$,

$$\begin{aligned}((\lambda_x\,\Omega)\cdot l)\,\rho\,\sigma &= \alpha_{s\to s}(\alpha^{-1}_{s\to s}(\lambda\kappa\colon Comp_s.\,\Omega\,\rho[\kappa/x]))\,(l\,\rho)\,\sigma \\ &= \Omega\,\rho[(l\,\rho)/x]\,\sigma \\ &= \bot \\ &= \alpha_{s\to s}\,\bot\,(l\,\rho)\,\bot \\ &= (\Omega\cdot l)\,\rho\,\sigma,\end{aligned}$$

and thus, for all $l \in L_s$, $(\lambda_x\,\Omega)\cdot l = \Omega\cdot l$, by extensionality in the metalanguage. I view the lack of extensionality as an expected property of models of TIE, rather than as a defect of $\mathcal{L}$.

Since application is by-name instead of by-value, we can give an equivalent definition of the operation *rec* that does not explicitly mention environments.

**Lemma 4.4.5** *An equivalent definition of the operation rec is*

$$rec_x\, l = \mu l'\colon L_s.\,(\lambda_{x,s}\, l) \cdot_{s,s} l'$$
$$(x \in I_s).$$

**Proof.** For $l, l' \in L_s$, $\rho \in Env$ and $\sigma \in Sto$,

$$\begin{aligned}((\lambda_x\, l)\cdot l')\,\rho\,\sigma &= \alpha_{s\to s}\,(\alpha^{-1}_{s\to s}\,\lambda\kappa\colon Comp_s.\,(l\,\rho[\kappa/x]))\,(l'\,\rho)\,\sigma\\ &= l\,\rho[(l'\,\rho)/x]\,\sigma.\end{aligned}$$

Thus for all $l, l' \in L_s$,

$$\begin{aligned}(\lambda_x\, l)\cdot l' &= \lambda\rho\colon Env.\,((\lambda_x\, l)\cdot l')\,\rho\\ &= \lambda\rho\colon Env.\,(l\,\rho[(l'\,\rho)/x]),\end{aligned}$$

by extensionality and $\eta$-conversion. □

The previous lemma motivates the following definition of a family of contextual least fixed point constraints for TIE.

**Definition 4.4.6** The family of contextual least fixed point constraints $\Delta$ is defined by

$$\Delta_s = \{\, (rec_x\, v) \equiv \bigsqcup\{\, rec^n_x \mid n \in \omega \,\} \mid x \in I_s \,\},$$

for some $v \in V_s$, where the $\omega$-chain $rec^n_x$ in $OT(\{v\})_s$ is defined by

$$\begin{aligned}rec^0_x &= \Omega,\\ rec^{n+1}_x &= (\lambda_x\, v)\cdot rec^n_x.\end{aligned}$$

The next lemma shows that a complete ordered algebra is a $\Delta$-contextually least fixed point model iff *rec* is the expected least fixed point operation. An immediate consequence is that $\mathcal{L}$ is a $\Delta$-contextually least fixed point model.

**Lemma 4.4.7** *A complete ordered algebra $\mathcal{A}$ is a $\Delta$-contextually least fixed point model iff for all $x \in I_s$, $s \in S$,*

$$rec_x\, a = \bigsqcup_{n\in\omega} r^n_x(a), \text{ for all } a \in A_s,$$

*where the $\omega$-chain $r^n_x(a)$ in $A_s$ is defined by:*

$$\begin{aligned}r^0_x(a) &= \bot,\\ r^{n+1}_x(a) &= (\lambda_x\, a)\cdot r^n_x(a).\end{aligned}$$

**Proof.** A simple induction over $n$ shows that for all $n \in \omega$, $rec_x^n\langle a\rangle = r_x^n(a)$, for all $a \in A_s$. Thus,

$$(rec_x\, v)_{\mathcal{A}} = \bigsqcup_{n\in\omega} rec^n_{x\,\mathcal{A}} \text{ iff } (rec_x\, a) = \bigsqcup_{n\in\omega} rec_x^n\langle a\rangle, \text{ for all } a \in A_s$$
$$\text{iff } (rec_x\, a) = \bigsqcup_{n\in\omega} r_x^n(a), \text{ for all } a \in A_s,$$

as required. □

Now, we define notions of program ordering and equivalence for TIE. It is natural to take the closed terms of program sort as *programs*, $Val|P$ as the cpo of *program behaviours*, and to define the *behaviour* of a program to be the result of evaluating it in the undefined environment and empty store.

**Definition 4.4.8** The continuous function $h\colon L|P \to Val|P$ is defined by:

$h_p\, l = let\ v\colon Val_p, \sigma\colon Sto\ be\ (l \perp empty)\ in\ ifdef\ \sigma\ then\ v.$

The behaviour of a program $t \in T_p$ is then $h_p(M_p\, t)$. Define a relation $\preceq^0$ over $T$ by: $t_1 \preceq^0_s t_2$ iff for all derived operators $c[v]$ of type $s \to p$, $p \in P$, such that both $c\langle t_1\rangle$ and $c\langle t_2\rangle$ are closed,

$$h_p(M_p\, c\langle t_1\rangle) \sqsubseteq_{Val_p} h_p(M_p\, c\langle t_2\rangle).$$

Let $\approx^0 = \preceq^0 \cap \succeq^0$.

It is easy to see that the terms $\star$ and *if true then* $\star$ *else* $x$ *fi* of sort **1** are assigned equal meanings by $\mathcal{L}$, and thus are equivalent under $\approx^0$. This shows that programs can be equivalent to nonprograms, or, in other words, that the property of being a program is not preserved by $\approx^0$, but must be explicitly verified to hold after applying $\approx^0$ transformations to a program. This situation is normal for languages with block structure.

Although $\preceq^0$ and $\approx^0$ are obviously reflexive and substitutive, their transitivity is not immediately clear, since if $t_1 \preceq^0_s t_2 \preceq^0_s t_3$ and $c\langle t_1\rangle$ and $c\langle t_3\rangle$ are closed, it does not follow that $c\langle t_2\rangle$ is also closed, as can be seen from the example of the previous paragraph. Furthermore, lemma 4.1.1, and thus much of the theory developed in chapters 5 and 7, does not directly apply to $\preceq^0$ and $\approx^0$, since this lemma makes no mention of identifiers and their scopes. Fortunately, we can give alternative definitions of these relations via lemma 4.1.1, thus showing their transitivity in the process. We proceed as follows. Take the set of all terms of program sort as *programs*, $Val|P$ (again) as the cpo of *program behaviours*, and define the *behaviour* of a program $t \in T_p$ to be $h_p(M_p\, t)$, for the function $h$ defined above.

**Definition 4.4.9** Define a pre-ordering $\leq$ over $L|P$ by

$$l_1 \leq_p l_2 \text{ iff } h_p\, l_1 \sqsubseteq_{Val_p} h_p\, l_2,$$

and a pre-ordering $\preceq$ over $T|P$ by

$$t_1 \preceq_p t_2 \text{ iff } M_p\, t_1 \leq_p M_p\, t_2.$$

Let $\approx$ be the equivalence relation over $T|P$ that is induced by $\preceq$.

Then, by lemma 4.1.1, $\preceq^c$ is an $\Omega$-least substitutive pre-ordering over $\mathcal{T}$, $\leq^c$ is a unary-substitutive inductive pre-ordering over $\mathcal{L}$,

$$t_1 \preceq^c_s t_2 \text{ iff } M_s\, t_1 \leq^c_s M_s\, t_2,$$

for all $t_1, t_2 \in T_s$, $s \in S$, and $\mathcal{L}$ is $\preceq^c$-inequationally correct. Furthermore, $\approx^c$ is the congruence over $\mathcal{T}$ that is induced by $\preceq^c$, and $\mathcal{L}$ is $\approx^c$-correct.

**Lemma 4.4.10** *For every finite set of identifiers $X \subseteq I$ and sort $s \in S$, there is a derived operator $c^X[v]$ of type $s \to s$ such that for all $t \in T_s$, none of the identifiers in $X$ are free in $c^X\langle t\rangle$, all of the free identifiers (if any) of $c^X\langle t\rangle$ are also free in $t$, and*

$$M_s\, c^X\langle t\rangle \perp = M_s\, t \perp.$$

**Proof.** By induction on the size of $X$. For the case $|X| = 0$, simply let $c^X[v] = v$. For the induction step, suppose $X = Y \cup \{z\}$, for $z \in I_{s'}$, and let $c^X[v]$ be

$$(\lambda_{z,s}\, c^Y) \cdot_{s',s} \Omega_{s'}.$$

Let $t \in T_s$. Clearly $c^X$ has the desired identifier closure properties, and for all $\sigma \in Sto$,

$$\begin{aligned}
M_s\, c^X\langle t\rangle \perp \sigma &= ((\lambda_z\, (M_s\, c^Y\langle t\rangle)) \cdot \perp) \perp \sigma \\
&= \alpha_{s' \to s}(\alpha^{-1}_{s' \to s}(\lambda\kappa\colon Comp_{s'}.\, M_s\, c^Y\langle t\rangle \perp[k/z])) \perp \sigma \\
&= M_s\, c^Y\langle t\rangle \perp[\perp/z]\, \sigma \\
&= M_s\, c^Y\langle t\rangle \perp \sigma \\
&= M_s\, t \perp \sigma.
\end{aligned}$$

The lemma then follows by extensionality. □

**Lemma 4.4.11** $\preceq^0 = \preceq^c$ *and* $\approx^0 = \approx^c$

**Proof.** The latter equality will follow from the former, and clearly $\preceq^c \subseteq \preceq^0$. For the opposite inclusion, suppose that $t_1 \preceq^0_s t_2$, and let $c[v]$ be a derived operator of type $s \to p$, $p \in P$. By lemma 4.4.10, there is a derived operator $c'[v']$ of type $p \to p$ such that both $c'\langle c\langle t_1\rangle\rangle$ and $c'\langle c\langle t_2\rangle\rangle$ are closed, and

$$M_p\, c'\langle c\langle t_i\rangle\rangle \perp = M_p\, c\langle t_i\rangle \perp,$$

for $i = 1, 2$. Thus $c'\langle c\rangle[v]$ is a derived operator of type $s \to p$, and

$$h_p(M_p\, c\langle t_1\rangle) = h_p(M_p\, (c'\langle c\rangle)\langle t_1\rangle) \sqsubseteq h_p(M_p\, (c'\langle c\rangle)\langle t_2\rangle) = h_p(M_p\, c\langle t_2\rangle),$$

by the assumption that $t_1 \preceq^0_s t_2$. □

I conjecture that $\mathcal{L}$ is not $\approx^c$-fully abstract (and thus not $\preceq^c$-inequationally fully abstract) since

$$M_1\ (new\ \star); \star \neq M_1\ \star,$$

but it appears that

$$(new\ \star); \star \approx^c_1 \star.$$

In the remainder of this section, we investigate a call-by-value version of TIE. First, the isomorphism equations for $\to$ that are used in the definition of *Val* should be changed to

$$\alpha_{s_1 \to s_2}\colon Val_{s_1 \to s_2} \cong Val_{s_1} \to Comp_{s_2},$$

for all $s_1, s_2 \in S$. Second, the definitions of the operations $\lambda$ and $\cdot$ should be changed to

$$\begin{aligned} \lambda_{x,s_2}\, l = {} & \lambda \rho\colon Env.\, \lambda \sigma\colon Sto. \\ & \quad \langle \alpha^{-1}_{s_1 \to s_2}(\lambda v\colon Val_{s_1}.\, (l\, \rho[\lambda \sigma\colon Sto.\, \langle v, \sigma\rangle / x])), \\ & \quad \sigma\rangle \\ & \qquad (x \in I_{s_1}), \end{aligned}$$

and

$$\begin{aligned} l_1 \cdot_{s_1,s_2} l_2 = {} & \lambda \rho\colon Env.\, \lambda \sigma\colon Sto. \\ & \quad let\ v_1\colon Val_{s_1 \to s_2}, \sigma'\colon Sto\ be\ (l_1\, \rho\, \sigma) \\ & \quad in\ let\ v_2\colon Val_{s_1}, \sigma''\colon Sto\ be\ (l_2\, \rho\, \sigma') \\ & \qquad in\ (\alpha_{s_1 \to s_2}\, v_1\, v_2\, \sigma''). \end{aligned}$$

Now both arguments of $\cdot$ are evaluated, the first followed by the second.

Unfortunately, the change from call-by-name to call-by-value has at least three unpleasant consequences. The first is that the derived conditional operator (given immediately after the definition of TIE's signature) is no longer suitable, and I conjecture that no replacement exists.

The second is that we lose lemma 4.4.5, and thus the family of contextual least fixed point constraints $\Delta$ is not appropriate for the changed language; again, there does not appear to be a suitable replacement. As a partial solution to this problem, we might consider making do with a family of (ordinary) least fixed point constraints. Unfortunately, we run into problems again, since the following "definition" of a family of least fixed point constraints $\Phi$ is invalid:

$$\Phi_s = \{\, rec_x\, t \equiv \bigsqcup\{\, rec_x^n\, t \mid n \in \omega \,\} \mid x \in I_s, t \in T_s \,\},$$

where $rec_x^n\, t$ is defined by

$$\begin{aligned} rec_x^0\, t &= \Omega, \\ rec_x^{n+1}\, t &= [rec_x^n\, t/x]t. \end{aligned}$$

Due to the renaming of identifiers that is involved in substitution, $rec_x^n\, t$ is not always an $\omega$-chain in $OT_s$.

The third problem is that we loose the proofs of lemmas 4.4.10 and 4.4.11, and the relations $\approx^0$ and $\approx^c$ (and thus $\preceq^0$ and $\preceq^c$) appear, in fact, to be unequal. More seriously, it is unclear whether $\preceq^0$ and $\approx^0$ are even transitive. Consider the terms $\star$ and $x; \star$ of sort $\mathbf{1}$, for $x \in I_{\mu\nu.\nu}$. It is easy to see that they are distinguished by $\approx_{\mathbf{1}}^c$, since

$$h_{\mathbf{1}}(M_{\mathbf{1}}\,(x;\star)) = \bot \neq (\alpha_{\mathbf{1}}^{-1}\,\star) = h_{\mathbf{1}}(M_{\mathbf{1}}\,\star).$$

On the other hand, I see no way of causing $x; \star$ to diverge in a closed context, without also causing $\star$ to diverge in that context, and thus it seems that they are equivalent under $\approx_{\mathbf{1}}^0$. Here, it is essential that the sort $\mu\nu.\nu$ is *uninhabited*, i.e., that there does not exist a closed, convergent, term $t$ of sort $\mu\nu.\nu$, since if such a $t$ did exist then our pair of terms would be distinguished by the context $c[v] = rec_x\,(v; t)$. Perhaps an ad hoc solution to this problem can be found by disallowing uninhabited types.

I hope that some of these problems can be solved by giving identifiers and their scopes formal significance in signatures, and working with models that have environments as part of their formal structure. In such a theory, terms would be identified up to the renaming of bound variables, solving the problem with $\Phi$. Perhaps the problem of defining derived operators can be solved by working with two kinds of derived operators: ones that can capture free identifiers and ones that cannot. The other problems seem more difficult, and may require more changes, but I hope that this proposal is a step in the right direction.

# 5 Conditions for the Existence of Fully Abstract Models

In this chapter, we give necessary and sufficient conditions for the existence of correct and fully abstract, least fixed point, complete ordered algebras. As usual, we consider the three kinds of correctness and full abstraction, equational (ordinary), inequational and contextual, and the two kinds of least fixed point models, ordinary and contextual. The condition for the existence of inequationally fully abstract, (ordinarily) least fixed point, complete ordered algebras is the cornerstone of these results: it is developed first, using a general term model construction, and the other conditions are derived from it. The condition for the existence of equationally fully abstract, least fixed point models will be employed in chapter 6 to show that such models do not exist for two natural nondeterministic programming languages. The condition for the existence of inequationally fully abstract, least fixed point models will be used in chapter 7 to develop a useful model-theoretic condition, which is used to show the existence of inequationally fully abstract models for the languages introduced in chapter 4.

We also prove theorems concerning the existence of initial objects and the nonexistence of terminal objects in various categories of correct and fully abstract, least fixed point, complete ordered algebras, and show the existence of nonisomorphic inductively reachable, inequationally fully abstract, least fixed point, complete ordered algebras.

As an aid to understanding and appreciating these results, we begin by considering the simpler case of inequationally correct and fully abstract ordered algebras. In the following, let $\preceq$ be an $\Omega$-least substitutive pre-ordering over $\mathcal{T}$. Clearly $\mathcal{OT}$ is initial in the category of $\preceq$-inequationally correct ordered algebras, together with monotonic homomorphisms, and, by theorem 2.4.15, $\mathcal{OT}/\preceq$ is initial in the full subcategory of $\preceq$-inequationally fully abstract ordered algebras. By corollary 2.4.18, every reachable ordered algebra $\mathcal{A}$ is order-isomorphic to $\mathcal{OT}/\preceq_{\mathcal{A}}$. Thus $\mathcal{OT}/\preceq$ is the unique (up to order-isomorphism) reachable, $\preceq$-inequationally fully abstract, ordered algebra and, again by theorem 2.4.15, it is terminal in the category of reachable, $\preceq$-inequationally correct, ordered algebras, together with monotonic morphisms.

As we will see in the following sections, the situation is considerably more complicated for least fixed point, complete ordered algebras and continuous homomorphisms.

## 5.1 Inequational Full Abstraction

In this section, we give a necessary and sufficient condition for the existence of $\preceq$-inequationally fully abstract, $\Phi$-least fixed point, complete ordered algebras, and show that if the category of such ordered algebras and continuous homomorphisms is nonempty that it has an initial object.

Theorem 5.1.4 is the main result: a $\preceq$-inequationally fully abstract, $\Phi$-least fixed point, complete ordered algebra exists iff $\preceq$ satisfies $\overline{\Phi}$. The "only if" direction of this theorem is straightforward. For the "if" direction, we construct a $\preceq$-inequationally fully abstract, $\Phi$-least fixed point, complete ordered algebra $\mathcal{I}(\preceq, \overline{\Phi})$ via the quotienting and completion constructions of section 2.4. The ordered algebra $\mathcal{OT}/\preceq$ is $\preceq$-inequationally fully abstract and satisfies the constraints of $\overline{\Phi}$ but is not, in general, complete, and thus we must embed it into a complete ordered algebra in such a way that at least the lub's corresponding to the constraints of $\overline{\Phi}$ are preserved. It is not always possible to preserve all existing lub's in this process, and the most we can do, in general, is preserve exactly the lub's corresponding to $\overline{\Phi}$. Furthermore, by preserving only the necessary lub's, we succeed in producing an initial object in the category of $\preceq$-inequationally fully abstract, $\Phi$-least fixed point, complete ordered algebras, together with continuous homomorphisms.

**Lemma 5.1.1** *Suppose $\Phi$ is a closed family of least fixed point constraints and $\preceq$ is an $\Omega$-least substitutive pre-ordering over $\mathcal{T}$ that satisfies $\Phi$. Define an $S$-indexed family $\Gamma$ of sets of subsets of $OT/\preceq$ by*

$$\Gamma_s = \{\, qt_s T' \mid t \equiv \bigsqcup T' \in \Phi_s \,\}.$$

*Then $\Gamma$ is a family of subsets of $\mathcal{OT}/\preceq$, and $\mathcal{OT}/\preceq$ is $\Gamma$-complete.*

**Proof.** Clearly $\Gamma$ consists of sets of directed subsets of $OT/\preceq$. Let $a \in (OT/\preceq)_s$, $s \in S$; we must show that $\{a\} \in \Gamma_s$. Since $qt$ is surjective, there is a $t \in OT_s$ such that $qt_s\, t = a$. Furthermore, by lemma 3.2.5, $t \equiv \bigsqcup\{t\} \in \Phi_s$, and thus

$$\{a\} = \{qt_s\, t\} = qt_s\,\{t\} \in \Gamma_s.$$

Now, suppose $\sigma \in \Sigma$ has type $s_1 \times \cdots \times s_n \to s'$ and $t_i \equiv \bigsqcup T'_i \in \Phi_{s_i}$, $1 \le i \le n$. Then,

$$\begin{aligned} \sigma((qt_{s_1} T'_1) \times \cdots \times (qt_{s_n} T'_n)) &= qt_{s'}\, \sigma(T'_1 \times \cdots \times T'_n) \\ &\in \Gamma_{s'}, \end{aligned}$$

since

$$\sigma\langle t_1,\ldots,t_n\rangle \equiv \bigsqcup \sigma(T_1' \times \cdots \times T_n') \in \Phi_{s'}.$$

Thus, $\Gamma$ is indeed a family of subsets of $\mathcal{OT}/\preceq$.

Suppose $t \equiv \bigsqcup T' \in \Phi_s$, $s \in S$; we must show that $qt_s T'$ has a lub in $(OT/\preceq)_s$. By assumption, $t$ is a lub of $T'$ in $\langle T_s, \preceq_s\rangle$, and thus, by corollary 2.4.17, $qt_s t$ is the lub of $qt_s T'$ in $(OT/\preceq)_s$. Suppose $\sigma \in \Sigma$ has type $s_1 \times \cdots \times s_n \to s'$ and $t_i \equiv \bigsqcup T_i' \in \Phi_{s_i}$, $1 \le i \le n$. Then,

$$\begin{aligned}
\sigma\langle \bigsqcup qt_{s_1} T_1', \ldots, \bigsqcup qt_{s_n} T_n'\rangle &= \sigma\langle qt_{s_1} t_1, \ldots, qt_{s_n} t_n\rangle \\
&= qt_{s'} \sigma\langle t_1, \ldots, t_n\rangle \\
&= \bigsqcup qt_{s'} \sigma(T_1' \times \cdots \times T_n') \\
&= \bigsqcup \sigma((qt_{s_1} T_1') \times \cdots \times (qt_{s_n} T_n')).
\end{aligned}$$

Thus $\mathcal{OT}/\preceq$ is indeed $\Gamma$-complete. □

We now give a definition that is based upon lemma 5.1.1 and theorem 2.4.2.

**Definition 5.1.2** Let $\Phi$ be a closed family of least fixed point constraints and $\preceq$ be an $\Omega$-least substitutive pre-ordering over $\mathcal{T}$ that satisfies $\Phi$. The complete ordered algebra $\mathcal{I}(\preceq,\Phi)$ is defined to be $(\mathcal{OT}/\preceq)^\Gamma$, where $\Gamma$ is defined as in the statement of lemma 5.1.1.

**Theorem 5.1.3** *Suppose $\Phi$ is a closed family of least fixed point constraints and $\preceq$ is an $\Omega$-least substitutive pre-ordering over $\mathcal{T}$ that satisfies $\Phi$.*

(i) *$\mathcal{I}(\preceq,\Phi)$ is a $\preceq$-inequationally fully abstract, $\Phi$-least fixed point, complete ordered algebra.*

(ii) *If $\mathcal{A}$ is a $\preceq'$-inequationally fully abstract, $\Phi$-least fixed point, complete ordered algebra, for an $\Omega$-least substitutive pre-ordering $\preceq'$ over $\mathcal{T}$ such that $\preceq \subseteq \preceq'$, then there is a unique continuous homomorphism $h: \mathcal{I}(\preceq,\Phi) \to \mathcal{A}$.*

**Proof.** Let $\Gamma$ be the family of subsets of $\mathcal{OT}/\preceq$ that was defined in the statement of lemma 5.1.1.

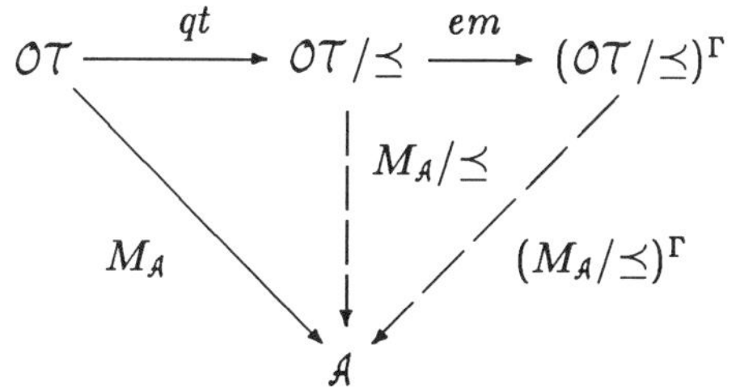

We begin by showing (i). Clearly $(\mathcal{OT}/\preceq)^\Gamma$ is a complete ordered algebra. To see that it is $\preceq$-inequationally fully abstract, let $t_1, t_2 \in T_s$, $s \in S$. Then,

$$\begin{aligned} t_1 \preceq_s t_2 \ \text{ iff } \ & qt_s\, t_1 \sqsubseteq_s qt_s\, t_2 \\ \text{iff } \ & em_s(qt_s\, t_1) \sqsubseteq_s em_s(qt_s\, t_2), \end{aligned}$$

since $em$ is an order-embedding. To see that $(\mathcal{OT}/\preceq)^\Gamma$ satisfies $\Phi$, suppose that $t \equiv \bigsqcup T' \in \Phi_s$, $s \in S$. By assumption, $t$ is a lub of $T'$ in $\langle T_s, \preceq_s \rangle$, and thus, by corollary 2.4.17, $qt_s\, t = \bigsqcup qt_s\, T'$. Then,

$$em_s(qt_s\, t) = em_s \bigsqcup qt_s\, T' = \bigsqcup em_s(qt_s\, T'),$$

since $em$ is $\Gamma$-continuous.

Next, we consider (ii). If $t_1, t_2 \in S$, $s \in S$, then

$$t_1 \preceq_s t_2 \Rightarrow t_1 \preceq'_s t_2 \Rightarrow M_s\, t_1 \sqsubseteq_s M_s\, t_2.$$

Thus (†) there is a unique monotonic homomorphism $M_{\mathcal{A}}/\preceq$ from $\mathcal{OT}/\preceq$ to $\mathcal{A}$ such that $(M_{\mathcal{A}}/\preceq) \circ qt = M_{\mathcal{A}}$. Furthermore, $M_{\mathcal{A}}/\preceq$ is $\Gamma$-continuous, since if $t \equiv \bigsqcup T' \in \Phi_s$, $s \in S$, then

$$\begin{aligned} (M_{\mathcal{A}}/\preceq)_s \bigsqcup qt_s\, T' &= (M_{\mathcal{A}}/\preceq)_s(qt_s\, t) \\ &= M_{\mathcal{A}_s}\, t \\ &= \bigsqcup M_{\mathcal{A}_s}\, T' \\ &= \bigsqcup (M_{\mathcal{A}}/\preceq)_s(qt_s\, T'). \end{aligned}$$

Thus (‡) there is a unique continuous homomorphism $(M_{\mathcal{A}}/\preceq)^\Gamma$ from $(\mathcal{OT}/\preceq)^\Gamma$ to $\mathcal{A}$ such that $(M_{\mathcal{A}}/\preceq)^\Gamma \circ em = M_{\mathcal{A}}/\preceq$. For uniqueness, suppose $h\colon (\mathcal{OT}/\preceq)^\Gamma \to \mathcal{A}$ is a continuous homomorphism. By the initiality of $\mathcal{OT}$, we know that $(h \circ em) \circ qt = M_{\mathcal{A}}$, and thus by (†) that $h \circ em = M_{\mathcal{A}}/\preceq$. The fact that $h = (M_{\mathcal{A}}/\preceq)^\Gamma$ then follows from (‡). □

**Theorem 5.1.4** *Suppose $\Phi$ is a family of least fixed point constraints and $\preceq$ is an $\Omega$-least substitutive pre-ordering over $\mathcal{T}$. A $\preceq$-inequationally fully abstract, $\Phi$-least fixed point, complete ordered algebra exists iff $\preceq$ satisfies $\overline{\Phi}$.*

**Proof.** The "if" direction follows immediately from theorem 5.1.3. For the "only if" direction, suppose $\mathcal{A}$ is a $\preceq$-inequationally fully abstract, $\Phi$-least fixed point, complete ordered algebra. By lemma 3.2.7, $\mathcal{A}$ also satisfies $\overline{\Phi}$. Suppose $t \equiv \bigsqcup T' \in \overline{\Phi}_s$, $s \in S$. Then $M_s\, t = \bigsqcup M_s\, T'$, and thus $t$ is an ub of $T'$ in $\langle T_s, \preceq_s \rangle$. Suppose $t''$ is also an ub of $T'$. Then $M_s\, t''$ is an ub of $M_s\, T'$, and so $M_s\, t \sqsubseteq_s M_s\, t''$. But this, in turn, implies that $t \preceq_s t''$, showing that $t$ is a lub of $T'$ in $\langle T_s, \preceq_s \rangle$, as required. □

**Corollary 5.1.5** *If the category of $\preceq$-inequationally fully abstract, $\Phi$-least fixed point, complete ordered algebras, together with continuous homomorphisms, is nonempty then it has an initial object, $\mathcal{I}(\preceq, \overline{\Phi})$.*

**Proof.** Immediate from theorems 5.1.3 and 5.1.4. □

We conclude this section with the corollary that $\mathcal{I}(\preceq, \overline{\Phi})$ is always inductively reachable. Thus, if the category of inductively reachable $\preceq$-inequationally fully abstract, $\Phi$-least fixed point, complete ordered algebras, together with continuous homomorphisms, is nonempty then it has $\mathcal{I}(\preceq, \overline{\Phi})$ as an initial object.

**Corollary 5.1.6** *If $\Phi$ is a closed family of least fixed point constraints and $\preceq$ is an $\Omega$-least substitutive pre-ordering over $\mathcal{T}$ that satisfies $\Phi$ then $\mathcal{I}(\preceq, \Phi)$ is inductively reachable.*

**Proof.** By lemma 2.3.33, it is sufficient to show that $\mathcal{I}(\preceq, \Phi)$ and $R(\mathcal{I}(\preceq, \Phi))$ are order-isomorphic. Since $\mathcal{I}(\preceq, \Phi)$ is initial in the category of $\preceq$-inequationally fully abstract, $\Phi$-least fixed point, complete ordered algebras, together with continuous homomorphisms (corollary 5.1.5), it is sufficient to show that $R(\mathcal{I}(\preceq, \Phi))$ is also initial in this category. It is easy to see that $R(\mathcal{I}(\preceq, \Phi))$ is a $\preceq$-inequationally fully abstract, $\Phi$-least fixed point, complete ordered algebra, since $R(\mathcal{I}(\preceq, \Phi)) \preceq \mathcal{I}(\preceq, \Phi)$. Let $i$ be the inclusion from $R(I(\preceq, \Phi))$ to $I(\preceq, \Phi)$, so that $i$ is a continuous homomorphism from $R(\mathcal{I}(\preceq, \Phi))$ to $\mathcal{I}(\preceq, \Phi)$. Suppose $\mathcal{A}$ is a $\preceq$-inequationally fully abstract, $\Phi$-least fixed point, complete ordered algebra, and let $h\colon \mathcal{I}(\preceq, \Phi) \rightarrow \mathcal{A}$ be the unique continuous homomorphism. Then $h \circ i$ is the unique continuous homomorphism from $R(\mathcal{I}(\preceq, \Phi))$ to $\mathcal{A}$, by lemma 2.3.31. □

### 5.2 More Existence Results

This section consists of two corollaries of theorem 5.1.4. In the first, we show that inequationally fully abstract, complete ordered algebras always exist and give a necessary and sufficient condition for the existence of inequationally correct, least fixed point, complete ordered algebras. In the second, we give necessary and sufficient conditions for the existence of equationally fully abstract (respectively, equationally correct), least fixed point, complete ordered algebras, and equationally fully abstract, complete ordered algebras, as well as showing that equationally correct, complete ordered algebras always exist.

**Corollary 5.2.1** *Let $\preceq$ be an $\Omega$-least substitutive pre-ordering over $\mathcal{T}$ and $\Phi$ a family of least fixed point constraints.*

(i) *A $\preceq$-inequationally fully abstract, complete ordered algebra exists.*

(ii) *A $\preceq$-inequationally correct, $\Phi$-least fixed point, complete ordered algebra exists iff there exists an $\Omega$-least substitutive pre-ordering $\preceq'$ over $\mathcal{T}$ such that $\preceq' \subseteq \preceq$ and $\preceq'$ satisfies $\overline{\Phi}$.*

**Proof.** (i) By lemma 3.2.6, the least closed family of least fixed point constraints, $\overline{\emptyset}$, consists of exactly the singleton constraints $t \equiv \bigsqcup\{t\}$, $t \in T_s$, $s \in S$. Thus $\preceq$ satisfies $\overline{\emptyset}$, and the result follows by theorem 5.1.4.

(ii) ($\Rightarrow$) Suppose $\mathcal{A}$ is a $\preceq$-inequationally correct, $\Phi$-least fixed point, complete ordered algebra. Then $\preceq_{\mathcal{A}} \subseteq \preceq$. Further, $\mathcal{A}$ is $\preceq_{\mathcal{A}}$-inequationally fully abstract, and thus, by theorem 5.1.4, $\preceq_{\mathcal{A}}$ satisfies $\overline{\Phi}$. ($\Leftarrow$) By theorem 5.1.4, there is a $\preceq'$-inequationally fully abstract, $\Phi$-least fixed point, complete ordered algebra, and, since $\preceq' \subseteq \preceq$, $\mathcal{A}$ is $\preceq$-inequationally correct. □

It is easy to find artificial examples of $\preceq$ and $\Phi$ such that no $\preceq$-inequationally correct, $\Phi$-least fixed point, complete ordered algebras exist. It would be quite surprising, however, if natural examples existed.

**Corollary 5.2.2** *Let $\approx$ be a congruence over $\mathcal{T}$ and $\Phi$ be a family of least fixed point constraints.*

(i) *A $\approx$-fully abstract, $\Phi$-least fixed point, complete ordered algebra exists iff there is an $\Omega$-least substitutive pre-ordering $\preceq$ over $\mathcal{T}$ such that $\approx\, = \,\preceq \cap \succeq$ and $\preceq$ satisfies $\overline{\Phi}$.*

(ii) *A $\approx$-fully abstract, complete ordered algebra exists iff there is an $\Omega$-least substitutive pre-ordering $\preceq$ over $\mathcal{T}$ such that $\approx\, = \,\preceq \cap \succeq$.*

(iii) *A $\approx$-correct, $\Phi$-least fixed point, complete ordered algebra exists iff there is an $\Omega$-least substitutive pre-ordering $\preceq$ over $\mathcal{T}$ such that $\preceq \cap \succeq \,\subseteq\, \approx$ and $\preceq$ satisfies $\overline{\Phi}$.*

(iv) *A $\approx$-correct, complete ordered algebra exists.*

**Proof.** (i) ($\Rightarrow$) Suppose $\mathcal{A}$ is a $\approx$-fully abstract, $\Phi$-least fixed point, complete ordered algebra. Then $\approx\, = \,\preceq_{\mathcal{A}} \cap \succeq_{\mathcal{A}}$. Further, $\mathcal{A}$ is $\preceq_{\mathcal{A}}$-inequationally fully abstract, and thus, by theorem 5.1.4, $\preceq_{\mathcal{A}}$ satisfies $\overline{\Phi}$. ($\Leftarrow$) By theorem 5.1.4, there exists a $\preceq$-inequationally fully abstract, $\Phi$-least fixed point, complete ordered algebra $\mathcal{A}$, and, since $\approx\, = \,\preceq \cap \succeq$, $\mathcal{A}$ is $\approx$-fully abstract.

(ii) Follows from (i), with $\Phi = \emptyset$.

(iii) ($\Rightarrow$) Suppose $\mathcal{A}$ is a $\approx$-correct, $\Phi$-least fixed point, complete ordered algebra. Then $\approx_{\mathcal{A}} \subseteq \approx$. Further, $\mathcal{A}$ is $\approx_{\mathcal{A}}$-fully abstract, and thus, by (i), there is an $\Omega$-least substitutive pre-ordering $\preceq$ over $\mathcal{T}$ such that

$$\preceq \cap \succeq = \approx_{\mathcal{A}} \subseteq \approx$$

and $\preceq$ satisfies $\overline{\Phi}$. ($\Leftarrow$) Let $\approx' = \preceq \cap \succeq$. By (i), there exists a $\approx'$-fully abstract, $\Phi$-least fixed point, complete ordered algebra $\mathcal{A}$, and, since

$$\approx' = \preceq \cap \succeq \subseteq \approx,$$

$\mathcal{A}$ is $\approx$-correct.

(iv) Since $\preceq^{\Omega}$ is a partial ordering, $\preceq^{\Omega} \cap \succeq^{\Omega}$ is the least congruence over $\mathcal{T}$ (no distinct terms are congruent). Thus $\preceq^{\Omega} \cap \succeq^{\Omega} \subseteq \approx$, and the result follows by applying (iii), with $\preceq = \preceq^{\Omega}$ and $\Phi = \emptyset$. □

By lemma 2.2.13, we know that not every congruence $\approx$ over $\mathcal{T}$ is induced by an $\Omega$-least substitutive pre-ordering, and thus, by corollary 5.2.2 (ii), $\approx$-fully abstract, complete ordered algebras do not always exist. It is unclear whether there are naturally occurring congruences that are not induced by such pre-orderings. Similarly, it is not difficult to find artificial examples of $\approx$ and $\Phi$ such that no $\approx$-correct, $\Phi$-least fixed point, complete ordered algebras exist. It would be surprising, however, if natural examples existed.

Corollary 5.2.2 (i) is the basis for the negative results of chapter 6.

## 5.3 Contextual Full Abstraction and Least Fixed Point Models

In this section, we show that inductively reachable, $\approx$-fully abstract, $\Delta^*$-least fixed point, complete ordered algebras, for congruences $\approx$ over $\mathcal{T}$ and families of contextual least fixed point constraints $\Delta$, are also $\approx$-contextually fully abstract, $\Delta$-contextually least fixed point, complete ordered algebras. Thus $\approx$-contextually fully abstract, $\Delta$-contextually least fixed point, complete ordered algebras exist exactly when $\approx$-fully abstract, $\Delta^*$-least fixed point, complete ordered algebras do.

**Theorem 5.3.1** *Suppose $\mathcal{A}$ is an inductively reachable complete ordered algebra and $\approx$ is a congruence over $\mathcal{T}$. Then $\mathcal{A}$ is $\approx$-fully abstract iff $\mathcal{A}$ is $\approx$-contextually fully abstract.*

**Proof.** The "if" direction is obvious. (The hypothesis of inductive reachability is not needed.) For the "only if" direction, first note that, by theorem 3.1.5, $\mathcal{A}$ is $\approx$-contextually correct. Thus, we need only show that for all derived operators $c_1[v_1, \ldots, v_n]$ and $c_2[v_1, \ldots, v_n]$ of type $s_1 \times \cdots \times s_n \to s'$: if $c_1\langle t_1, \ldots, t_n\rangle \approx_{s'} c_2\langle t_1, \ldots, t_n\rangle$, for all $t_i \in T_{s_i}$, $1 \leq i \leq n$, then $c_{1\mathcal{A}} = c_{2\mathcal{A}}$. We show this by induction on the arity $n$ of $c_1$ and $c_2$. The case $n = 0$ holds since $\mathcal{A}$ is $\approx$-fully abstract. For the induction step, suppose that $c_1[v_1, \ldots, v_{n+1}]$ and $c_2[v_1, \ldots, v_{n+1}]$ are derived operators of type $s_1 \times \cdots \times s_{n+1} \to s'$, and that $c_1\langle t_1, \ldots, t_{n+1}\rangle \approx_{s'} c_2\langle t_1, \ldots, t_{n+1}\rangle$, for all $t_i \in T_{s_i}$, $1 \leq i \leq n+1$. We show by induction over $A_{s_{n+1}}$ that for all $a_{n+1} \in A_{s_{n+1}}$,

$$c_1\langle a_1, \ldots, a_{n+1}\rangle = c_2\langle a_1, \ldots, a_{n+1}\rangle, \text{ for all } a_i \in A_{s_i}, 1 \leq i \leq n. \tag{5.1}$$

Let $A'$ be the set of all $a_{n+1} \in A_{s_{n+1}}$ such that (5.1). Suppose $t \in T_{s_{n+1}}$; we must show that $M_{s_{n+1}}\, t \in A'$. Then $(c_1\langle v_1, \ldots, v_n, t\rangle)[v_1, \ldots, v_n]$ and $(c_2\langle v_1, \ldots, v_n, t\rangle)[v_1, \ldots, v_n]$ are derived operators of type $s_1 \times \cdots \times s_n \to s'$, and, by the inductive hypothesis on $n$, for all $a_i \in A_{s_i}$, $1 \leq i \leq n$,

$$\begin{aligned} c_1\langle a_1, \ldots, a_n, M_{s_{n+1}}\, t\rangle &= (c_1\langle v_1, \ldots, v_n, t\rangle)\langle a_1, \ldots, a_n\rangle \\ &= (c_2\langle v_1, \ldots, v_n, t\rangle)\langle a_1, \ldots, a_n\rangle \\ &= c_2\langle a_1, \ldots, a_n, M_{s_{n+1}}\, t\rangle. \end{aligned}$$

Now, suppose $D \subseteq A'$ is a directed set; we must show that $\bigsqcup D \in A'$. Suppose $a_i \in A_{s_i}$, $1 \leq i \leq n$. Then,

$$\begin{aligned} c_1\langle a_1, \ldots, a_n, \bigsqcup D\rangle &= \bigsqcup c_1(\{a_1\} \times \cdots \times \{a_n\} \times D) \\ &= \bigsqcup c_2(\{a_1\} \times \cdots \times \{a_n\} \times D) \\ &= c_2\langle a_1, \ldots, a_n, \bigsqcup D\rangle, \end{aligned}$$

since $\mathcal{A}$ is complete. □

**Theorem 5.3.2** *If $\Delta$ is a family of contextual least fixed point constraints and $\mathcal{A}$ is an inductively reachable complete ordered algebra then $\mathcal{A}$ satisfies $\Delta$ iff $\mathcal{A}$ satisfies the family of least fixed point constraints $\Delta^*$.*

**Proof.** The "only if" direction follows by lemma 3.2.11. For the "if" direction, it is sufficient to show that for all distinct context variables $v_i \in V_{s'_i}$, $1 \leq i \leq n$, $c \in T(\{v_1, \ldots, v_n\})_s$ and directed sets $C' \subseteq OT(\{v_1, \ldots, v_n\})_s$: if

$$M_s\, c\langle t_1, \ldots, t_n\rangle = \bigsqcup_{c' \in C'} M_s\, c'\langle t_1, \ldots, t_n\rangle,$$

for all $t_i \in T_{s'_i}$, $1 \leq i \leq n$, then

$$c_{\mathcal{A}} = \bigsqcup_{c' \in C'} c'_{\mathcal{A}}.$$

We show this by induction on $n$. The case $n = 0$ is trivial. For the induction step, suppose that $v_i \in V_{s'_i}$, $1 \leq i \leq n+1$, $c \in T(\{v_1, \ldots, v_{n+1}\})_s$, $C' \subseteq OT(\{v_1, \ldots, v_{n+1}\})_s$ is a directed set, and

$$M_s\, c\langle t_1, \ldots, t_{n+1}\rangle = \bigsqcup_{c' \in C'} M_s\, c'\langle t_1, \ldots, t_{n+1}\rangle,$$

for all $t_i \in T_{s'_i}$, $1 \leq i \leq n+1$. We show by induction over $A_{s'_{n+1}}$ that for all $a_{n+1} \in A_{s'_{n+1}}$,

$$c\langle a_1, \ldots, a_{n+1}\rangle = \bigsqcup_{c' \in C'} c'\langle a_1, \ldots, a_{n+1}\rangle, \text{ for all } a_i \in A_{s'_i}, 1 \leq i \leq n. \tag{5.2}$$

Let $A'$ be the set of all $a_{n+1} \in A_{s'_{n+1}}$ such that (5.2). Suppose $t' \in T_{s'_{n+1}}$; we must show that $M_{s'_{n+1}}\, t' \in A'$. Then,

$$c\langle v_1, \ldots, v_n, t'\rangle \in T(\{v_1, \ldots, v_n\})_s,$$

and

$$\{\, c'\langle v_1, \ldots, v_n, t'\rangle \mid c' \in C' \,\} \subseteq OT(\{v_1, \ldots, v_n\})_s$$

is a directed set. Further, for all $t_i \in T_{s'_i}$, $1 \leq i \leq n$,

$$\begin{aligned} M_s(c\langle v_1, \ldots, v_n, t'\rangle)\langle t_1, \ldots, t_n\rangle &= M_s\, c\langle t_1, \ldots, t_n, t'\rangle \\ &= \bigsqcup_{c' \in C'} M_s\, c'\langle t_1, \ldots, t_n, t'\rangle \\ &= \bigsqcup_{c' \in C'} M_s(c'\langle v_1, \ldots, v_n, t'\rangle)\langle t_1, \ldots, t_n\rangle. \end{aligned}$$

Thus, by the inductive hypothesis on $n$,

$$\begin{aligned} c\langle a_1, \ldots, a_n, M_{s'_{n+1}}\, t'\rangle &= (c\langle v_1, \ldots, v_n, t'\rangle)\langle a_1, \ldots, a_n\rangle \\ &= \bigsqcup_{c' \in C'} (c'\langle v_1, \ldots, v_n, t'\rangle)\langle a_1, \ldots, a_n\rangle \\ &= \bigsqcup_{c' \in C'} c'\langle a_1, \ldots, a_n, M_{s'_{n+1}}\, t'\rangle, \end{aligned}$$

for all $a_i \in A_{s'_i}$, $1 \leq i \leq n$. Now, suppose $D \subseteq A'$ is a directed set; we must show that $\bigsqcup D \in A'$. Let $a_i \in A_{s'_i}$, $1 \leq i \leq n$. Then,

$$\begin{aligned} c\langle a_1, \ldots, a_n, \bigsqcup D\rangle &= \bigsqcup_{d \in D} c\langle a_1, \ldots, a_n, d\rangle \\ &= \bigsqcup_{d \in D} \bigsqcup_{c' \in C'} c'\langle a_1, \ldots, a_n, d\rangle \\ &= \bigsqcup_{c' \in C'} \bigsqcup_{d \in D} c'\langle a_1, \ldots, a_n, d\rangle \\ &= \bigsqcup_{c' \in C'} c'\langle a_1, \ldots, a_n, \bigsqcup D\rangle, \end{aligned}$$

as required. □

**Corollary 5.3.3** *Suppose $\approx$ is a congruence over $\mathcal{T}$ and $\Delta$ is a family of contextual least fixed point constraints. If $\mathcal{A}$ is a $\approx$-fully abstract, $\Delta^*$-least fixed point, complete ordered algebra then $R(\mathcal{A})$ is a $\approx$-contextually fully abstract, $\Delta$-contextually least fixed point, complete ordered algebra.*

**Proof.** Since $R(\mathcal{A}) \preceq \mathcal{A}$, $R(\mathcal{A})$ is also a $\approx$-fully abstract, $\Delta^*$-least fixed point, complete ordered algebra. The result then follows from theorems 5.3.1 and 5.3.2. □

**Corollary 5.3.4** *Suppose $\approx$ is a congruence over $\mathcal{T}$ and $\Delta$ is a family of contextual least fixed point constraints. Then, there exists a $\approx$-contextually fully abstract, $\Delta$-contextually least fixed point, complete ordered algebra iff there exists a $\approx$-fully abstract, $\Delta^*$-least fixed point, complete ordered algebra iff there exists an $\Omega$-least substitutive pre-ordering $\preceq$ over $\mathcal{T}$ such that $\approx = \preceq \cap \succeq$ and $\preceq$ satisfies $\overline{\Delta^*}$.*

**Proof.** Immediate from lemma 3.2.11, corollary 5.3.3 and corollary 5.2.2 (i). □

## 5.4 Categorical Properties

In this section, we prove theorems concerning the existence of initial objects and the nonexistence of terminal objects in various categories of correct and fully abstract, least fixed point, complete ordered algebras, and show the existence of nonisomorphic inductively reachable, inequationally fully abstract, least fixed point, complete ordered algebras.

To begin with, we name the categories we will be considering. Let $\mathbf{L}(\Phi)$ be the category of $\Phi$-least fixed point, complete ordered algebras, together with continuous homomorphisms. Define the following full subcategories of $\mathbf{L}(\Phi)$.

| Category | Objects |
|---|---|
| $\mathbf{C}(\approx, \Phi)$ | $\approx$-correct |
| $\mathbf{FA}(\approx, \Phi)$ | $\approx$-fully abstract |
| $\mathbf{IC}(\preceq, \Phi)$ | $\preceq$-inequationally correct |
| $\mathbf{IFA}(\preceq, \Phi)$ | $\preceq$-inequationally fully abstract |

In addition, let $\mathbf{RL}(\Phi)$, $\mathbf{RC}(\approx, \Phi)$, $\mathbf{RFA}(\approx, \Phi)$, $\mathbf{RIC}(\preceq, \Phi)$, and $\mathbf{RIFA}(\preceq, \Phi)$ be the full subcategories of $\mathbf{L}(\Phi)$, $\mathbf{C}(\approx, \Phi)$, etc., whose objects are inductively reachable. Note that $\mathbf{FA}(\approx, \Phi)$ (respectively, $\mathbf{RFA}(\approx, \Phi)$) is a subcategory of $\mathbf{C}(\approx, \Phi)$ (respectively,

$\mathbf{RC}(\approx, \Phi)$), and $\mathbf{IFA}(\preceq, \Phi)$ (respectively, $\mathbf{RIFA}(\preceq, \Phi)$) is a subcategory of $\mathbf{IC}(\preceq, \Phi)$ (respectively, $\mathbf{RIC}(\preceq, \Phi)$).

In section 5.1, we learned that if the category $\mathbf{IFA}(\preceq, \Phi)$ is nonempty then it has an initial object, $\mathcal{I}(\preceq, \overline{\Phi})$. We now prove analogous theorems for our other categories. Theorem 5.4.1 shows that $\mathbf{L}(\Phi)$ always has an initial object $\mathcal{A}$, and that if $\mathbf{C}(\approx, \Phi)$ (respectively, $\mathbf{IC}(\preceq, \Phi)$) is nonempty then it also has $\mathcal{A}$ as an initial object.

**Theorem 5.4.1** *Suppose $\Phi$ is a family of least fixed point constraints and let $\preceq^0$ be the least $\Omega$-least substitutive pre-ordering over $\mathcal{T}$ that satisfies $\overline{\Phi}$.*

(i) *$\mathcal{I}(\preceq^0, \overline{\Phi})$ is initial in $\mathbf{L}(\Phi)$.*

(ii) *If $\mathbf{C}(\approx, \Phi)$ is nonempty, for a congruence $\approx$ over $\mathcal{T}$, then it has $\mathcal{I}(\preceq^0, \overline{\Phi})$ as an initial object.*

(iii) *If $\mathbf{IC}(\preceq, \Phi)$ is nonempty, for an $\Omega$-least substitutive pre-ordering $\preceq$ over $\mathcal{T}$, then it has $\mathcal{I}(\preceq^0, \overline{\Phi})$ as an initial object.*

**Proof.** We begin by showing that such a $\preceq^0$ exists. Let $X$ be the set of all $\preceq$ such that $\preceq$ is an $\Omega$-least substitutive pre-ordering over $\mathcal{T}$ that satisfies $\overline{\Phi}$. Then $X$ is nonempty, since the greatest $\Omega$-least substitutive pre-ordering over $\mathcal{T}$ (every term is less than every other term) satisfies $\overline{\Phi}$, and it is easy to see that $\bigcap X$ is the least $\Omega$-least substitutive pre-ordering over $\mathcal{T}$ that satisfies $\overline{\Phi}$.

(i) Clearly $\mathcal{I}(\preceq^0, \overline{\Phi})$ is an object of $\mathbf{L}(\Phi)$. Suppose $\mathcal{A}$ is also a $\Phi$-least fixed point, complete ordered algebra. Then $\mathcal{A}$ is $\preceq_{\mathcal{A}}$-inequationally fully abstract, and, by lemma 3.2.7, $\mathcal{A}$ satisfies $\overline{\Phi}$. By theorem 5.1.4, $\preceq_{\mathcal{A}}$ satisfies $\overline{\Phi}$, and thus, by the leastness of $\preceq^0$, $\preceq^0 \subseteq \preceq_{\mathcal{A}}$. The existence of the unique continuous homomorphism from $\mathcal{I}(\preceq^0, \overline{\Phi})$ to $\mathcal{A}$ then follows from theorem 5.1.3.

(ii) By (i), it is sufficient to show that $\mathcal{I}(\preceq^0, \overline{\Phi})$ is an object of $\mathbf{C}(\approx, \Phi)$, i.e., that it is $\approx$-correct. Let $\approx^0 = \preceq^0 \cap \succeq^0$. Then $\mathcal{I}(\preceq^0, \overline{\Phi})$ is $\approx^0$-fully abstract, and thus it is sufficient to show that $\approx^0 \subseteq \approx$. By corollary 5.2.2 (iii), there is an $\Omega$-least substitutive pre-ordering $\preceq$ over $\mathcal{T}$ such that $\preceq \cap \succeq \subseteq \approx$ and $\preceq$ satisfies $\overline{\Phi}$. Then, by the leastness of $\preceq^0$, $\preceq^0 \subseteq \preceq$, and thus

$$\approx^0 = \preceq^0 \cap \succeq^0 \subseteq \preceq \cap \succeq \subseteq \approx.$$

(iii) By (i), it is sufficient to show that $\mathcal{I}(\preceq^0, \overline{\Phi})$ is an object of $\mathbf{IC}(\preceq, \Phi)$, i.e., that it is $\preceq$-inequationally correct. Thus it is sufficient to show that $\preceq^0 \subseteq \preceq$. By corollary 5.2.1 (ii), there is an $\Omega$-least substitutive pre-ordering $\preceq'$ over $\mathcal{T}$ such that $\preceq' \subseteq \preceq$ and $\preceq'$ satisfies $\overline{\Phi}$. Then, by the leastness of $\preceq^0$, $\preceq^0 \subseteq \preceq'$, and thus $\preceq^0 \subseteq \preceq$. □

**Theorem 5.4.2** *Suppose $\Phi$ is a family of least fixed point constraints and $\approx$ is a congruence over $\mathcal{T}$. If $\mathbf{FA}(\approx, \Phi)$ is nonempty then it has $\mathcal{I}(\preceq^0, \overline{\Phi})$ as an initial object, where $\preceq^0$ is the least $\Omega$-least substitutive pre-ordering over $\mathcal{T}$ such that $\preceq^0$ satisfies $\overline{\Phi}$ and $\approx \; = \; \preceq^0 \cap \succeq^0$.*

**Proof.** We begin by showing that such a $\preceq^0$ exists. Let $X$ be the set of all $\Omega$-least substitutive pre-orderings over $\mathcal{T}$ that satisfy $\overline{\Phi}$ and induce $\approx$. Then $X$ is nonempty, by corollary 5.2.2 (i), and it is easy to see that $\bigcap X$ may be taken as $\preceq^0$.

Clearly $\mathcal{I}(\preceq^0, \overline{\Phi})$ is an object of $\mathbf{FA}(\approx, \Phi)$. Suppose $\mathcal{A}$ is also a $\approx$-fully abstract, $\Phi$-least fixed point, complete ordered algebra. Then $\approx \; = \; \preceq_{\mathcal{A}} \cap \succeq_{\mathcal{A}}$, and, by theorem 5.1.4, $\preceq_{\mathcal{A}}$ satisfies $\overline{\Phi}$. By the leastness of $\preceq^0$, $\preceq^0 \subseteq \preceq_{\mathcal{A}}$, and thus, by theorem 5.1.3, there is a unique continuous homomorphism from $\mathcal{I}(\preceq^0, \overline{\Phi})$ to $\mathcal{A}$. □

We now turn our attention to the subcategories of inductively reachable objects: $\mathbf{RC}(\approx, \Phi)$, $\mathbf{RFA}(\approx, \Phi)$, $\mathbf{RIC}(\preceq, \Phi)$ and $\mathbf{RIFA}(\preceq, \Phi)$. Since $\mathcal{I}(\preceq, \overline{\Phi})$ is always inductively reachable, all of these categories have initial objects whenever they are nonempty.

The next theorem shows, perhaps surprisingly, that $\mathbf{RIFA}(\preceq, \Phi)$ can have nonisomorphic objects.

**Theorem 5.4.3** *There is a signature $\Sigma$, an $\Omega$-least substitutive pre-ordering $\preceq$ over $\mathcal{T}$ and a family of least fixed point constraints $\Phi$ such that $\mathbf{RIFA}(\preceq, \Phi)$ has nonisomorphic objects.*

**Proof.** Let $\Sigma$ over $S = \{\star\}$ consist of the following nullary operators: $\Omega_\star$, $x$ and $n$, $n \in \omega$. Since there is only one sort, we drop the sort subscripts from carriers, relations, etc., below. Define ordered algebras $\mathcal{A}$ and $\mathcal{B}$ as follows. Their carriers are defined by

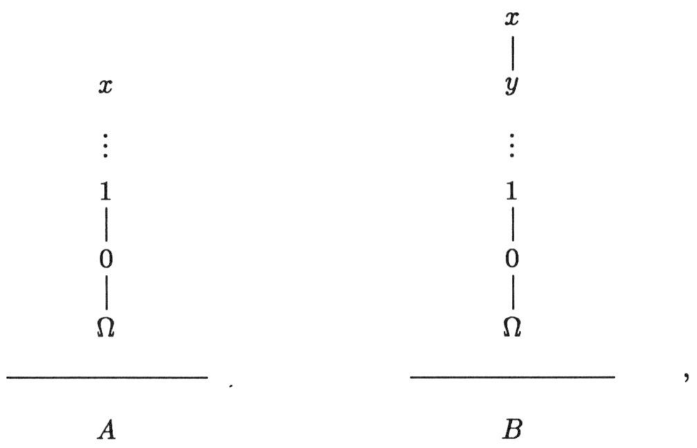

so that $x = \bigsqcup_A \omega$ and $y = \bigsqcup_B \omega$. Their operations are interpreted by themselves. It is easy to see that $\mathcal{A}$ and $\mathcal{B}$ are non order-isomorphic inductively reachable, complete ordered algebras. Furthermore, $\preceq_{\mathcal{A}} = \preceq_{\mathcal{B}}$. Thus the theorem holds with $\preceq = \preceq_{\mathcal{A}}$ and $\Phi = \emptyset$. $\square$

We now consider the existence of terminal objects in our categories of inductively reachable objects. Theorem 5.4.4 shows that $\mathbf{RFA}(\approx, \Phi)$ can be nonempty yet lack a terminal object. Thus, even when $\mathbf{RFA}(\approx, \Phi)$ is nonempty, $\mathbf{RC}(\approx, \Phi)$ can lack a terminal object. The situation is less clear for $\mathbf{RIFA}(\preceq, \Phi)$ and $\mathbf{RIC}(\preceq, \Phi)$. Theorem 5.4.5 shows that $\mathbf{RIC}(\preceq, \Phi)$ can lack a terminal object, even when $\mathbf{RIFA}(\preceq, \Phi)$ is nonempty. It is open, however, whether $\mathbf{RIFA}(\preceq, \Phi)$ always has a terminal object whenever it is nonempty; I conjecture that it always does.

**Theorem 5.4.4** *There is a signature $\Sigma$, a congruence $\approx$ over $\mathcal{T}$ and a family of least fixed point constraints $\Phi$ such that $\mathbf{RFA}(\approx, \Phi)$ is nonempty but lacks a terminal object.*

**Proof.** Let $\Sigma$ over $S = \{\star\}$ consist of the nullary operators $\Omega_\star$, $x$ and $y$. Since there is only one sort, we drop the sort subscripts from carriers, relations, etc., below. Define ordered algebras $\mathcal{A}$ and $\mathcal{B}$ as follows. Their carriers are defined by

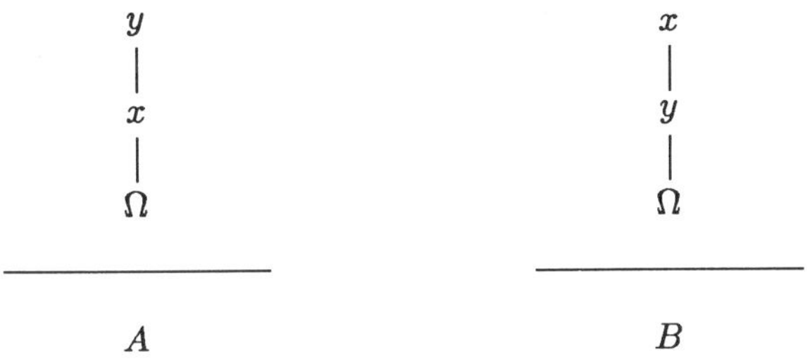


,

and their operations are interpreted by themselves. Clearly $\mathcal{A}$ and $\mathcal{B}$ are inductively reachable complete ordered algebras. Furthermore, $\approx_{\mathcal{A}} = \approx_{\mathcal{B}}$, and, in particular, $x \not\approx_{\mathcal{A}} y$. Thus $\mathcal{A}$ and $\mathcal{B}$ are $\mathbf{RFA}(\approx, \Phi)$ objects, where $\approx = \approx_{\mathcal{A}}$ and $\Phi = \emptyset$. Suppose, toward a contradiction, that $\mathcal{C}$ is terminal in $\mathbf{RFA}(\approx, \Phi)$, and let $f: \mathcal{A} \to \mathcal{C}$ and $g: \mathcal{B} \to \mathcal{C}$ be the unique continuous homomorphisms. But then

$$M_C\, x = f\, x \sqsubseteq_C f\, y = M_C\, y$$

and

$$M_C\, y = g\, y \sqsubseteq_C g\, x = M_C\, x,$$

showing that $M_C\, x = M_C\, y$—a contradiction. $\square$

**Theorem 5.4.5** *There is a signature $\Sigma$, an $\Omega$-least substitutive pre-ordering $\preceq$ over $\mathcal{T}$ and a family of least fixed point constraints $\Phi$ such that* **RIFA**$(\preceq, \Phi)$ *is nonempty but* **RIC**$(\preceq, \Phi)$ *lacks a terminal object. In particular, there is a* **RIC**$(\preceq, \Phi)$ *object that cannot be collapsed, via a continuous homomorphism, to any* **RIFA**$(\preceq, \Phi)$ *object.*

**Proof.** Let $\Sigma$ over $S = \{\star\}$ consist of the following nullary operators: $\Omega_\star$, $x$, $y$ and $n$, $n \in \omega$. Since there is only one sort, we drop the sort subscripts from carriers, relations, etc., below. Define $\preceq$ over $\mathcal{T}$ by

,

and let $\Phi = \emptyset$. Then $\mathcal{I}(\preceq, \overline{\Phi})$ is a **RIFA**$(\preceq, \Phi)$ object. Define an ordered algebra $\mathcal{A}$ as follows. Its carrier is defined by

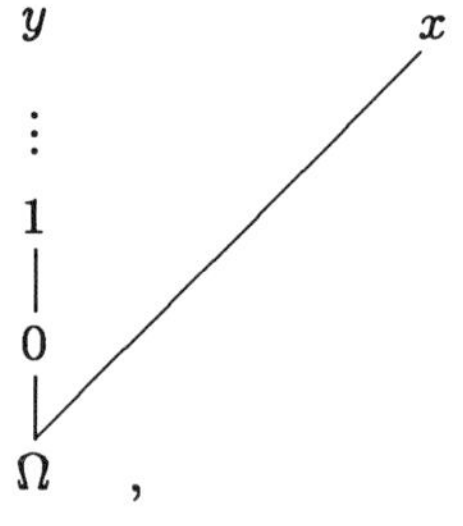


,

and its operations are interpreted by themselves. It is easy to see that $\mathcal{A}$ is an inductively reachable complete ordered algebra. Furthermore, $\mathcal{A}$ is $\preceq$-inequationally correct, and thus is a **RIC**$(\preceq, \Phi)$ object. Suppose, toward a contradiction, that $\mathcal{B}$ is a **RIFA**$(\preceq, \Phi)$ object, and that $h: \mathcal{A} \to \mathcal{B}$ is a continuous homomorphism. Then $M_{\mathcal{B}}\, y = \bigsqcup M_{\mathcal{B}}\, \omega$. By inequational full abstraction, $M_{\mathcal{B}}\, x$ is an ub of $M_{\mathcal{B}}\, \omega$, and thus $M_{\mathcal{B}}\, y \sqsubseteq_{\mathcal{B}} M_{\mathcal{B}}\, x$. But this implies that $y \preceq x$—a contradiction. Finally, suppose toward a contradiction that **RIC**$(\preceq, \Phi)$ has a terminal object, $\mathcal{C}$. Then $\mathcal{C}$ is $\preceq$-inequationally fully abstract, since **RIFA**$(\preceq, \Phi)$ is nonempty. But, by the above, this yields a contradiction. □

**Conjecture 5.4.6** *The category* $\mathbf{RIFA}(\preceq, \Phi)$ *always has a terminal object, whenever it is nonempty.*

My reasons for making this conjecture are largely negative: my attempts at finding a counterexample have failed. To prove the conjecture, it would be sufficient to show that inequational full abstraction is preserved by arbitrary coproducts in the category of inductively reachable complete ordered algebras, together with continuous homomorphisms. Then the terminal object would be the coproduct of representatives of all of the isomorphism classes in $\mathbf{RIFA}(\preceq, \Phi)$. (The number of isomorphism classes in $\mathbf{RIFA}(\preceq, \Phi)$ is bounded, since every element of an inductively reachable complete ordered algebra is the lub of a (not necessarily directed) set of denotable elements.)

# 6 Negative Results

This chapter consists of proofs of the nonexistence of fully abstract models of two nondeterministic imperative programming languages: one with random assignment and the other with infinite output streams. We give operational semantics for these languages, define notions of program equivalence in terms of these semantics, and use the condition for the existence of equationally fully abstract, least fixed point, complete ordered algebras given in chapter 5 in order to prove the negative results. No model-theoretic reasoning is involved in these proofs.

The language with random assignment is taken from [AptPlo] (with minor variations). Our proof of the nonexistence of fully abstract models of this language is a simplification of theirs. Our treatment of the language with infinite output streams is motivated by Abramsky's negative result for a nondeterministic applicative language with infinite streams [Abr3].

## 6.1 A Language with Random Assignment

In this section, we study a nondeterministic imperative programming language with random assignment statements ($x{:=}?$), which nondeterministically choose natural numbers and assign them to identifiers. The language also includes binary nondeterministic choice (*or*), which nondeterministically selects one of its arguments to be executed, as well as the usual null (*skip*), assignment ($x{:=}n$, etc.), sequencing (;), conditional and iteration statements. We begin by defining the language's syntax, i.e., its signature.

**Definition 6.1.1** Let $I$ be a countably infinite set of *identifiers*, and the set of *boolean expressions* $Exp$ be

$$\{\, x{\equiv}0 \mid x \in I \,\} \cup \{\, x{\not\equiv}0 \mid x \in I \,\}.$$

Define a signature $\Sigma$ over $S = \{\star\}$ with the following operators:

(i) $\Omega_\star$, *skip*, $x{:=}n$, $x{:=}x{+}1$, $x{:=}x{-}1$, $x{:=}y$ and $x{:=}?$ of type $\star$, for all $x, y \in I$ and $n \in \omega$;

(ii) *while* $E$ *do*$-$*od* of type $\star \to \star$, for all $E \in Exp$; and

(iii) ; , *or*, and *if* $E$ *then*$-$*else*$-$*fi* of type $\star \times \star \to \star$, for all $E \in Exp$.

We let ; and *or* associate to the right, and drop the single sort $\star$ from carriers, relations, etc., below.

**Definition 6.1.2** Let the set of *states* *Sta* be $I \to N$. For $\sigma \in Sta$, $x \in I$ and $n \in N$, define $\sigma[x] \in N$ and $\sigma[n/x] \in Sta$ by:

$$\sigma[x] = \sigma\, x;$$
$$\sigma[n/x]\, y = \begin{cases} n & \text{if } y = x, \\ \sigma\, y & \text{otherwise.} \end{cases}$$

Define an evaluation map for boolean expressions $\mathcal{E}\colon Exp \to Sta \to Tr$ by:

$$\mathcal{E}\; x{\equiv}0\; \sigma = \begin{cases} tt & \text{if } \sigma[x] = 0, \\ \mathit{ff} & \text{if } \sigma[x] \neq 0; \end{cases}$$
$$\mathcal{E}\; x{\not\equiv}0\; \sigma = \begin{cases} tt & \text{if } \sigma[x] \neq 0, \\ \mathit{ff} & \text{if } \sigma[x] = 0. \end{cases}$$

**Definition 6.1.3** We define a transition system for our language as follows. Its set of *configurations* $\Gamma$ is $(T \times Sta) \cup Sta$. Its transition relation $\to$ is the least binary relation over $\Gamma$ satisfying the following conditions, for all $x, y \in I$, $n \in \omega$, $E \in Exp$, $t, t_1, t_1', t_2 \in T$ and $\sigma, \sigma' \in Sta$:

$$\langle \Omega, \sigma\rangle \to \langle \Omega, \sigma\rangle,$$

$$\langle skip, \sigma\rangle \to \sigma,$$

$$\langle x{:=}n, \sigma\rangle \to \sigma[n/x],$$

$$\langle x{:=}x{+}1, \sigma\rangle \to \sigma[\sigma[x]+1/x],$$

$$\begin{array}{ll} \langle x{:=}x{-}1, \sigma\rangle \to \sigma[\sigma[x]-1/x] & (\sigma[x] \neq 0), \\ \langle x{:=}x{-}1, \sigma\rangle \to \sigma & (\sigma[x] = 0), \end{array}$$

$$\langle x{:=}y, \sigma\rangle \to \sigma[\sigma[y]/x],$$

$$\langle x{:=}?, \sigma\rangle \to \sigma[n/x],$$

$$\begin{array}{ll} \langle \textit{while } E \textit{ do } t \textit{ od}, \sigma\rangle \to \langle t; \textit{while } E \textit{ do } t \textit{ od}, \sigma\rangle & (\mathcal{E}\; E\; \sigma = tt), \\ \langle \textit{while } E \textit{ do } t \textit{ od}, \sigma\rangle \to \sigma & (\mathcal{E}\; E\; \sigma = \mathit{ff}), \end{array}$$

$$\frac{\langle t_1, \sigma\rangle \to \langle t_1', \sigma'\rangle}{\langle t_1; t_2, \sigma\rangle \to \langle t_1'; t_2, \sigma'\rangle}, \qquad \frac{\langle t_1, \sigma\rangle \to \sigma'}{\langle t_1; t_2, \sigma\rangle \to \langle t_2, \sigma'\rangle},$$

$$\langle t_1 \textit{ or } t_2, \sigma\rangle \to \langle t_1, \sigma\rangle, \qquad \langle t_1 \textit{ or } t_2, \sigma\rangle \to \langle t_2, \sigma\rangle,$$

$$\langle \textit{if } E \textit{ then } t_1 \textit{ else } t_2 \textit{ fi}, \sigma\rangle \to \langle t_1, \sigma\rangle \qquad (\mathcal{E}\, E\, \sigma = tt),$$
$$\langle \textit{if } E \textit{ then } t_1 \textit{ else } t_2 \textit{ fi}, \sigma\rangle \to \langle t_2, \sigma\rangle \qquad (\mathcal{E}\, E\, \sigma = \mathit{ff}).$$

**Definition 6.1.4** The family $\to_n$, $n \in \omega$, of binary relations over $\Gamma$ is defined by:

$$\gamma_1 \to_0 \gamma_2 \quad \text{iff} \quad \gamma_1 = \gamma_2,$$
$$\gamma_1 \to_{n+1} \gamma_2 \quad \text{iff} \quad \gamma_1 \to_n \gamma' \to \gamma_2, \text{ for some } \gamma' \in \Gamma.$$

We say that $\gamma$ *may diverge*, written $\gamma \uparrow$, iff there exists a $\vec{\gamma} \in \Gamma^\omega$ such that $\vec{\gamma}_0 = \gamma$, and $\vec{\gamma}_i \to \vec{\gamma}_{i+1}$, for all $i \in \omega$.

Thus, $\gamma_1 \to^* \gamma_2$ iff there exists an $n \in \omega$ such that $\gamma_1 \to_n \gamma_2$.

Next, we define notions of program behaviour and equivalence for our language.

**Definition 6.1.5** The evaluation map

$$\mathcal{O}: T \to \mathit{Sta} \to \mathcal{P}(\mathit{Sta} \cup \{\bot\})$$

(for some $\bot \notin \mathit{Sta}$) is defined by:

$$\mathcal{O}\, t\, \sigma = \{\, \sigma' \mid \langle t, \sigma\rangle \to^* \sigma' \,\} \cup \{\, \bot \mid \langle t, \sigma\rangle \uparrow \,\}.$$

Define an equivalence relation $\approx$ over $T$ by:

$$t_1 \approx t_2 \text{ iff } \mathcal{O}\, t_1 = \mathcal{O}\, t_2.$$

Thus, $\approx^c$ is a congruence over $\mathcal{T}$. The next lemma shows that $\approx$ is already a congruence.

**Lemma 6.1.6** $\approx^c = \approx$

**Proof.** By lemma 2.2.25, it is sufficient to show that $\approx$ is substitutive. We only show substitutivity under ; and *while E do—od*, leaving the *or* and *if E then—else—fi* cases, which are simpler, to the reader.

For ;, suppose that $t_1 \approx t_1'$ and $t_2 \approx t_2'$; we must show that $t_1; t_2 \approx t_1'; t_2'$. By the symmetry of $\approx$, it is sufficient to show that

$$\frac{\langle t_1; t_2, \sigma\rangle \to^* \sigma'}{\langle t_1'; t_2', \sigma\rangle \to^* \sigma'}, \text{ for all } \sigma, \sigma' \in \mathit{Sta}, \tag{6.1}$$

and

$$\frac{\langle t_1; t_2, \sigma\rangle \uparrow}{\langle t_1'; t_2', \sigma\rangle \uparrow}, \text{ for all } \sigma \in \mathit{Sta}. \tag{6.2}$$

For (6.1), if $\langle t_1; t_2, \sigma\rangle \to^\star \sigma'$ then there is a $\sigma''$ such that $\langle t_1, \sigma\rangle \to^\star \sigma''$ and $\langle t_2, \sigma''\rangle \to^\star \sigma'$. Thus, from the assumption that $t_i \approx t'_i$, $i = 1, 2$, it follows that $\langle t'_1, \sigma\rangle \to^\star \sigma''$ and $\langle t'_2, \sigma''\rangle \to^\star \sigma'$, and thus that $\langle t'_1; t'_2, \sigma\rangle \to^\star \sigma'$. For (6.2), if $\langle t_1; t_2, \sigma\rangle \uparrow$ then either $\langle t_1, \sigma\rangle \uparrow$ or there is a $\sigma'$ such that $\langle t_1, \sigma\rangle \to^\star \sigma'$ and $\langle t_2, \sigma'\rangle \uparrow$. In the first case, $\langle t'_1, \sigma\rangle \uparrow$, by the assumption, and thus $\langle t'_1; t'_2, \sigma\rangle \uparrow$. In the second case, $\langle t'_1, \sigma\rangle \to^\star \sigma'$ and $\langle t'_2, \sigma'\rangle \uparrow$, showing that $\langle t'_1; t'_2, \sigma\rangle \uparrow$.

For *while E do—od*, $E \in Exp$, suppose that $t \approx t'$; we must show that

$$\textit{while } E \textit{ do } t \textit{ od} \approx \textit{while } E \textit{ do } t' \textit{ od}.$$

By the symmetry of $\approx$, it is sufficient to show that

$$\frac{\langle \textit{while } E \textit{ do } t \textit{ od}, \sigma\rangle \to^\star \sigma'}{\langle \textit{while } E \textit{ do } t' \textit{ od}, \sigma\rangle \to^\star \sigma'}, \text{ for all } \sigma, \sigma' \in Sta, \tag{6.3}$$

and

$$\frac{\langle \textit{while } E \textit{ do } t \textit{ od}, \sigma\rangle \uparrow}{\langle \textit{while } E \textit{ do } t' \textit{ od}, \sigma\rangle \uparrow}, \text{ for all } \sigma \in Sta. \tag{6.4}$$

For (6.3), it is sufficient to show that for all $n \in \omega$,

$$\frac{\langle \textit{while } E \textit{ do } t \textit{ od}, \sigma\rangle \to_n \sigma'}{\langle \textit{while } E \textit{ do } t' \textit{ od}, \sigma\rangle \to^\star \sigma'}, \text{ for all } \sigma, \sigma' \in Sta.$$

We prove this by course of values induction over $n$. Suppose that

$$\langle \textit{while } E \textit{ do } t \textit{ od}, \sigma\rangle \to_n \sigma'.$$

If $\mathcal{E}\ E\,\sigma = \mathit{ff}$ then $\sigma = \sigma'$ and

$$\langle \textit{while } E \textit{ do } t' \textit{ od}, \sigma\rangle \to^\star \sigma'.$$

So, assume that $\mathcal{E}\ E\,\sigma = tt$. Then there is a $\sigma''$ and an $m < n$ such that $\langle t, \sigma\rangle \to^\star \sigma''$,

$$\begin{aligned}\langle \textit{while } E \textit{ do } t \textit{ od}, \sigma\rangle &\to \langle t; \textit{while } E \textit{ do } t \textit{ od}, \sigma\rangle \\ &\to^\star \langle \textit{while } E \textit{ do } t \textit{ od}, \sigma''\rangle,\end{aligned}$$

and

$$\langle \textit{while } E \textit{ do } t \textit{ od}, \sigma''\rangle \to_m \sigma'.$$

The result then follows from the assumption that $t \approx t'$ and the inductive hypothesis on $m$. For (6.4), note that for all $\sigma$ and $\vec{\gamma} \in \Gamma^\omega$, if $\vec{\gamma}_0 = \langle \textit{while } E \textit{ do } t \textit{ od}, \sigma\rangle$, and $\vec{\gamma}_i \to \vec{\gamma}_{i+1}$, for all $i \in \omega$, then either $\langle t, \sigma\rangle \uparrow$ or there exists an $i > 0$ and a $\sigma'$ such that $\langle t, \sigma\rangle \to^\star \sigma'$ and $\vec{\gamma}_i = \langle \textit{while } E \textit{ do } t \textit{ od}, \sigma'\rangle$. Thus, if $\langle \textit{while } E \textit{ do } t \textit{ od}, \sigma\rangle \uparrow$ then we can choose a $\vec{\gamma}' \in \Gamma^\omega$ such that $\vec{\gamma}'_0 = \langle \textit{while } E \textit{ do } t' \textit{ od}, \sigma\rangle$, and $\vec{\gamma}'_i \to \vec{\gamma}'_{i+1}$, for all $i \in \omega$. □

Next, we define a family of least fixed point constraints $\Phi$ for our language, and prove that complete ordered algebras satisfy $\Phi$ iff they give the usual least fixed point meanings to while-loops.

**Definition 6.1.7** Let the family of least fixed point constraints $\Phi$ be

$$\{\, \mathit{while}\ E\ \mathit{do}\ t\ \mathit{od} \equiv \bigsqcup\{\, W^n(E,t) \mid n \in \omega \,\} \mid E \in \mathit{Exp}, t \in T \,\},$$

where $W^n(E,t)$ is the $\omega$-chain in $OT$ defined by

$$\begin{aligned} W^0(E,t) &= \Omega, \\ W^{n+1}(E,t) &= \mathit{if}\ E\ \mathit{then}\ t; W^n(E,t)\ \mathit{else}\ \mathit{skip}\ \mathit{fi}. \end{aligned}$$

**Lemma 6.1.8** *A complete ordered algebra $\mathcal{A}$ is a $\Phi$-least fixed point model iff for all $E \in Exp$ and $t \in T$,*

$$M\ \mathit{while}\ E\ \mathit{do}\ t\ \mathit{od} = \bigsqcup_{n \in \omega} w^n(E,t),$$

*where $w^n(E,t)$ is the $\omega$-chain in $A$ defined by*

$$\begin{aligned} w^0(E,t) &= \bot, \\ w^{n+1}(E,t) &= \mathit{if}\ E\ \mathit{then}\ (M\,t); w^n(E,t)\ \mathit{else}\ \mathit{skip}\ \mathit{fi}. \end{aligned}$$

**Proof.** A simple induction on $n$ shows that for all $n \in \omega$, $M\,W^n(E,t) = w^n(E,t)$, and thus

$$M\ \mathit{while}\ E\ \mathit{do}\ t\ \mathit{od} = \bigsqcup_{n \in \omega} M\,W^n(E,t) \ \text{ iff } \ M\ \mathit{while}\ E\ \mathit{do}\ t\ \mathit{od} = \bigsqcup_{n \in \omega} w^n(E,t),$$

as required. □

We can now prove the main result of this section: there is no fully abstract, least fixed point model for our programming language.

**Theorem 6.1.9** *There does not exist a $\approx$-fully abstract, $\Phi$-least fixed point, complete ordered algebra.*

**Proof.** Suppose, toward a contradiction, that such an ordered algebra does exist. Then, by corollary 5.2.2 (i), there is an $\Omega$-least substitutive pre-ordering $\preceq$ over $\mathcal{T}$ such that $\approx\, = \,\preceq \cap \succeq$ and $\preceq$ satisfies $\overline{\Phi}$. Let the term $t$ be

$$x{:=}?;\ \mathit{while}\ x{\neq}0\ \mathit{do}\ x{:=}x{-}1\ \mathit{od},$$

and the $\omega$-chain $t'_n$ in $OT$ be defined by

$$x{:=}?; W^n(x{\not\equiv}0, x{:=}x{-}1).$$

Then $t$ is a lub of $t'_n$ in $\langle T, \preceq\rangle$, since $t{\equiv}\bigsqcup\{ t'_n \mid n \in \omega\} \in \overline{\Phi}$ and $\preceq$ satisfies $\overline{\Phi}$. But $t \approx x{:=}0$, $t'_0 \approx \Omega$ and $t'_{n+1} \approx x{:=}0\ \mathit{or}\ \Omega$, for all $n \in \omega$, which implies that $x{:=}0$ is a lub of $\{\Omega, x{:=}0\ \mathit{or}\ \Omega\}$ in $\langle T, \preceq\rangle$, and thus that $x{:=}0 \approx x{:=}0\ \mathit{or}\ \Omega$—a contradiction. □

An apparently stronger result is actually proved in [AptPlo]: there does not exist a $\Phi$-least fixed point, complete ordered algebra $\mathcal{A}$, together with a continuous *full abstraction function*, i.e., a continuous function $h$ from $A$ to a cpo $B$ with the property that

$$t_1 \approx t_2 \text{ iff } h(M\,t_1) = h(M\,t_2),$$

for all $t_1, t_2 \in T$. Corollary 7.1.2 shows, however, that if a full abstraction function exists for a least fixed point model of a programming language then a fully abstract, least fixed point model also exists for that language. Thus their result follows, by a language-independent corollary, from theorem 6.1.9.

On the other hand, the negative result of [AptPlo] is stronger than ours in the following respect. As an essential part of our theory, we have included the constant $\Omega$ in our language, and required that it be interpreted as the least element of any model. Furthermore, it is easy to see that any term that diverges in all states, such as

$$x{:=}0;\ \mathit{while}\ x{\equiv}0\ \mathit{do}\ \mathit{skip}\ \mathit{od},$$

is equivalent to $\Omega$, and thus must also have the value $\perp$ in any model. Thus our theorem 6.1.9 leaves open the possibility that a fully abstract, least fixed point model exists in which such divergent terms have a non-$\perp$ meaning. The negative result of [AptPlo] shows, however, that no such models exist.

## 6.2 A Nondeterministic Language with Infinite Output Streams

In this section, we study a nondeterministic imperative programming language with output statements (*output* $x$), which write the values of identifiers into potentially infinite-length output streams. Otherwise the language is the same as that of section 6.1, with the exception that random assignment statements are not included.

**Definition 6.2.1** Let the sets $I$ of *identifiers* and $Exp$ of *boolean expressions* be the same as in section 6.1. The signature $\Sigma$ is also the same, with the exception that the family of constants $x{:=}?$, $x \in I$, is replaced by the family *output* $x$, $x \in I$. The set *Sta* of *states* and its associated operations are as in definition 6.1.2. We define a transition system for our language as follows. Its set of *configurations* $\Gamma$ is

$$(T \times Sta \times N^\star) \cup (Sta \times N^\star),$$

where the element $\delta \in N^\star$ in a configuration $\gamma$ is intended to be the output produced before reaching $\gamma$. Its transition relation $\rightarrow$ is the least binary relation over $\Gamma$ satisfying the following conditions, for all $x, y \in I$, $E \in Exp$, $n \in \omega$, $t, t_1, t_1', t_2 \in T$, $\sigma, \sigma' \in Sta$ and $\delta, \delta' \in N^\star$:

$$\langle \Omega, \sigma, \delta \rangle \rightarrow \langle \Omega, \sigma, \delta \rangle,$$

$$\langle skip, \sigma, \delta \rangle \rightarrow \langle \sigma, \delta \rangle,$$

$$\langle x{:=}n, \sigma, \delta \rangle \rightarrow \langle \sigma[n/x], \delta \rangle,$$

$$\langle x{:=}x{+}1, \sigma, \delta \rangle \rightarrow \langle \sigma[\sigma[x] + 1/x], \delta \rangle,$$

$$\begin{array}{ll} \langle x{:=}x{-}1, \sigma, \delta \rangle \rightarrow \langle \sigma[\sigma[x] - 1/x], \delta \rangle & (\sigma[x] \neq 0), \\ \langle x{:=}x{-}1, \sigma, \delta \rangle \rightarrow \langle \sigma, \delta \rangle & (\sigma[x] = 0), \end{array}$$

$$\langle x{:=}y, \sigma, \delta \rangle \rightarrow \langle \sigma[\sigma[y]/x], \delta \rangle,$$

$$\langle output\ x, \sigma, \delta \rangle \rightarrow \langle \sigma, \delta\, \langle \sigma[x] \rangle \rangle,$$

$$\begin{array}{ll} \langle while\ E\ do\ t\ od, \sigma, \delta \rangle \rightarrow \langle t; while\ E\ do\ t\ od, \sigma, \delta \rangle & (\mathcal{E}\ E\ \sigma = tt), \\ \langle while\ E\ do\ t\ od, \sigma, \delta \rangle \rightarrow \langle \sigma, \delta \rangle & (\mathcal{E}\ E\ \sigma = ff), \end{array}$$

$$\frac{\langle t_1, \sigma, \delta \rangle \rightarrow \langle t_1', \sigma', \delta' \rangle}{\langle t_1; t_2, \sigma, \delta \rangle \rightarrow \langle t_1'; t_2, \sigma', \delta' \rangle}, \qquad \frac{\langle t_1, \sigma, \delta \rangle \rightarrow \langle \sigma', \delta' \rangle}{\langle t_1; t_2, \sigma, \delta \rangle \rightarrow \langle t_2, \sigma', \delta' \rangle},$$

$$\langle t_1\ or\ t_2, \sigma, \delta \rangle \rightarrow \langle t_1, \sigma, \delta \rangle, \qquad \langle t_1\ or\ t_2, \sigma, \delta \rangle \rightarrow \langle t_2, \sigma, \delta \rangle,$$

$$\begin{array}{ll} \langle if\ E\ then\ t_1\ else\ t_2\ fi, \sigma, \delta \rangle \rightarrow \langle t_1, \sigma, \delta \rangle & (\mathcal{E}\ E\ \sigma = tt), \\ \langle if\ E\ then\ t_1\ else\ t_2\ fi, \sigma, \delta \rangle \rightarrow \langle t_2, \sigma, \delta \rangle & (\mathcal{E}\ E\ \sigma = ff). \end{array}$$

**Definition 6.2.2** The function $out: \Gamma \rightarrow N^\star$ is defined by:

$$out\ \langle t, \sigma, \delta \rangle = \delta,$$

$$out\ \langle \sigma, \delta \rangle = \delta.$$

For $\gamma \in \Gamma$ and $\delta \in N^\infty$, we say that $\gamma$ *may diverge with output* $\delta$, written $\gamma \uparrow \delta$, iff there is a $\vec{\gamma} \in \Gamma^\omega$ such that $\vec{\gamma}_0 = \gamma$, $\vec{\gamma}_i \rightarrow \vec{\gamma}_{i+1}$, for all $i \in \omega$, and $\delta = \bigcup_{i \in \omega} out\ \vec{\gamma}_i$.

It is easy to see that $out\ \gamma_1 \subseteq out\ \gamma_2$ if $\gamma_1 \rightarrow \gamma_2$.

Next, we define notions of program behaviour and equivalence for our language.

**Definition 6.2.3** The evaluation map

$$\mathcal{O}: T \rightarrow Sta \rightarrow \mathcal{P}[(Sta \times N^{\star}) \cup (\{\bot\} \times N^{\infty})]$$

(for some $\bot \notin Sta$) is defined by:

$$\mathcal{O}\ t\ \sigma = \{\ \langle \sigma', \delta\rangle \mid \langle t, \sigma, \langle\,\rangle\rangle \rightarrow^{\star} \langle \sigma', \delta\rangle\ \} \cup \{\ \langle \bot, \delta\rangle \mid \langle t, \sigma, \langle\,\rangle\rangle \uparrow \delta\ \}.$$

Define an equivalence relation $\approx$ over $T$ by:

$$t_1 \approx t_2 \text{ iff } \mathcal{O}\ t_1 = \mathcal{O}\ t_2.$$

Thus, $\approx^c$ is a congruence over $\mathcal{T}$. The next lemma shows that $\approx$ is already a congruence.

**Lemma 6.2.4** $\approx^c = \approx$

**Proof.** The proof is similar to that of lemma 6.1.6, and uses the fact that if $t_1 \approx t_2$ then

$$\langle t_1, \sigma, \delta\rangle \rightarrow^{\star} \langle \sigma', \delta'\rangle \text{ iff } \langle t_2, \sigma, \delta\rangle \rightarrow^{\star} \langle \sigma', \delta'\rangle$$

and

$$\langle t_1, \sigma, \delta\rangle \uparrow \delta'' \text{ iff } \langle t_2, \sigma, \delta\rangle \uparrow \delta'',$$

for all $\sigma, \sigma' \in Sta$, $\delta, \delta' \in N^{\star}$ and $\delta'' \in N^{\infty}$. □

**Definition 6.2.5** The while-loop approximations $W^n(E, t)$ and the family of least fixed point constraints $\Phi$ have the same formal definitions as in definition 6.1.7.

We can now prove the main result of this section: there is no fully abstract, least fixed point model of our programming language.

**Theorem 6.2.6** *There does not exist a $\approx$-fully abstract, $\Phi$-least fixed point, complete ordered algebra.*

**Proof.** Suppose, toward a contradiction, that such an ordered algebra does exist. By corollary 5.2.2 (i), there is an $\Omega$-least substitutive pre-ordering $\preceq$ over $\mathcal{T}$ such that $\approx = \preceq \cap \succeq$ and $\preceq$ satisfies $\overline{\Phi}$. Let the term $t$ be

$$
\begin{array}{l}
x{:=}1;\\
y{:=}0;\\
\textit{while } x{\not\equiv}0 \textit{ do } y{:=}y{+}1 \textit{ or } x{:=}0 \textit{ od};\\
\textit{while } y{\not\equiv}0 \textit{ do output } x;\, y{:=}y{-}1 \textit{ od};\\
\Omega,
\end{array}
$$

so that $\mathcal{O}\, t\, \sigma = \{\, \langle \bot, 0^n \rangle \mid n \in \omega \,\}$, where $0^n$ is the sequence of zeroes of length $n$. Let $t'$ be

$$x{:=}0;\ \textit{while } x{\equiv}0 \textit{ do output } x \textit{ od},$$

and define an $\omega$-chain $t''_n$ in $OT$ by

$$x{:=}0;\ W^n(x{\equiv}0, \textit{output } x).$$

Then $\mathcal{O}\, t'\, \sigma = \{\langle \bot, 0^\omega \rangle\}$, where $0^\omega$ is the infinite sequence of zeroes, and $\mathcal{O}\, t''_n\, \sigma = \{\langle \bot, 0^n \rangle\}$, for all $n \in \omega$. Now, $t \textit{ or } t'$ is a lub of the $\omega$-chain $t \textit{ or } t''_n$ in $\langle T, \preceq \rangle$, since

$$(t \textit{ or } t') \equiv \bigsqcup\{\, t \textit{ or } t''_n \mid n \in \omega \,\} \in \overline{\Phi},$$

and $\preceq$ satisfies $\overline{\Phi}$. But $t \textit{ or } t''_n \approx t$, for all $n \in \omega$, and thus $t \textit{ or } t' \approx t$—a contradiction. □

# 7 Obtaining Fully Abstract Models from Correct Models

In this chapter, we investigate two approaches to obtaining fully abstract models from correct ones. In section 7.1, we use the condition for the existence of inequationally fully abstract models of chapter 5 in order to develop useful necessary and sufficient conditions involving the existence of correct models. In section 7.2, we consider the possibility of collapsing correct models, via continuous homomorphisms, to fully abstract ones. We show that this is not always possible—indeed the natural continuous function model $\mathcal{E}$ of PCF provides a counterexample—but give sufficient conditions for the possibility of collapsing inductively reachable correct models, via continuous homomorphisms, to inductively reachable fully abstract models, and, more generally, for collapsing the reachable inductive subalgebras of correct models to inductively reachable fully abstract models. Both of these approaches yield fully abstract models for the languages introduced in chapter 4 and, more generally, for languages whose notions of program ordering and equivalence are defined as abstractions of models using the technique of section 4.1.

In the case of PCF, we are able to continuously collapse $R(\mathcal{E})$ to an inductively reachable, inequationally fully abstract, least fixed point, complete ordered algebra $\mathcal{A}$. Furthermore, with some language specific work, we are able to show that $\mathcal{A}$ is (up to order-isomorphism) the only object of the category of such models, and is an order-extensional, standard, combinatory algebra. Thus, $\mathcal{A}$ is Milner's fully abstract model, and we have a pleasing, algebraic solution to Mulmuley's problem of relating $\mathcal{E}$ and $\mathcal{A}$.

## 7.1 Model-Theoretic Conditions

The following theorem gives two model-theoretic necessary and sufficient conditions for the existence of inequationally fully abstract, least fixed point, complete ordered algebras. Their necessity is obvious; theorem 5.1.4 is used to show their sufficiency. A corollary of this theorem gives two model-theoretic necessary and sufficient conditions for the existence of equationally fully abstract, least fixed point, complete ordered algebras.

**Theorem 7.1.1** *Let $\preceq$ be an $\Omega$-least substitutive pre-ordering over $\mathcal{T}$ and $\Phi$ be a family of least fixed point constraints. The following conditions are equivalent.*

(i) *A $\preceq$-inequationally fully abstract, $\Phi$-least fixed point, complete ordered algebra exists.*

(ii) *There is a $\Phi$-least fixed point, complete ordered algebra $\mathcal{A}$, together with an inductive pre-ordering $\leq$ over $A$, such that*

$$t_1 \preceq_s t_2 \text{ iff } M_s\, t_1 \leq_s M_s\, t_2,$$

*for all $t_1, t_2 \in T_s$, $s \in S$.*

(iii) *There is a $\Phi$-least fixed point, complete ordered algebra $\mathcal{A}$, together with a continuous function $h$ from $A$ to a cpo $B$, such that*

$$t_1 \preceq_s t_2 \text{ iff } h_s(M_s\, t_1) \sqsubseteq_s h_s(M_s\, t_2),$$

*for all $t_1, t_2 \in T_s$, $s \in S$.*

**Proof.** We show that (ii) $\Rightarrow$ (i), (i) $\Rightarrow$ (iii) and (iii) $\Rightarrow$ (ii).

(ii) $\Rightarrow$ (i) By theorem 5.1.4, it is sufficient to show that $\preceq$ satisfies $\overline{\Phi}$. Suppose $t \equiv \bigsqcup T' \in \overline{\Phi}_s$, $s \in S$. By lemma 3.2.7, $\mathcal{A}$ satisfies $\overline{\Phi}$, and thus $M_s\, t = \bigsqcup M_s\, T'$. Since $\sqsubseteq_A \subseteq \leq$, it then follows that $M_s\, t$ is an ub of $M_s\, T'$ in $\langle A_s, \leq_s \rangle$, and thus that $t$ is an ub of $T'$ in $\langle T_s, \preceq_s \rangle$. Suppose $t''$ is also an ub of $T'$ in $\langle T_s, \preceq_s \rangle$. Then $M_s\, t''$ is an ub of $M_s\, T'$ in $\langle A_s, \leq_s \rangle$, and, since $\leq$ is inductive,

$$M_s\, t = \bigsqcup M_s\, T' \leq M_s\, t''.$$

Thus $t \preceq_s t''$, showing that $t$ is indeed a lub of $T'$ in $\langle T_s, \preceq_s \rangle$.

(i) $\Rightarrow$ (iii) Simply take $\mathcal{A}$ to be a $\preceq$-inequationally fully abstract, $\Phi$-least fixed point, complete ordered algebra, and let $h$ be the identity function from $A$ to $B = A$.

(iii) $\Rightarrow$ (ii) Let $\leq$ be $\leq_h$. Then,

$$\begin{aligned} t_1 \preceq_s t_2 \quad &\text{iff} \quad h_s(M_s\, t_1) \sqsubseteq_s h_s(M_s\, t_2) \\ &\text{iff} \quad M_s\, t_1 \leq_s M_s\, t_2, \end{aligned}$$

for $t_1, t_2 \in T_s$, $s \in S$. □

**Corollary 7.1.2** *Let $\approx$ be a congruence over $\mathcal{T}$ and $\Phi$ be a family of least fixed point constraints. The following conditions are equivalent.*

(i) *A $\approx$-fully abstract, $\Phi$-least fixed point, complete ordered algebra exists.*

(ii) *There is a $\Phi$-least fixed point, complete ordered algebra $\mathcal{A}$, together with an inductive pre-ordering $\leq$ over $A$, such that*

$$t_1 \approx_s t_2 \text{ iff } M_s\, t_1 \, (\leq \cap \geq)_s \, M_s\, t_2,$$

*for all* $t_1, t_2 \in T_s$, $s \in S$.

(iii) *There is a* $\Phi$*-least fixed point, complete ordered algebra* $\mathcal{A}$*, together with a continuous function* $h$ *from* $A$ *to a cpo* $B$*, such that*

$$t_1 \approx_s t_2 \text{ iff } h_s(M_s\, t_1) = h_s(M_s\, t_2),$$

*for all* $t_1, t_2 \in T_s$, $s \in S$.

**Proof.** We show that (ii) $\Rightarrow$ (i), (i) $\Rightarrow$ (iii) and (iii) $\Rightarrow$ (ii).

(ii) $\Rightarrow$ (i) Define a pre-ordering $\preceq$ over $T$ by

$$t_1 \preceq_s t_2 \text{ iff } M_s\, t_1 \leq_s M_s\, t_2,$$

so that $\preceq$ induces $\approx$. Then by lemma 2.3.36, $\preceq^c$ is an $\Omega$-least substitutive pre-ordering over $\mathcal{T}$, $\leq^c$ is a unary-substitutive inductive pre-ordering over $\mathcal{A}$, and

$$t_1 \preceq_s^c t_2 \text{ iff } M_s\, t_1 \leq_s^c M_s\, t_2,$$

for all $t_1, t_2 \in T_s$, $s \in S$. Furthermore, by lemma 2.2.26, $\preceq^c$ also induces $\approx$. Thus, by condition (ii) of theorem 7.1.1, a $\approx$-fully abstract, $\Phi$-least fixed point, complete ordered algebra exists.

(i) $\Rightarrow$ (iii) Simply take $\mathcal{A}$ to be a $\approx$-fully abstract, $\Phi$-least fixed point, complete ordered algebra, and let $h$ be the identity function from $A$ to $B = A$.

(iii) $\Rightarrow$ (ii) Simply let $\leq = \leq_h$. $\square$

Note the subtlety in the proof that condition (ii) implies condition (i) of the corollary: the pre-ordering $\preceq$ is not necessarily substitutive, and thus $\preceq^c$, which also induces $\approx$, must be used instead.

Condition (iii) of corollary 7.1.2 states that there exists a correct, least fixed point model, together with a continuous "full abstraction function", for a programming language. It was suggested in [AptPlo] that condition (iii) might be weaker than condition (i); the corollary shows that this is false. See the end of section 6.1 for an application of this result.

Condition (ii) of theorem 7.1.1 is especially useful since it allows us to conclude that fully abstract models exist for the languages of chapter 4 and, more generally, for any language whose notion of program ordering is defined via lemma 4.1.1. We consider the case of PCF in detail. Let $S$, $P$, $\Sigma$, $\mathcal{E}$, $\Delta$, $\preceq$, $\leq$ and $\approx$ be as in section 4.3. We can apply condition (ii), with $\Delta^*$, $\mathcal{E}$, $\preceq^c$ and $\leq^c$ substituted for $\Phi$, $\mathcal{A}$, $\preceq$ and

$\leq$, respectively, and conclude that a $\preceq^c$-inequationally fully abstract, $\Delta^*$-least fixed point, complete ordered algebra exists. Then $\mathcal{I}(\preceq^c, \overline{\Delta^*})$ is initial in the category of such complete ordered algebras, by corollary 5.1.5, is inductively reachable, by corollary 5.1.6, and is thus a $\approx^c$-contextually fully abstract, $\Delta$-contextually least fixed point, complete ordered algebra, by theorems 5.3.1 and 5.3.2.

Milner and Berry have shown that there exists a unique (up to order-isomorphism) extensional, combinatorial, standard, $\preceq^c$-inequationally fully abstract, $\Delta$-contextually least fixed point, complete ordered algebra $\mathcal{A}$, and, furthermore, that $\mathcal{A}$ is order-extensional and inductively reachable, since its carrier is $\omega$-algebraic and all of its finite (isolated) elements are denotable [Mil2][Ber1][BerCurLév]. In the remainder of this section, we prove a pleasing companion result: $\mathcal{I}(\preceq^c, \overline{\Delta^*})$ is, up to order-isomorphism, the unique inductively reachable, $\preceq^c$-inequationally fully abstract, $\Delta$-contextually least fixed point, complete ordered algebra, and thus $\mathcal{I}(\preceq^c, \overline{\Delta^*}) = \mathcal{A}$.

**Theorem 7.1.3** *Inductively reachable, $\approx^c$-fully abstract, complete ordered algebras are combinatory algebras.*

**Proof.** By theorem 3.1.5, $\mathcal{E}$ is $\approx^c$-contextually correct, and, by theorem 5.3.1, all inductively reachable, $\approx^c$-fully abstract, complete ordered algebras $\mathcal{A}$ are $\approx^c$-contextually fully abstract. Thus all universally quantified equations (expressed by pairs of derived operators) which hold in $\mathcal{E}$ also hold in $\mathcal{A}$. The result then follows from the fact that $\mathcal{E}$ is a combinatory algebra. □

**Theorem 7.1.4** *Inductively reachable, $\preceq^c$-inequationally fully abstract, complete ordered algebras are standard.*

**Proof.** Let $\mathcal{A}$ be such an ordered algebra; we must show that conditions (i)–(iii) of definition 4.3.8 hold.

(i) Since $\mathcal{E}$ is standard and $\preceq_{\mathcal{E}\,bool} = \preceq^c_{bool}$, by lemma 4.3.16, it is easy to see that $\Omega_{bool\,\mathcal{A}}$, $tt_{\mathcal{A}}$ and $f\!f_{\mathcal{A}}$ are distinct and form all of $M_{bool}T_{bool}$, and that for all $a_1, a_2 \in M_{bool}T_{bool}$, $a_1 \sqsubseteq_{bool} a_2$ iff $a_1 = \Omega_{bool}$ or $a_1 = a_2$. But then $A_{bool} = M_{bool}T_{bool}$, since $M_{bool}T_{bool}$ is flat and $\mathcal{A}$ is inductively reachable.

(ii) Similar to (i).

(iii) Holds since $\mathcal{E}$ is standard and $\approx^c$-contextually correct, and $\mathcal{A}$ is $\approx^c$-contextually fully abstract. □

From the previous two theorems, we can conclude that $\mathcal{I}(\preceq^c, \overline{\Delta^\star})$ is a standard, combinatory algebra. We now show that it is also order-extensional, adapting techniques of Milner [Mil2] and Berry [Ber1] to our framework.

**Definition 7.1.5** For $x \in I_{nat \to nat}$ and $y \in I_{nat}$, let $F \in T_{(nat \to nat) \to nat \to nat}$ be

$$[x][y](if_{nat} \cdot (zero? \cdot y) \cdot 0 \cdot (succ \cdot (x \cdot (pred \cdot y)))).$$

For all $n \in \omega$ and $s \in S$, define $\Psi_n^s \in T_{s \to s}$ by

$$\begin{aligned}
\Psi_0^{nat} &= \Omega_{nat \to nat};\\
\Psi_{n+1}^{nat} &= F \cdot \Psi_n^{nat};\\
\Psi_n^{bool} &= [x]x, \text{for } x \in I_{bool};\\
\Psi_n^{s_1 \to s_2} &= [x][y](\Psi_n^{s_2} \cdot (x \cdot (\Psi_n^{s_1} \cdot y))), \text{for } x \in I_{s_1 \to s_2}, y \in I_{s_1}.
\end{aligned}$$

For $s \in S$, define $ID_s \in T_{s \to s}$ by

$$\begin{aligned}
ID_{nat} &= Y_{nat \to nat} \cdot F;\\
ID_{bool} &= [x]x, \text{for } x \in I_{bool};\\
ID_{s_1 \to s_2} &= [x][y](ID_{s_2} \cdot (x \cdot (ID_{s_1} \cdot y))), \text{for } x \in I_{s_1 \to s_2}, y \in I_{s_1}.
\end{aligned}$$

For an algebra $\mathcal{A}$, we write $\psi_n^s$ for $M_{s \to s} \Psi_n^s \in A_{s \to s}$ and $id_s$ for $M_{s \to s} ID_s \in A_{s \to s}$.

Expanding the identifier abstractions, one can see that for all $s \in S$, $\Psi_n^s$ is an $\omega$-chain in $OT_{s \to s}$, and $ID_s \equiv \bigsqcup\{ \Psi_n^s \mid n \in \omega \} \in (\overline{\Delta^\star})_{s \to s}$.

From [Mil2] and [Ber1], it is known that the $\psi_n^s$ represent a chain of projections with finite range in $E_{s \to s}$ whose lub is the identify function, which is represented by $id_s$. In the sequel, however, we only need the following portion of this information.

**Lemma 7.1.6** (i) *For all $s \in S$ and $n \in \omega$, $\{ \psi_n^s \cdot e \mid e \in E_s \}$ is finite.*

(ii) *For all $s \in S$ and $e \in E_s$, $id_s \cdot e = e$.* □

**Lemma 7.1.7** *If $\mathcal{A}$ is an inductively reachable, $\approx^c$-fully abstract, $\Delta$-contextually least fixed point, complete ordered algebra, and $a \in A_s$, $s \in S$, then $a = \bigsqcup_{n \in \omega}(\psi_n^s \cdot a)$.*

**Proof.** Let $\Delta'$ be the family of contextual least fixed point constraints defined by

$$\Delta'_s = \{(ID_s \cdot v) \equiv \bigsqcup\{ \Psi_n^s \cdot v \mid n \in \omega \}\},$$

for some $v \in V_s$. Then $\mathcal{A}$ satisfies $\Delta'$, by theorem 5.3.2 and since $(\Delta')^\star \subseteq \overline{\Delta^\star}$. Furthermore, $(ID_s \cdot v)_{\mathcal{A}} = v_{\mathcal{A}}$, since $(ID_s \cdot v)_{\mathcal{E}} = v_{\mathcal{E}}$ (lemma 7.1.6), $\mathcal{E}$ is $\approx^c$-contextually correct, and $\mathcal{A}$ is $\approx^c$-contextually fully abstract. Thus for all $a \in A_s$,

$$a = id_s \cdot a = \bigsqcup_{n \in \omega} (\psi^s_n \cdot a),$$

as required. □

The proof of the following lemma makes use of the internal structure of $\mathcal{I}(\preceq^c, \overline{\Delta^\star})$, in contrast to the other proofs of the section.

**Lemma 7.1.8** *Let $\mathcal{A} = \mathcal{I}(\preceq^c, \overline{\Delta^\star})$. For all $n \in \omega$ and $a \in A_s$, $\psi^s_n \cdot a$ is denotable.*

**Proof.** Let $\Gamma$ be the family of subsets of $\mathcal{OT}/\preceq^c$ that is defined from $\overline{\Delta^\star}$ in the manner of lemma 5.1.1, so that $\mathcal{A} = (\mathcal{OT}/\preceq^c)^\Gamma$. Then, for all $qt_s T' \in A_s$,

$$\begin{aligned}
\psi^s_n \cdot (qt_s T') &= (M_{s\to s} \Psi^s_n) \cdot (qt_s T') \\
&= (em_{s\to s}(qt_{s\to s} \Psi^s_n)) \cdot (qt_s T') \\
&= cl(\{qt_{s\to s} \Psi^s_n\}) \cdot cl(qt_s T') \\
&= cl(\{ (qt_{s\to s} \Psi^s_n) \cdot (qt_s t') \mid t' \in T' \}) \qquad \text{(lemma 2.4.13)} \\
&= cl(\{ qt_s(\Psi^s_n \cdot t') \mid t' \in T' \}).
\end{aligned}$$

But $\{ qt_s(\Psi^s_n \cdot t') \mid t' \in T' \}$ is finite, since $\{ M_{\mathcal{E}\,s}(\Psi^s_n \cdot t') \mid t' \in T' \}$ is finite, by lemma 7.1.6. Thus, by lemma 2.4.12, there exists a $t' \in T'$ such that

$$\begin{aligned}
cl(\{ qt_s(\Psi^s_n \cdot t') \mid t' \in T' \}) &= cl(\{qt_s(\Psi^s_n \cdot t')\}) \\
&= em_s(qt_s(\Psi^s_n \cdot t')) \\
&= M_s(\Psi^s_n \cdot t'),
\end{aligned}$$

as required. □

**Theorem 7.1.9** *$\mathcal{I}(\preceq^c, \overline{\Delta^\star})$ is order-extensional.*

**Proof.** Let $\mathcal{A} = \mathcal{I}(\preceq^c, \overline{\Delta^\star})$ and suppose that $a_1, a_2 \in A_{s_1\to s_2}$ are such that (†) $a_1 \cdot a' \sqsubseteq_{s_2} a_2 \cdot a'$, for all $a' \in A_{s_1}$. By lemma 7.1.7, to show that $a_1 \sqsubseteq_{s_1\to s_2} a_2$ it is sufficient to show that $\psi^{s_1\to s_2}_n \cdot a_1 \sqsubseteq_{s_1\to s_2} \psi^{s_1\to s_2}_n \cdot a_2$, for all $n \in \omega$. By lemma 7.1.8, $\psi^{s_1\to s_2}_n \cdot a_1$ and $\psi^{s_1\to s_2}_n \cdot a_2$ are denotable. Furthermore, for all denotable $a' \in A_{s_1}$,

$$\begin{aligned}
(\psi^{s_1\to s_2}_n \cdot a_1) \cdot a' &= \psi^{s_2}_n \cdot (a_1 \cdot (\psi^{s_1}_n \cdot a')) \\
&\sqsubseteq \psi^{s_2}_n \cdot (a_2 \cdot (\psi^{s_1}_n \cdot a')) \\
&= (\psi^{s_1\to s_2}_n \cdot a_2) \cdot a',
\end{aligned}$$

by (†) and since $\mathcal{A}$ is a combinatory algebra. Thus, by the obvious semantic restatement of theorem 4.3.17, $\psi_n^{s_1 \to s_2} \cdot a_1 \sqsubseteq_{s_1 \to s_2} \psi_n^{s_1 \to s_2} \cdot a_2$, as required. □

Combining theorems 7.1.3, 7.1.4 and 7.1.9, we have that $\mathcal{I}(\preceq^c, \overline{\Delta^\star})$ is a standard, order-extensional, combinatory algebra. It remains to show the promised uniqueness result.

The following lemma, which we will also use in the next section, is taken from the proof of theorem 4.6 of [Plo1].

**Lemma 7.1.10** (i) *If $h\colon \mathcal{A} \to \mathcal{B}$ is a homomorphism over algebras, $\mathcal{A}$ is extensional, and $h_{nat}$ and $h_{bool}$ are injections then $h$ is an injection.*

(ii) *If $h\colon \mathcal{A} \to \mathcal{B}$ is a monotonic homomorphism over ordered algebras, $\mathcal{A}$ is order-extensional, and $h_{nat}$ and $h_{bool}$ are order-embeddings then $h$ is an order-embedding.*

**Proof.** We prove (ii), leaving (i), which is similar, to the reader. Let $s = s_1 \to \cdots \to s_n \to p$, for $n \geq 1$, $s_i \in S$, $1 \leq i \leq n$, and $p \in P$, and suppose $h_s\, a \sqsubseteq_s h_s\, a'$. Then for all $a_i \in A_{s_i}$, $1 \leq i \leq n$,

$$\begin{aligned} h_p(a \cdot a_1 \cdot \cdots \cdot a_n) &= (h_s\, a) \cdot (h_{s_1}\, a_1) \cdot \cdots \cdot (h_{s_n}\, a_n) \\ &\sqsubseteq (h_s\, a') \cdot (h_{s_1}\, a_1) \cdot \cdots \cdot (h_{s_n}\, a_n) \\ &= h_p(a' \cdot a_1 \cdot \cdots \cdot a_n), \end{aligned}$$

so that

$$a \cdot a_1 \cdot \cdots \cdot a_n \sqsubseteq_p a' \cdot a_1 \cdot \cdots \cdot a_n,$$

since $h_p$ is an order-embedding. Thus $a \sqsubseteq_s a'$, since $\mathcal{A}$ is order-extensional. □

**Theorem 7.1.11** *$\mathcal{I}(\preceq^c, \overline{\Delta^\star})$ is the unique (up to order-isomorphism) inductively reachable, $\preceq^c$-inequationally fully abstract, $\Delta$-contextually least fixed point, complete ordered algebra.*

**Proof.** Let $\mathcal{A} = \mathcal{I}(\preceq^c, \overline{\Delta^\star})$ and $h$ be the unique continuous homomorphism from $\mathcal{A}$ to another such ordered algebra, $\mathcal{B}$. We show that $h$ is a surjective order-embedding. Suppose that $a_1, a_2 \in A_p$, $p \in P$, and $h_p\, a_1 \sqsubseteq_p h_p\, a_2$. Since $\mathcal{A}$ is standard, there exist terms $t_1, t_2 \in T_p$ such that $M_p\, t_i = a_i$, for $i = 1, 2$. Then,

$$M_{\mathcal{B}\,p}\, t_1 = h_p(M_{\mathcal{A}\,p}\, t_1) \sqsubseteq_p h_p(M_{\mathcal{A}\,p}\, t_2) = M_{\mathcal{B}\,p}\, t_2,$$

showing that $a_1 = M_{\mathcal{A}\,p}\, t_1 \sqsubseteq_p M_{\mathcal{A}\,p}\, t_2 = a_2$. Thus $h_{nat}$ and $h_{bool}$ are order-embeddings, and, by lemma 7.1.10, we can conclude that $h$ itself is an order-embedding. It remains to show that $h$ is surjective. If $h_s\,A' \subseteq B_s$ is directed, for $A' \subseteq A_s$, then $A'$ is also directed, since $h$ is an order-embedding, and thus $h_s \bigsqcup A' = \bigsqcup h_s\,A'$. Thus $h\,\mathcal{A}$ is an inductive subalgebra of $\mathcal{B}$, and, since $\mathcal{B}$ is inductively reachable, $h\,\mathcal{A} = \mathcal{B}$. □

**Corollary 7.1.12** *All inductively reachable, $\preceq^c$-inequationally fully abstract, $\Delta$-contextually least fixed point, complete ordered algebras are standard, order-extensional, combinatory algebras.*

**Proof.** Such an ordered algebra is standard and combinatorial, by theorems 7.1.4 and 7.1.3, and is order-isomorphic to $\mathcal{I}(\preceq^c, \overline{\Delta^*})$, by theorem 7.1.11. But $\mathcal{I}(\preceq^c, \overline{\Delta^*})$ is order-extensional, by theorem 7.1.9, and order-extensionality is obviously preserved by order-isomorphisms. □

## 7.2 Collapsing Correct Models into Fully Abstract Models

Given a correct, least fixed point, complete ordered algebra, it is natural to consider collapsing it, via a continuous homomorphism, into a fully abstract, least fixed point, complete ordered algebra. This, of course, is not always possible, since fully abstract models do not always exist. But, is it always possible when such models do exist? The answer is "no"; in fact neither of the following conditions are sufficient to guarantee that a $\preceq$-inequationally correct, $\Phi$-least fixed point, complete ordered algebra $\mathcal{A}$ can be continuously collapsed into a $\preceq$-inequationally fully abstract, $\Phi$-least fixed point, complete ordered algebra:

(i) $\mathcal{A}$ is inductively reachable, and there exist $\preceq$-inequationally fully abstract, $\Phi$-least fixed point, complete ordered algebras;

(ii) $\preceq$ is related to an inductive pre-ordering $\leq$ over $A$ according to condition (ii) of theorem 7.1.1, so that $\preceq$-inequationally fully abstract, $\Phi$-least fixed point, complete ordered algebras exist.

We shall see, however, that the conjunction of these conditions is sufficient. Theorem 5.4.5 shows that (i) is not sufficient, and we now present a theorem of Plotkin's (unpublished) that shows the insufficiency of (ii).

For the next theorem and the remarks that follow, let $P$, $S$, $\Sigma$, $\mathcal{E}$, $\Delta$, $\preceq$, $\approx$, $\leq$, *portest*$_i$ and *por* be as in section 4.3.

**Theorem 7.2.1** *$\mathcal{E}$ cannot be collapsed, via a homomorphism, to a $\approx^c$-fully abstract algebra. In particular, $\mathcal{E}$ cannot be collapsed, via a continuous homomorphism, to a $\preceq^c$-inequationally fully abstract, $\Delta^*$-least fixed point, complete ordered algebra.*

**Proof.** We give two proofs of the theorem. The first is due to Plotkin, and the second to the author.

(i) Suppose, toward a contradiction, that $h$ is a homomorphism from $\mathcal{E}$ to a $\approx^c$-fully abstract algebra $\mathcal{A}$. Since $\mathcal{E}$ is standard and $\approx_{\mathcal{E}}|P = \approx_{\mathcal{A}}|P$ (lemma 4.3.16), it follows that $h_{nat}$ and $h_{bool}$ are injections, and thus that $h$ itself is an injection, by lemma 7.1.10. But then $\approx_{\mathcal{E}} = \approx_{\mathcal{A}} = \approx^c$, contradicting the fact that $\mathcal{E}$ is not $\approx^c$-fully abstract.

(ii) It is sufficient to show that there does not exist a congruence $\equiv$ over $\mathcal{E}$ such that

$$t_1 \approx^c_s t_2 \text{ iff } M_s\, t_1 \equiv_s M_s\, t_2,$$

for all $t_1, t_2 \in T_s$, $s \in S$. Suppose, toward a contradiction, that such a congruence $\equiv$ exists. Let $s'$ be the sort $(bool \to bool \to bool) \to nat$. Then,

$$\begin{aligned} & portest_1 \approx^c_{s'} portest_2 \\ \Rightarrow\ & M_{s'}\, portest_1 \equiv_{s'} M_{s'}\, portest_2 \\ \Rightarrow\ & M_{nat}\, 1 = (M_{s'}\, portest_1) \cdot por \equiv_{nat} (M_{s'}\, portest_2) \cdot por = M_{nat}\, 2 \\ \Rightarrow\ & 1 \approx^c_{nat} 2, \end{aligned}$$

which is a contradiction. □

A consequence of this theorem is that $\mathcal{E}$ and $\leq^c$ provide an alternative proof of lemma 2.3.34; in particular, $\leq^c$ is unary-substitutive but not substitutive.

Next we show that, whenever they are possible, continuous collapses can be carried out using the inductive quotienting construction of section 2.4.

**Lemma 7.2.2** *Let $\preceq$ be an $\Omega$-least substitutive pre-ordering over $\mathcal{T}$, $\Phi$ be a family of least fixed point constraints, $\mathcal{A}$ be a $\Phi$-least fixed point, complete ordered algebra, and $\leq$ be a substitutive inductive pre-ordering over $\mathcal{A}$ such that*

$$t_1 \preceq_s t_2 \textit{ iff } M_s\, t_1 \leq_s M_s\, t_2,$$

*for all $t_1, t_2 \in T_s$, $s \in S$. Then $\mathcal{A}$ can be collapsed, via the continuous homomorphism $qt$, to the $\preceq$-inequationally fully abstract, $\Phi$-least fixed point, complete ordered algebra $\mathcal{A}//\leq$.*

**Proof.** For the inequational full abstraction of $\mathcal{A}//\leq$, let $t_1, t_2 \in T_s$, $s \in S$. Then,

$$\begin{aligned} t_1 \preceq_s t_2 \ \text{ iff }\ & M_{\mathcal{A}s}\, t_1 \leq_s M_{\mathcal{A}s}\, t_2 \\ \text{ iff }\ & qt_s(M_{\mathcal{A}s}\, t_1) \sqsubseteq_{(\mathcal{A}//\leq)_s} qt_s(M_{\mathcal{A}s}\, t_2) \\ \text{ iff }\ & M_{(\mathcal{A}//\leq)_s}\, t_1 \sqsubseteq_{(\mathcal{A}//\leq)_s} M_{(\mathcal{A}//\leq)_s}\, t_2. \end{aligned}$$

To see that $\mathcal{A}//\leq$ satisfies $\Phi$, let $t \equiv \bigsqcup T' \in \Phi_s$, $s \in S$. Then,

$$\begin{aligned} M_{(\mathcal{A}//\leq)_s} t &= qt_s(M_{\mathcal{A}_s} t) \\ &= qt_s \bigsqcup M_{\mathcal{A}_s} T' \\ &= \bigsqcup qt_s(M_{\mathcal{A}_s} T') \\ &= \bigsqcup M_{(\mathcal{A}//\leq)_s} T', \end{aligned}$$

as required. □

**Lemma 7.2.3** *Let $\mathcal{A}$ be a $\Phi$-least fixed point, complete ordered algebra. The following two conditions are equivalent.*

(i) *There is a $\preceq$-inequationally fully abstract, $\Phi$-least fixed point, complete ordered algebra $\mathcal{B}$, together with a continuous homomorphism $h: \mathcal{A} \to \mathcal{B}$.*

(ii) *There is a substitutive inductive pre-ordering $\leq$ over $\mathcal{A}$ such that for all $t_1, t_2 \in T_s$, $s \in S$,*

$$t_1 \preceq_s t_2 \textit{ iff } M_s t_1 \leq_s M_s t_2.$$

**Proof.** For (i) $\Rightarrow$ (ii), let $\leq$ be $\leq_h$. Then $\leq$ is a substitutive inductive pre-ordering over $\mathcal{A}$, and for $t_1, t_2 \in T_s$, $s \in S$,

$$\begin{aligned} t_1 \preceq_s t_2 \quad &\text{iff} \quad M_{\mathcal{B}_s} t_1 \sqsubseteq_s M_{\mathcal{B}_s} t_2 \\ &\text{iff} \quad h_s(M_{\mathcal{A}_s} t_1) \sqsubseteq_s h_s(M_{\mathcal{A}_s} t_2) \\ &\text{iff} \quad M_{\mathcal{A}_s} t_1 \leq_s M_{\mathcal{A}_s} t_2. \end{aligned}$$

For (ii) $\Rightarrow$ (i), simply apply lemma 7.2.2. □

Now we are able to give a sufficient condition for the possibility of collapsing inductively reachable, inequationally correct models, via continuous homomorphisms, to inequationally fully abstract models, and, more generally, for collapsing the reachable inductive subalgebras of inequationally correct models to inequationally fully abstract models.

**Theorem 7.2.4** *Suppose $\preceq$ is an $\Omega$-least substitutive pre-ordering over $\mathcal{T}$, $\Phi$ is a family of least fixed point constraints, $\mathcal{A}$ is a $\Phi$-least fixed point, complete ordered algebra, and $\leq$ is an inductive pre-ordering over $A$ with the property that*

$$t_1 \preceq_s t_2 \textit{ iff } M_s t_1 \leq_s M_s t_2,$$

*for all $t_1, t_2 \in T_s$, $s \in S$. Let $\leq'$ be the restriction of $\leq^c$ to $R(A)$. Then $R(\mathcal{A})$ can be collapsed, via the continuous homomorphism $qt$, to the inductively reachable, $\preceq$-inequationally fully abstract, $\Phi$-least fixed point, complete ordered algebra $R(\mathcal{A})//\leq'$.*

**Proof.** By lemmas 2.3.14, 2.3.12 and 2.3.35, $\leq'$ is a substitutive inductive pre-ordering over $R(\mathcal{A})$, and, by lemma 2.3.37,

$$t_1 \preceq_s t_2 \text{ iff } M_s\, t_1 \leq_s^c M_s\, t_2 \text{ iff } M_s\, t_1 \leq_s' M_s\, t_2,$$

for all $t_1, t_2 \in T_s$, $s \in S$. Thus, by lemma 7.2.2, $R(\mathcal{A})$ can be collapsed, via the continuous homomorphism $qt$, to the $\preceq$-inequationally fully abstract, $\Phi$-least fixed point, complete ordered algebra $R(\mathcal{A})//\leq'$, and, by lemma 2.4.21, $R(\mathcal{A})//\leq'$ is inductively reachable. □

Note the following special cases of theorem 7.2.4. If $\leq$ is already unary-substitutive then $R(\mathcal{A})$ can be collapsed to $R(\mathcal{A})//\leq'$, where $\leq'$ is simply the restriction of $\leq$ to $R(A)$. If $\leq$ is unary-substitutive and $\mathcal{A}$ is inductively reachable then $\mathcal{A}$ itself can be collapsed to $\mathcal{A}//\leq$, since $\leq$ is in fact substitutive.

Theorem 7.2.4 can be immediately applied to the languages of chapter 4 and, more generally, to languages whose notions of program ordering are defined via lemma 4.1.1. Consider, e.g., the case of PCF. Let $S$, $\Sigma$, $\mathcal{E}$, $\Delta$, $\preceq$, $\leq$ and $\approx$ be as in section 4.3. Then $R(\mathcal{E})$ can be collapsed, via the continuous homomorphism $qt$, to the inductively reachable, $\preceq^c$-inequationally fully abstract, $\Delta^*$-least fixed point, complete ordered algebra $R(\mathcal{E})//\leq'$, where $\leq'$ is the restriction of $\leq^c$ to $R(E)$. Furthermore, $R(\mathcal{E})//\leq'$ is also $\approx^c$-fully abstract, and thus, by theorems 5.3.1 and 5.3.2, is $\approx^c$-contextually fully abstract and $\Delta$-contextually least fixed point. Finally, theorem 7.1.11 allows us to conclude that $R(\mathcal{E})//\leq'$ is order-isomorphic to $\mathcal{I}(\preceq^c, \overline{\Delta^*})$, and is thus a standard, order-extensional, combinatory algebra, by corollary 7.1.12. Summarizing, we have the following corollary.

**Corollary 7.2.5** *$R(\mathcal{E})$ can be collapsed, via a continuous homomorphism, to $\mathcal{I}(\preceq^c, \overline{\Delta^*})$.*
□

We can also prove the following equational variant of theorem 7.2.4.

**Corollary 7.2.6** *Suppose $\approx$ is a congruence over $\mathcal{T}$, $\Phi$ is a family of least fixed point constraints, $\mathcal{A}$ is a $\Phi$-least fixed point, complete ordered algebra, and $h$ is a continuous function from $A$ to a cpo $B$, such that*

$$t_1 \approx_s t_2 \textit{ iff } h_s(M_s\, t_1) = h_s(M_s\, t_2),$$

*for all* $t_1, t_2 \in T_s$, $s \in S$. *Then* $R(\mathcal{A})$ *can be collapsed, via the continuous homomorphism* $qt$, *to the inductively reachable,* $\approx$*-fully abstract,* $\Phi$*-least fixed point, complete ordered algebra* $R(\mathcal{A})//\leq'$, *where* $\leq'$ *is the restriction of* $(\leq_h)^c$ *to* $R(A)$.

**Proof.** Define a pre-ordering $\preceq$ over $T$ by

$$t_1 \preceq_s t_2 \text{ iff } M_s\, t_1\, (\leq_h)_s\, M_s\, t_2,$$

so that $\preceq$ induces $\approx$ (but $\preceq$ may not be substitutive!). Then, by lemma 2.3.36, $\preceq^c$ is an $\Omega$-least substitutive pre-ordering over $\mathcal{T}$, $(\leq_h)^c$ is a unary-substitutive inductive pre-ordering over $\mathcal{A}$,

$$t_1 \preceq_s^c t_2 \text{ iff } M_s\, t_1\, (\leq_h)_s^c\, M_s\, t_2,$$

for all $t_1, t_2 \in T_s$, $s \in S$, and, by lemma 2.2.26, $\preceq^c$ also induces $\approx$. The desired result follows by theorem 7.2.4. □

# 8 Conclusion

In the preceding chapters, we have developed a theory of fully abstract models of programming languages and applied this theory to several programming languages. On the basis of these examples, it seems likely that the theory will yield proofs of the existence or nonexistence of fully abstract models of a wide variety of programming languages. I expect, for example, that the existence of fully abstract models for the Algol-like language of [HalMeyTra] can be shown using the methods of chapter 7, and that the nonexistence of fully abstract models of the fair parallel programming language of [Plo2] can be shown using the techniques of chapter 6. In this final chapter, we consider the theory's limitations and the corresponding possibilities for further research.

The cornerstone of the theory is its class of models: complete ordered algebras. This was a natural and rewarding choice, but there are many other important classes of models, narrower and wider, that should also be studied. Examples include: universal algebras whose carriers are cpo's with additional order-theoretic structure, e.g., consistently-complete $\omega$-algebraic cpo's; models based on weaker notions of continuity [Plo2]; categorical models [Leh][Abr2]; and models definable in particular metalanguages (and thus, in a formal sense, natural). The extension of the theory to these classes of models will probably involve the development of new quotienting and completion constructions.

An essential feature of the theory is the inclusion of the undefined constants $\Omega$ in all signatures, and the corresponding requirements that they be interpreted as $\perp$ in models, and be least elements in notions of program ordering. Unfortunately, this feature limits the applicability of the theory. There are programming languages, such as the parallel programming language of [HenPlo1], whose notions of program ordering do not have least elements, and, thus, whose inequationally correct models cannot have denotable least elements. (Our theory should be applicable, however, to the language of [HenPlo1] minus the somewhat peculiar coroutine construct.) There may even be naturally occurring languages for which equationally fully abstract models exist, but such that there do not exist such models with denotable least elements. It is thus desirable to develop a theory in which the undefined constants are not required. This would be a radical departure from the current theory, however, and it is unclear how to proceed.

As we indicated in chapter 4, our treatment of programming languages with block structure, such as TIE and the lambda calculus variant of PCF, is only partially satisfactory, for the following reasons. First, we are unable to construct environment models for these languages, i.e., models that have identifier environments as formal components. Second, our theory is not directly applicable to notions of program ordering and equivalence that are defined in terms of the behaviour of closed terms of program sort, as opposed to all such terms. Third, there apparently do not exist suitable families of least fixed point constraints for certain languages with recursion, such as the call-by-value version of TIE. Removing the first of these defects, and giving program identifiers and their scopes formal status in signatures, is the first step toward the removal of the second and third defects.

Notions of program equivalence are often defined as abstractions of operational semantics, as with the languages of chapter 6. Unfortunately, the condition for the existence of inequationally fully abstract models of section 7.1, which was the basis for our positive results, is model-theoretic in nature and is expressed in terms of program orderings instead of equivalences. It would thus be useful to develop conditions for the existence of fully abstract models that are directly applicable to operationally defined program equivalences.

In section 7.2, we gave useful sufficient conditions for the possibility of collapsing inductively reachable correct models, via continuous homomorphisms, to fully abstract models, and, more generally, for collapsing the reachable inductive subalgebras of correct models to fully abstract models. We also showed that it is not always possible to collapse correct models in such a way. Useful sufficient conditions for the possibility of collapsing non-inductively reachable correct models should be developed.

In section 5.4, we began the study of various categories of correct and fully abstract models, proving theorems concerning the existence and nonexistence of initial and terminal objects, respectively. Much remains to be learned about the structure of these categories, and thus this study should continue. In particular, it would be nice to resolve conjecture 5.4.6.

Finally, more should be learned about the internal structure of the conservative completions of posets and ordered algebras of section 2.4. In particular, conjecture 2.4.11 should be settled.

# Bibliography


[ADJ1] J. Goguen, J. Thatcher, E. Wagner and J. Wright. Initial algebra semantics and continuous algebras. *J. ACM* 24, 1, 1977.

[ADJ2] J. Wright, E. Wagner and J. Thatcher. A uniform approach to inductive posets and inductive closure. *Theoretical Computer Science* 7, 1978.

[Abr1] S. Abramsky. Experiments, powerdomains and fully abstract models for applicative multiprogramming. *Proc. Conference on Foundations of Computation Theory*, Lecture Notes in Computer Science, vol. 158, Springer-Verlag, 1983.

[Abr2] S. Abramsky. On semantic foundations for applicative multiprogramming. *Proc. 10th ICALP*, Lecture Notes in Computer Science, vol. 154, Springer-Verlag, 1983.

[Abr3] S. Abramsky. Semantic foundations of applicative multiprogramming. *Proc. Workshop on Semantics of Programming Languages*, Programming Methodology Group, University of Göteborg and Chalmers University of Technology, 1983.

[AptPlo] K. Apt and G. Plotkin. Countable nondeterminism and random assignment. *J. ACM*, to appear.

[Ber1] G. Berry. *Modèles complètement adéquats et stables des lambda-calculs typés.* Thèse de Doctorat d'Etat, Université Paris VII, 1979.

[Ber2] G. Berry. *Some syntactic and categorical constructions of lambda-calculus models.* Technical report No. 80, INRIA, 1981.

[BerCur] G. Berry and P.-L. Curien. Sequential algorithms on concrete data structures. *Theoretical Computer Science* 20, 1982.

[BerCurLév] G. Berry, P.-L. Curien and J.-J. Lévy. Full abstraction for sequential languages: the state of the art. In M. Nivat and J. Reynolds (editors), *Algebraic Methods in Semantics*, Cambridge University Press, 1985.

[Bro] S. Brookes. A fully abstract semantics and a proof system for an ALGOL-like language with sharing. *Proc. Conference on Mathematical Foundations of Programming Semantics*, Kansas State University, 1985.

[CouNiv] B. Courcelle and M. Nivat. Algebraic families of interpretations. *Proc. 17th IEEE Symposium on Foundations of Computer Science*, 1976.

[CouRao] B. Courcelle and J.-C. Raoult. Completions of ordered magmas. *Fundamenta Informaticae* 3, 1, 1980.

[HalMeyTra] J. Halpern, A. Meyer and B. Trakhtenbrot. The semantics of local storage, or What makes the free-list free? *Proc. 11th ACM Symposium on Principles of Programming Languages*, 1984.

[Hen] M. Hennessy. A term model for synchronous processes. *Information and Control* 51, 1, 1981.

[HenPlo1] M. Hennessy and G. Plotkin. Full abstraction for a simple parallel programming language. *Proc. 8th MFCS*, Lecture Notes in Computer Science, vol. 74, Springer-Verlag, 1979.

[HenPlo2] M. Hennessy and G. Plotkin. A term model for CCS. *Proc. 9th MFCS*, Lecture Notes in Computer Science, vol. 88, Springer-Verlag, 1980.

[Grä] G. Grätzer. *Universal Algebra.* Springer-Verlag, 1979.

[Leh] D. Lehmann. Categories for fixed point semantics. *Proc. 17th IEEE Symposium on Foundations of Computer Science*, 1976.

[Mar] G. Markowsky. Chain-complete posets and directed sets with applications. *Algebra Univ.* 6, 1976.

[Mil1] R. Milner. Processes: a mathematical model of computing agents. *Proc. Logic Colloquium '73*, North Holland, 1975.

[Mil2] R. Milner. Fully abstract models of typed λ-calculi. *Theoretical Computer Science* 4, 1977.

[Mil3] R. Milner. *A Calculus of Communicating Systems.* Springer-Verlag, 1980.

[Mul] K. Mulmuley. *Full abstraction and semantic equivalence.* The MIT Press, 1987.

[Nel] E. Nelson. Z-continuous algebras. *Continuous Lattices*, Lecture Notes in Mathematics, vol. 871, Springer-Verlag, 1981.

[Plo1] G. Plotkin. LCF considered as a programming language. *Theoretical Computer Science* 5, 1977.

[Plo2] G. Plotkin. A powerdomain for countable nondeterminism. *Proc. 9th ICALP*, Lecture Notes in Computer Science, vol. 140, Springer-Verlag, 1982.

[Plo3] G. Plotkin. *Domains.* Lecture Notes, Department of Computer Science, University of Edinburgh, 1980.

[Sco] D. Scott. The lattice of flow diagrams. *Proc. Symposium on Semantics of Algorithmic Languages*, Lecture Notes in Mathematics, vol. 188, Springer-Verlag, 1971.

[SmyPlo] M. Smyth and G. Plotkin. The category-theoretic solution of recursive domain equations. *SIAM J. Computing* 11, 4, 1982.

[Stou] A. Stoughton. *Fully Abstract Models of Programming Languages.* Ph.D. Thesis, Technical Report CST–40–86, Computer Science Department, University of Edinburgh, 1986.

[Stoy] J. Stoy. *Denotational Semantics: The Scott-Strachey Approach to Programming Language Theory.* The MIT Press, 1977.

# Index of Definitions